U0369356

"十四五" 國家重點出版物出版規劃項目

The Tsinghua University Warring States Bamboo Manuscripts: Studies and Translations 3

《清華大學藏戰國竹簡》研究與英譯3

The Yi Yin Manuscripts and Related Texts

伊尹諸篇

Zhou Boqun

周博群 著譯

Edited by the Research and Conservation Center
for Unearthed Texts, Tsinghua University
清華大學出土文獻研究與保護中心 編

清華大學出版社
Tsinghua University Press
北京

内 容 簡 介

　　2008 年 7 月，清華大學從境外搶救入藏了一批戰國時期竹簡，學界稱之為"清華簡"。清華簡的內容多為早期的經史類典籍，其中除了可與《尚書》等傳世古書對照的篇目外，更多的則是已失傳兩千年之久的前所未見的佚篇，對於準確認識先秦古籍的原貌、重建中國早期歷史均有重要學術價值。清華簡所帶來的新知識以及對傳統文化認識的更新，已經引起了海內外學術界以及社會各界的廣泛關注，對中華優秀傳統文化的傳承與創新性發展具有重要的意義。

　　本書的主要內容是對清華簡中與商湯及伊尹相關篇目(《赤鳩之集湯之屋》《尹至》《尹誥》《湯在啻門》《湯處於湯丘》《殷高宗問於三壽》)的英譯及背景知識介紹，同時對戰國時期歷史敘事的文學特徵提供了一些見解。主要讀者為海內外從事早期中國研究的學者以及對中國古代文明有興趣的一般讀者。

圖書在版編目 (CIP) 數據

《清華大學藏戰國竹簡》研究與英譯. 3, 伊尹諸篇：
英文 / 清華大學出土文獻研究與保護中心；周博群著
譯. -- 北京：清華大學出版社, 2024. 9. -- ISBN 978-
7-302-67048-3

　　Ⅰ. K877.54
　　中國國家版本館CIP數據核字第2024551GT9號

責任編輯：梁　斐
封面設計：王紅衛　劉星池
責任校對：趙麗敏
責任印製：楊　艷

出版發行：清華大學出版社
　　　　　　網　　　址：https://www.tup.com.cn, https://www.wqxuetang.com
　　　　　　地　　　址：北京清華大學學研大廈A座　　　　郵　　編：100084
　　　　　　社 總 機：010-83470000　　　　　　　　　　郵　　購：010-62786544
　　　　　　投稿與讀者服務：010-62776969, c-service@tup.tsinghua.edu.cn
　　　　　　質量反饋：010-62772015, zhiliang@tup.tsinghua.edu.cn
印 裝 者：三河市春園印刷有限公司
經　　銷：全國新華書店
成　　品：155mm×235mm　**印　　張**：16.75　**插　頁**：7　**字　　數**：279千字
版　　次：2024年9月第1版　　　　　　　　　　　**印　　次**：2024年9月第1次印刷
定　　價：188.00元

產品編號：102182-01

本叢書獲得了國家社科基金重大項目 "清華大學藏戰國竹簡的價值挖掘與傳承傳播研究"（20&ZD309）的資助

This book has received support from the Paleography and Chinese Civilization Inheritance and Development Program and the National Social Science Fund Key Program "Research on the Value and Transmission of the Tsinghua University Warring States Bamboo Manuscripts" (20&ZD309)

Contents

III

General Preface Ⅰ

Huang Dekuan 黃德寬

Since the beginning of the twentieth century, a series of important archaeological discoveries has greatly enriched contemporary scholars' understanding of ancient China. Among the many archaeological excavations, several discoveries of Warring State, Qin and Han manuscripts stand out as milestones: the Han-dynasty bamboo-slips unearthed at Yinqueshan 銀雀山, the silk manuscripts unearthed at Mawangdui 馬王堆, and the Warring States Chu 楚 manuscripts from Guodian 郭店. The publication of these ancient manuscripts has attracted the greatest interest from the scholarly world, and has had a profound influence on the development of contemporary Chinese scholarship. Scholars both at home and abroad have approached these new documents from different scholarly backgrounds to explore such different topics as ancient history, ancient literature and paleography, bringing manuscript studies to the forefront of contemporary scholarship.

The profound influence that the discovery of these manuscripts has had on contemporary Chinese scholarship is a sign of their extraordinary significance for the study of ancient China. As one of the great civilizations of the world, Chinese civilization has had a long and unbroken history, and its writing system is the only one in the world that is still in use today and that still maintains its ancient form. For this reason, there is a continuous tradition of literature written in Chinese characters, making China the richest source of literature in the world. Even though Chinese history saw the calamity of the burning of the books during the Qin dynasty (221–206 BCE), after the establishment of the Han dynasty Emperor Hui of Han 漢惠帝 (r. 194–186 BCE) abolished the Qin proscription on literature and thereafter there were continuous efforts during the remainder of the dynasty to restore pre-Qin literature. This established a firm foundation for the transmission of classical literature over the next two thousand years, throughout which time the sacred place of classical literature was never shaken.

In modern times, the prestige of the ancient classics was called into question by the rise of the new historiography of the "doubting antiquity" movement. Nevertheless, against the background of the "doubting antiquity" movement's attack on classical literature, repeated discoveries of such paleographic sources as the oracle-bone inscriptions and Western Zhou bronze inscriptions, as well as the Warring States, Qin and Han manuscripts had an especially important significance. In 1925, while teaching the course "New Evidence of Ancient History" at Tsinghua University's Institute of Sinology, Wang Guowei 王國維 (1877–1927) announced his famous principle of "dual evidence." In this, he found a middle ground between traditional scholars' excessive belief in antiquity and the modern excessive doubting of antiquity. What is more, he also demonstrated the value of combining "paper sources" and "underground sources."[1] Some of the Warring States, Qin and Han manuscripts discovered since the 1970s correspond to texts in the received literature, and these manuscripts have resolved certain questions of long standing concerning those texts; some have confirmed the authenticity and date of texts that have been doubted, while many others provide hitherto unknown sources for the literature of the period. More important still, these unearthed manuscripts allow an entirely new understanding of how ancient texts were created, transmitted, modified, and systematized.

These discoveries have also furthered the development of contemporary Chinese scholarship, especially as represented in the fields of history, literature and paleography. This has prompted the scholarly world in general

---

1 Wang Guowei 王國維, *Gu shi xin zheng: Wang Guowei zuihou de jiangyi* 古史新證——王國維最後的講義 (Beijing: Qinghua daxue chubanshe, 1994).

to rethink the history of Chinese scholarship. For instance, Li Xueqin 李學勤 (1933–2019) spoke of "leaving behind the doubting antiquity period,"[2] and proposed instead to "rewrite the history of scholarship" "based on new materials, new viewpoints, new methods, new heights, and under new historical conditions."[3] He also argued that "rewriting the history of scholarship should especially include a renewed emphasis on the history of twentieth century scholarship."[4] Qiu Xigui 裘錫圭 has proposed "reestablishing classical studies," suggesting that "the first of the recent reestablishments of Chinese classical studies began in the 1920s," when "doubting antiquity gradually became the main current of classical studies, to a considerable extent replacing traditional classicism." According to Qiu, because of the great amount of paleographic materials unearthed beginning in the 1950s — and especially of manuscripts discovered beginning in the 1970s — Chinese scholars then "began the second reestablishment of classical studies."[5] This rethinking of Chinese scholarship has not only had an enormous influence on scholars within China, but has also attracted the notice of Western scholars. In the Preface to his book *Rewriting Early Chinese Texts*, Edward L. Shaughnessy said:

"[Professor Li's call to leave behind the doubting antiquity period] has had a resounding effect in China, numerous books and articles published in the intervening ten years featuring the word 'rewriting.' Even in the West, the notion of rewriting China's early history, if not the word itself, inspired the recently

---

2   Li Xueqin 李學勤, *Zouchu yigu shidai* 走出疑古時代 (Shenyang: Liaoning daxue chubanshe, 1994).

3   Li Xueqin 李學勤, "Yigu sichao yu chonggou gu shi" 疑古思潮與重構古史, *Zhongguo wenhua yanjiu* 中國文化研究 1999.1: 4; rpt. Li Xueqin, *Chongxie xueshushi* 重寫學術史 (Shijiazhuang: Hebei Jiaoyu chubanshe, 2002), 2.

4   *Ibid.*

5   Qiu Xigui 裘錫圭, "Zhongguo gudianxue chongjian zhong yinggai zhuyi de wenti" 中國古典學重建中應該注意的問題, *Beijing daxue Zhongguo guwenxian yanjiu zhongxin jikan* 北京大學中國古文獻研究中心集刊 2 (2001): 4; "Chutu wenxian yu gudianxue chongjian" 出土文獻與古典學重建, *Chutu wenxian* 出土文獻 4 (2013): 1–18.

published *Cambridge History of Ancient China*."[6]

Expressions such as "leaving behind the doubting antiquity period," "rewriting the history of scholarship," and "reestablishing classical studies" surely show the great significance of these discoveries of Warring States, Qin and Han manuscripts.

In this context, the appearance of the Tsinghua University Warring States bamboo slips (commonly referred to as the "Tsinghua manuscripts") can be said to have "met the moment," and to have provided a further impetus to the "rewriting" of Chinese scholarship. In 2008, Li Xueqin encouraged Tsinghua University to salvage this corpus of invaluable manuscripts from the Hong Kong antique market. Based on AMS ^{14}C analysis, the bamboo slips can be dated to about 305±30 BCE, which is to say toward the end of the middle of the Warring States period. This is consistent with the opinion of the group of experts that Tsinghua University convened to evaluate them. As of the end of 2021, after more than ten years of work preserving, editing, and studying the more than 2,500 separate slips, eleven volumes, including sixty-one different texts, have already been published. We have already finished two-thirds of the editorial work, and the overall picture of these manuscripts is already perfectly clear.

The contents of the Tsinghua manuscripts are extremely rich. Just the texts already published include long-lost texts of chapters of the *Shang shu* 尚書 *Exalted Scriptures* and *Yi Zhou shu* 逸周書 *Leftover Zhou Scriptures*, Western Zhou poems not seen in the *Shi jing* 詩經 *Classic of Poetry*, historical materials of the Three Dynasties period through the Springs and Autumns and Warring States periods, as well as astronomical and hemerological texts. These texts touch on the core topics of Chinese civilization, and their publication has received the attention of scholars in all the related fields and has added invaluable new materials for the rewriting of ancient Chinese history.

---

6 Edward L. Shaughnessy, *Rewriting Early Chinese Texts* (Albany: SUNY Press, 2006), 1.

After having been buried for more than 2300 years, the Tsinghua slips have now finally been exposed to the light of day, allowing us to see something of the intellectual culture of the pre-Qin period; how fortunate this has been for those of us who study ancient China! Nevertheless, it is disappointing that these slips did not come to us by way of archaeological excavation, but rather were robbed from some unknown tomb, destroying the context from which they were taken and losing whatever other objects may have been buried in the same tomb. This has given us many problems in terms of preserving, editing and studying the slips, but the team at Tsinghua University's Research and Conservation Center for Unearthed Texts (清華大學出土文獻研究與保護中心) has worked very hard to preserve and edit them. We have made use of the most advanced technology to produce enhanced images of the texts; we have made every effort to put the slips, most of which came to us in great disarray, back in order; and, to the extent possible, we have attempted to return them to their original appearance. On this basis, the editorial team has produced transcriptions of the text, as well as notes on disputed characters, all of which has been published in the formal volumes that have made it possible for other scholars also to study the texts.

The publication of each of these volumes has stimulated wide attention within China and even abroad, such that both Chinese and foreign scholars have produced a great many studies of the manuscripts. At the same time that foreign scholars have written articles about the Tsinghua manuscripts, they have also translated some of them into foreign languages, making them available to those who are unable to read Chinese. However, these translations have been occasional, based on individual scholars' own interests. This suggested to us the need to organize a systematic effort to translate all of the manuscripts. But this is truly an intimidating project. After all, these texts are over 2300 years old, and even if the basic editorial work has been relatively well done, there are still many characters and phrases that still have not been explained, and for some of the manuscripts there is no scholarly consensus at all regarding their meaning. Because of this, one can imagine just how difficult it would be to translate these texts into a foreign language, not to mention one of a completely different culture. It demands that the translators not only thoroughly understand the language of the texts, but also their historical background. This requires the very greatest of scholarly competence.

Fortunately, the internationally renowned scholar Edward L. Shaughnessy has already succeeded in translating some of the Tsinghua manuscripts, and his translation of the *Yi Zhou shu* texts has allowed us to see the dawn of this work. In 2019, while Shaughnessy was visiting Tsinghua University, we proposed this translation project to him and invited him to join us in a cooperative effort. After careful deliberation and much communication back and forth, Shaughnessy has organized a team of translators and is working together with us to bring this giant project to fruition. At the beginning of 2020, when this effort was just taking shape, we agreed to work together to make available the results of our research on the manuscripts and to provide the best possible conditions for the translations. I myself organized the editorial team at Tsinghua University's Research and Conservation Center for Unearthed Texts to produce revised editions of the manuscripts, to reorganize them according to their contents, to provide more detailed notes, and to translate them into modern Chinese, to be made available to the English translators. Shaughnessy has been responsible for organizing the team of excellent international scholars to undertake the translations, and is responsible for the quality of their work. After considerable consultation, we have settled on the principles of translation, the format, the framework of the series, and the publisher. As of the end of 2021, this project is finally on the way forward, with the Tsinghua team and the English translation team both making progress toward the publication of the revised editions of the manuscripts and of the translations.

The translation and publication of the Tsinghua manuscripts is an enterprise of great significance, but it is also one that will require a long-term effort. We hope that this effort will advance still further the scholarship on the Tsinghua manuscripts, and we hope too that it will also contribute to scholarly cooperation between Chinese and foreign scholars. We sincerely hope both that all scholars will give enthusiastic aid and support to this project, and will provide criticism and suggestions.

For my part, I am extraordinarily pleased and honored to have the opportunity to work with Shaughnessy and his team to undertake this English translation. As the first volume of the series becomes available to readers, I am happy to express my highest admiration and gratitude to Shaughnessy and the international team of translators he has assembled. I also express heartfelt thanks to Tsinghua University for its wholehearted support of this project, as well as to Tsinghua University Press and to all those friends whose hard work has made possible the publication of these English translations.

General Preface Ⅱ

Edward L. Shaughnessy

Early in 2006, rumors about an important new cache of ancient bamboo-slip manuscripts began to circulate on the Hong Kong antiques market. This was but the latest in a rash of antiquities coming on the market as a result of tomb robbing in China that began in the early 1990s. Reprehensible though tomb robbing is, robbing both the ancients of their dignity and also modern science of knowledge about the context from which the antiquities came, cultural organs within China, especially museums and universities, have taken it upon themselves to "rescue" and repatriate these products of traditional Chinese civilization. This has been especially true of bamboo-slip manuscripts, the writings on which are regarded as the highest expression of this civilization. Thus, in 2008, Tsinghua University of Beijing dispatched a small group of select scholars led by Li Xueqin 李學勤 (1933–2019), at the time universally acknowledged as the leading expert on all aspects of early Chinese cultural history, to go to Hong Kong to examine this new cache of manuscripts. According to an account by Liu Guozhong 劉國忠, now a member of Tsinghua University's Research and Conservation Center for Unearthed Texts (清華大學出土文獻研究與保護中心), once Li determined the slips to be authentic, the university moved quickly to arrange for their purchase.[1]

The bamboo slips, totaling nearly 2,500 slips or fragments of slips in all, arrived at Tsinghua University in July 2008. When the plastic wrapping in

---

1   Liu Guozhong, *Introduction to the Tsinghua Bamboo-Strip Manuscripts,* tr. Christopher J. Foster and William N. French (Leiden: Brill, 2016), 51–54. Tsinghua University claimed that the slips had been donated by an anonymous alumnus.

which the slips had been transported to Beijing was opened, scholars there discovered that a form of mold was developing on many of them. They immediately commenced intensive efforts to preserve the slips; these efforts, which required almost three months, were ultimately successful.[2] A preliminary inventory conducted during the preservation work identified 2,388 slips or fragments bearing writing, to which unique serial numbers were assigned. Subsequent work with the slips turned up writing on another hundred or so pieces, such that the total number of fragments bearing writing is close to 2,500. Also at this time, pieces without writing were sent to the Peking University Accelerator Mass Spectrometry (AMS) Laboratory for ^{14}C testing; the result was a date of 305 BCE ± 30 years. This matched well the evaluation of both Tsinghua researchers and also a group of China's senior-most paleographers, who were brought to Beijing to evaluate the slips in October of 2008; they agreed that the calligraphy and format of the slips is consistent with other slips known to date to the end of the Middle Warring States period or the beginning of the Late Warring States period, i.e., roughly 300 BCE. The final step in the preservation work was the making of high-resolution photographs of the slips; thereafter, it was from these photographs that the Tsinghua editorial team would work, while the original slips were sealed away in a climate-controlled environment submerged in trays of distilled water.[3]

---

2 For a detailed narrative of this preservation work, see Liu, *Introduction to the Tsinghua Bamboo-Strip Manuscripts*, 54–69. Liu was one of three researchers tasked by Tsinghua to work with the original slips, and he kept a detailed diary of all of their efforts, so his account should be authoritative.

3 The tomb from which the slips came was almost certainly filled with water, providing an anaerobic environment conducive to the preservation of organic material such as bamboo. It is for this reason that slips such as these, once unearthed, are generally preserved submerged in water.

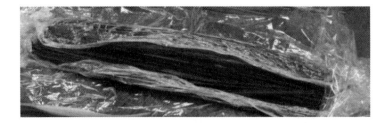

Tsinghua Slips arrive at Tsinghua University; 15 July 2008

Tsinghua Slips before and after being returned to natural color

Tsinghua Slips in trays of distilled water

During the preservation and photographic work, the editorial team was able to arrive at some preliminary understanding of the content of the slips. Nevertheless, it was only after that work was completed that editorial work could begin in earnest. The first order of business was to identify how many different discrete texts there were, and which slips belonged to which texts. Because the slips had been robbed from a tomb, when they arrived at Tsinghua University, they had become largely separated from their original context. Thus, the identification of texts depended on the sort of typological analysis that archaeologists usually employ: placing slips of similar length and width together; noting the locations of the straps that were used to bind them together (sometimes leaving a distinct mark on the bamboo, and usually marked as well by small notches on the side of the bamboo intended to keep the strap from sliding up and down on the slip); identifying paratextual features of the slips (placement of text above or below the top and bottom binding strap, the presence or absence of numbers indicating the sequence of the slips, the use and types of punctuation, as well as features on the reverse side of the slips including the presence or absence of titles, diagonal slash marks presumably made during the preparation of the slips, and occasional "ghost" characters left imprinted from other slips); and examination of the calligraphy (assuming that a discrete text would feature a consistent calligraphic hand). After placing slips into groups of these features, the editors turned finally to their content. In this regard, they were often able to rely on comparisons with received literature to identify text that continued from one slip to another. Often of crucial importance in this respect was sequence numbers found on the bottom or reverse side of numerous slips, a feature seen for the first time with the Tsinghua manuscripts.

In the course of this editorial work, the original approximately 2,500 fragments of slips have been rejoined into a total of 1,811 discrete slips, which the editors have further grouped into seventy-five different texts. The texts run the gamut from chapters of the *Shang shu* 尚書 *Exalted Scriptures* (also known as the *Classic of Documents*) and the *Yi Zhou shu* 逸周書 *Leftover Zhou Scriptures* to an anecdotal history of China from the early

Western Zhou (c. eleventh century BCE) to the early fourth century BCE and a chronicle of the capitals of the state of Chu 楚, from collections of poetry to an extensive handbook on milfoil divination, and include a great many discrete texts concerning the political philosophy of China's classical age, the Spring and Autumn and Warring States periods. The first volume, which includes nine of these texts, was published toward the end of 2010. Since then, the Tsinghua University Research and Conservation Center for Unearthed Texts has published the manuscripts at the rate of one volume per year, under the general title *Qinghua daxue cang Zhanguo zhujian* 清華大學藏戰國竹簡 *Warring States Bamboo Slips in the Collection of Tsinghua University*.[4] These are deluxe editions with full color photographs, exacting transcriptions, careful annotations, complete concordances for each volume, and tables of information regarding the physical features of each slip. Each new publication has generated great scholarly interest both in China and also abroad.

As just one indication of the great interest that the Tsinghua manuscripts hold, the first volume includes two texts that correspond to chapters of the *Shang shu*. These have conclusively resolved the greatest outstanding debate in the entire history of Chinese textual criticism: the question of the authenticity of the so-called *guwen* 古文 or "ancient script" chapters of that text. One of these manuscripts is entitled by the editors **Yin gao* 尹誥 *Announcement of Yin*.[5] It corresponds with the chapter "Xian you yi de"

---

4   For Volume One, see Li Xueqin 李學勤 ed.-in-chief, Qinghua daxue Chutu wenxian yanjiu yu baohu zhongxin 清華大學出土文獻研究與保護中心 ed., *Qinghua daxue cang Zhanguo zhujian (yi)* 清華大學藏戰國竹簡（壹）(Shanghai: Zhong Xi shuju, 2010).

5   *Qinghua daxue cang Zhanguo zhujian (yi)*, 4–5 (full-size photographs), 41–43 (double-size photographs), 132–134 (transcription and notes). In a similar manner, Volume Three of the Tsinghua manuscripts contains a three-part text, each part of which is self-titled as *Fu Yue zhi ming* 傅說之命 *The Command of Fu Yue*. This text corresponds with "Yue ming" 說命 "Command of Yue" chapter found in the *guwen Shang shu*. However, the contents of the Tsinghua *Fu Yue zhi ming* are completely different from the "Yue ming" chapter, again showing the spurious nature of the latter. See Li Xueqin 李學勤 ed.-in-chief, Qinghua daxue Chutu wenxian yanjiu yu baohu zhongxin 清華大學出土文獻研究與保護中心 ed., *Qinghua daxue cang Zhanguo zhujian (san)* 清華大學藏戰國竹簡（叁）(Shanghai: Zhong Xi shuju, 2012), 2–7 (full-size photographs), 29–51 (double-size photographs), 121–131 (transcription and notes).

咸有一德 "Both Had a Singular Virtue" found only in the *guwen* version of the *Shang shu*. A passage from the text is also quoted in the classic *Li ji* 禮記 *Record of Ritual*, where it is referred to as "Yin ji" 尹吉 (though *ji* 吉 "auspicious" is clearly a mistake for the graphically similar *gao* 告 "to announce" [itself an abbreviated form of the word *gao* 誥 "announcement"]).[6] This *Li ji* quotation is included in the *guwen Shang shu* version of the text, and is found also in the Tsinghua manuscript. However, everything else in the Tsinghua manuscript is completely different from the *guwen Shang shu* text. This seems to confirm that the *guwen Shang shu* text was fabricated, probably in the early fourth century CE, on the basis of this one early quotation and other materials then circulating, a hypothesis first proposed almost three hundred years ago.[7] The Tsinghua manuscript, on the other hand, represents the authentic early version of this chapter. The resolution of this question alone would serve to make the Tsinghua manuscripts one of the great discoveries of Chinese history. But there is much, much more as well. The panel of experts convened by Tsinghua University to examine the manuscripts in October 2008 was not exaggerating in the least when it said this about them:

> These Warring States bamboo slips are tremendously valuable
> historical artifacts, whose contents speak to the very core of

---

6   *Li ji zhengyi* 禮記正義, in *Shisan jing zhushu* 十三經注疏 (Beijing: Zhonghua shuju, 1980), 55 ("Zi yi" 緇衣), 420 (1648). It should be noted that there are two different early manuscripts of this text, and both of them write the name of the text quoted as *Yin gao* 尹誥; see Jingmen shi bowuguan 荊門市博物館 ed., *Guodian Chu mu zhujian* 郭店楚墓竹簡 (Beijing: Wenwu chubanshe, 1998), 17 (photograph), 129 (transcription); Ma Chengyuan 馬承源 ed.-in-chief, *Shanghai bowuguan cang Zhanguo Chu zhushu (yi)* 上海博物館藏戰國楚竹書（一）(Shanghai: Shanghai Guji chubanshe, 2001), 46 (photograph), 176 (transcription).

7   The first detailed presentation of this hypothesis was made by Yan Ruoqu 閻若璩 (1636–1704) in his *Shang shu guwen shuzheng* 尚書古文疏證, in *Huang Qing jingjie xubian* 皇清經解續編 (Jiangyin: Nanjing shuyuan, 1888), vols. 6–10. For Western-language studies of the issue, see Paul Pelliot, "Le *Chou King* en caractères anciens et le *Chang Chou che wen*," *Mémoires concernant l'Asie Orientale* 2 (1916): 123–177; Benjamin Elman, "Philosophy (*I-Li*) versus Philology (*K'ao-cheng*): The *Jen-hsin tao-hsin* Debate," *T'oung Pao* 2nd ser. 69.4–5 (1983): 175–222.

traditional Chinese culture. This is an unprecedented discovery, one which will inevitably attract the attention of scholars both here and abroad. It promises to have a lasting impact on many different disciplines, including but not limited to Chinese history, archaeology, paleography and philology.[8]

Tsinghua University established the Tsinghua University Research and Conservation Center for Unearthed Texts to study and preserve these manuscripts. Its first director was Li Xueqin. While the Center has very admirably fulfilled these responsibilities, in his Foreword to Liu Guozhong's *Introduction to the Tsinghua Bamboo-Strip Manuscripts*, Professor Li stressed that the further study of the manuscripts requires a collective endeavor.

> The significance of the Tsinghua slips cannot be overstated. It has fallen on us to preserve, edit, and eventually publish these manuscripts; what exciting research may come from these efforts is a question that must be answered in turn by the entire academic community.[9]

Liu Guozhong himself returned to this point in the conclusion to his work:

> The content of the Tsinghua slips can be very difficult to decipher. These are not manuscripts that can be explicated by only a handful of people over a short duration of study, but rather any comprehensive understanding of this collection will require careful analysis that spans a much longer period of time. Research on bamboo and silk manuscripts is at times very pragmatic and detail-oriented. Piecing together one slip, or one

---

8 "Report on Authentication" (鑒定意見), quoted at Liu, *Introduction to the Tsinghua Bamboo-Strip Manuscripts*, 72.
9 *Ibid.*, xii.

fragment of silk sheet, interpreting just one character or one sentence — each of these tasks requires much time and effort. Publication of the first volume of the Tsinghua slips was only possible due to the combined efforts of many scholars, who put much care and research into this project already. However, for this reason, publication of our editing report should mark only the first stage of research on the Tsinghua slips. Really it is only just the beginning. We hope that now many more scholars will conduct research on these remarkable artifacts, that you will join our team and help to bring study of the Tsinghua slips to a whole new level.[10]

It is in this spirit that early in the year 2020, the Research and Conservation Center for Unearthed Texts of Tsinghua University organized two separate projects to extend still further the research on these manuscripts. The first project, undertaken by scholars at Tsinghua University, is to produce "collated interpretations" (*jiaoshi* 校釋) volumes devoted to one or a group of related individual texts, summarizing scholarship on the texts published (largely, though not exclusively, in Chinese) in the years since their original publication; these volumes will not feature the same groupings of texts as the original publication *Tsinghua daxue cang Zhanguo zhujian*, but rather will group the texts based on various relationships (whether of content or codicology).[11] We expect this project to be complete in eighteen volumes. The second project is to produce English-language translations and studies of the manuscripts. These translations will be produced by a team of Western translators, the translator of each volume hand picked for their expertise with the contents of that volume. Each of these volumes of translation will mirror the "collated interpretations" volumes in terms of content, though the translations will not necessarily reflect the interpretations of the Tsing-

---

10 *Ibid.*, 208–209.
11 Huang Dekuan 黃德寬 ed.-in-chief, *Qinghua daxue cang Zhanguo zhujian jiaoshi* 清華大學藏戰國竹簡校釋 (Beijing: Shangwu yinshuguan, forthcoming).

hua editors, either in the original volumes or in the "collated interpretations" volumes. While the different contents of the different volumes will require somewhat different approaches, each volume will feature a general introduction placing the contents of the volume in their scholarly context, followed by carefully annotated translations of the individual text or texts. Each text will also be provided with a brief introduction discussing its significance, and will also feature translations of related texts from China's traditional literature when relevant. These volumes will be the work of the individual translator responsible for the volume, and will appear under his or her name.

In short, through the international collaboration of these two teams of scholars, and with the active support of the Tsinghua University Press, we look forward to sharing these Tsinghua Manuscripts with readers throughout the world. In closing, it is fitting to echo the sentiment of Liu Guozhong quoted above: "We hope that now many more scholars will conduct research on these remarkable artifacts, that you will join our team and help to bring study of the Tsinghua slips to a whole new level."

A Note on the Authenticity of the Tsinghua Manuscripts and the Ethics of Preserving Looted Cultural Artifacts

The publication of each successive volume of *Qinghua daxue cang Zhanguo zhujian* 清華大學藏戰國竹簡 *Warring States Bamboo Slips in the Collection of Tsinghua University* has demonstrated anew the conclusion reached by the panel of experts convened in October 2008 to evaluate the value of the manuscripts: "These Warring States bamboo slips are tremendously valuable historical artifacts, whose contents speak to the very core of traditional Chinese culture." Nevertheless, it cannot be denied that the value of the manuscripts is diminished by virtue of their having been robbed from some unknown tomb and then smuggled onto the antique market, with any information of either their provenience or provenance being unknown. Doubts have been expressed both in China and abroad about other collections of looted manuscripts, such as those of the Shanghai Museum and

Peking University,[12] though these have been met both in China and abroad by extensive discussions of authentication techniques.[13] With respect to the Tsinghua manuscripts, although as noted above Tsinghua University sent pieces of bamboo without writing to the Peking University Accelerator Mass Spectrometry (AMS) Laboratory for ^{14}C testing, and also invited a group of China's senior-most paleographers to authenticate the slips, both sorts of tests agreeing that the slips date to roughly 300 BCE, the publication of the first volume was also met by some doubts about the authenticity of the manuscripts.[14] As the volumes of *Qinghua daxue cang Zhanguo zhujian* have been published, there has developed a consensus among other scholars in China that the manuscripts are authentic, and do indeed date to the Warring States period.

Artifactual and archaeological evidence in support of the authenticity of the Tsinghua manuscripts has subsequently become available, corroborating the scientific and paleographic analyses. In 2010, Sun Peiyang 孫沛陽, working with the Peking University Han slips, discovered for the first time lines cut into the verso side of the slips, a feature that was subsequently found also on archaeologically excavated slips, such as those at Guodian 郭

---

12 For doubts regarding the Shanghai Museum manuscripts, see Xing Wen, "New Light on the *Li Ji* 禮記: The *Li Ji* and the Related Warring States period Guodian Bamboo Manuscripts," *Early China* 37 (2014): 522–523; and for those about the Peking University manuscripts, see Xing Wen 邢文, "Beida jian *Laozi* bianwei" 北大簡《老子》辨偽, *Guangming ribao* 光明日報, 8 August 2016; "Bianzheng zhi mei yu sandian toushi — Beida jian *Laozi* zai bianwei" 辯證之美與散點透視——北大簡《老子》再辨偽, *Guangming ribao*, 12 September 12 2016.

13 See Hu Pingsheng 胡平生, "Lun jianbo bianwei yu liushi jiandu qiangjiu" 論簡帛辨偽與流失簡牘搶救, *Chutu wenxian yanjiu* 出土文獻研究 9 (2010), 76–108; Christopher J. Foster, "Introduction to the Peking University Han Bamboo Strips: On the Authentication and Study of Purchased Manuscripts," *Early China* 40 (2017): 167–239.

14 Jiang Guanghui 姜廣輝, "'Qinghua jian' jianding keneng yao jingli yige changqi guocheng — Zai tan dui *Bao xun* pian de yiwen" "清華簡" 鑒定可能要經歷一個長期過程——再談對《保訓》篇的疑問, *Guangming ribao* 光明日報, 8 June 2009; Jiang Guanghui, "*Bao xun* yiwei xinzheng wuze"《保訓》疑偽新證五則, *Zhongguo zhexueshi* 中國哲學史 2010.3, 30–34; Jiang Guanghui, Fu Zan 付贊 and Qiu Mengyan 邱夢燕, "Qinghua jian *Qi ye* wei weizuo kao" 清華簡《耆夜》為偽作考, *Gugong bowuyuan yuankan* 故宮博物院院刊 4.168 (2013), 86–94; Jiang Guanghui, with Fu Zan, "Qinghua jian *Yin gao* xian yi" 清華簡《尹誥》獻疑, *Hunan daxue xuebao (shehui kexue ban)* 湖南大學學報（社會科學版）28.3 (2014), 109–114.

店.[15] While the exact function of these lines is still a topic of discussion, it is generally agreed that the lines were made in antiquity in the production of slips from the original bamboo stems. These verso lines are also found on the Tsinghua slips, and since they entered into the collection of Tsinghua University in 2008, two years before Sun Peiyang's discovery, this constitutes almost incontrovertible artifactual evidence for the authenticity of the slips.[16]

Even better evidence of the authenticity of the Tsinghua slips has come from a subsequent archaeological discovery. On 30 October 2020, archaeologists at the Jingzhou Museum 荊州博物館 excavated a tomb, numbered M46, at the Zaolinpu 棗林鋪 Paper Factory, with at least 535 inscribed bamboo slips in it. These slips can be divided into five different types, with nine discrete texts. One of these, which the excavators have given the title *Wu Wang Fuchai qi shi fa Yue* 吳王夫差起師伐越 *Fuchai, King of Wu, Raised Troops and Attacked Yue* matches very closely the Tsinghua manuscript entitled by the Tsinghua editors *Yue Gong qi shi* 越公其事 *May the Lord of Yue Attend*.[17] These are both lengthy texts, the Tsinghua version being written on seventy-five slips and the Zaolinpu version written on seventy-nine slips. While there are a number of variants between the two manuscripts, there is no doubt that they are one and the same text. Since the Tsinghua *Yue Gong qi shi* manuscript was published prior to the excavation of the Zaolinpu manuscript, the authenticity of which is beyond question, it could not have been copied from that text and so it too is almost surely authentic.[18] And since the slips of this one Tsinghua manuscript were embedded in

---

15 Sun Peiyang 孫沛陽, "Jiance bei hua xian chutan" 簡冊背劃綫初探, *Chutu wenxian yu guwenzi yanjiu* 出土文獻與古文字研究 4 (2011), 449–462. See, too, Li Tianhong 李天虹, "Hubei chutu Chu jian (wuzhong) geshi chuxi" 湖北出土楚簡（五種）格式初析, *Jiang Han kaogu* 江漢考古 2011.4, 102–106.

16 See Jia Lianxiang 賈連翔, *Zhanguo zhushu xingzhi ji xiangguan wenti yanjiu: Yi Qinghua Daxue cang Zhanguo zhujian wei zhongxin* 戰國竹書形制及相關問題研究——以清華大學藏戰國竹簡為中心 (Shanghai: Zhong Xi shuju, 2015), esp. 82–102.

17 See Zhao Xiaobin 趙曉斌, "Jingzhou Zaozhi jian *Wu Wang Fuchai qi shi fa Yue* yu Qinghua jian *Yue Gong qi shi*" 荊州棗紙簡《吳王夫差起師伐越》與清華簡《越公其事》, in *Qinghua Zhanguo Chujian Guoji xueshu yantaohui lunwenji* 清華戰國楚簡國際學術研討會論文集, Beijing, November 2021, 6–11.

18 It is interesting to note that the Zaolinpu text shows that the title given the Tsinghua text

mud together with the other slips when they arrived at Tsinghua University in 2008, it furthermore stands to reason that they too are authentic.

In addition to questions about the authenticity of the Tsinghua manuscripts, other scholars have raised questions about the ethics of working with looted materials. For instance, Paul R. Goldin has argued "when a looted artifact is repatriated by being purchased at great cost, the process only encourages more looting in the future,"[19] and he has suggested that scholars ought to refuse to study such materials. Scholars at the Research and Conservation Center for Unearthed Texts of Tsinghua University join scholars throughout China and abroad in decrying the scourge of tomb-robbing that has plagued the country for the last three decades. But they view the work they do to preserve, edit, and publish the manuscripts in their collection as both a scholarly and a moral responsibility. What is more, it is entirely consistent with the United Nations "Convention on the Means of Prohibiting and Preventing the Illicit Import, Export and Transfer of Ownership of Cultural Property" of 1970, Article 7 of which states:

> The States Parties to this Convention undertake:
>
> (a) To take the necessary measures, consistent with national legislation, to prevent museums and similar institutions within their territories from acquiring cultural property originating in another State Party which has been illegally exported after entry into force of this Convention, in the States concerned. Whenever possible, to inform a State of origin Party to this

---

by the Tsinghua editors was based on a faulty understanding of the final slip of that manuscript. The last four characters of the text are "*yue gong qi shi*" 越公其事, which the Tsinghua editors interpreted as the title, even though these characters followed immediately after the preceding phrase, and were not separated by a blank space as usually seen with titles. The Zaolinpu manuscript also writes "*yue gong qi shi ye*" 越公其事也 together-er with the preceding text, and what is more follows it with a section ending ∟ mark. See Zhao Xiaobin, "Jingzhou Zaozhi jian *Wu Wang Fuchai qi shi fa Yue* yu Qinghua jian *Yue Gong qi shi*," 11.

19 Paul R. Goldin, "*Heng Xian* and the Problem of Studying Looted Artifacts," *Dao* 12.2 (2013), 158.

Convention of an offer of such cultural property illegally removed from that State after the entry into force of this Convention in both States;

(b) (i) to prohibit the import of cultural property stolen from a museum or a religious or secular public monument or similar institution in another State Party to this Convention after the entry into force of this Convention for the States concerned, provided that such property is documented as appertaining to the inventory of that institution;

(ii) at the request of the State Party of origin, to take appropriate steps to recover and return any such cultural property imported after the entry into force of this Convention in both States concerned, provided, however, that the requesting State shall pay just compensation to an innocent purchaser or to a person who has valid title to that property. Requests for recovery and return shall be made through diplomatic offices. The requesting Party shall furnish, at its expense, the documentation and other evidence necessary to establish its claim for recovery and return. The Parties shall impose no customs duties or other charges upon cultural property returned pursuant to this Article. All expenses incident to the return and delivery of the cultural property shall be borne by the requesting Party.[20]

This international convention, to which China is a party, is concerned exclusively with the exportation of cultural artifacts beyond national boundaries. Since the Tsinghua manuscripts originated in China, it is the responsibility of relevant Chinese cultural institutions—such as Tsinghua

---

20 "Convention on the Means of Prohibiting and Preventing the Illicit Import, Export and Transfer of Ownership of Cultural Property of 1970," at: https://www.unesco.org/en/legal-affairs/convention-means-prohibiting-and-preventing-illicit-import-export-and-transfer-ownership-cultural

University—to make every effort to ensure that they do not leave the country. Within the country of origin, cultural and scholarly organizations have the right—and the responsibility—to preserve and make these manuscripts available to the broader public. It is this spirit that motivates the various publication projects of Tsinghua University's Research and Conservation Center for Unearthed Texts, very much including this series *The Tsinghua University Warring States Bamboo Manuscripts.*

Conventions

Manuscripts are based on Li Xueqin 李學勤 ed.-in-chief, Qinghua daxue Chutu wenxian yanjiu yu baohu zhongxin 清華大學出土文獻研究與保護中心 ed., *Qinghua daxue cang Zhanguo zhujian* 清華大學藏戰國竹簡, Vols. 1–8 (Shanghai: Zhong Xi shuju, 2010–2018) and Huang Dekuan 黄德寬 ed.-in-chief, Qinghua daxue Chutu wenxian yanjiu yu baohu zhongxin 清華大學出土文獻研究與保護中心 ed., *Qinghua daxue cang Zhanguo zhujian* 清華大學藏戰國竹簡, Vols. 9–15 (Shanghai: Zhong Xi shuju, 2019–) as the publication of record. Titles of texts are generally given as in that publication, with the following qualification: when a title is specified on the manuscript, it is rendered as written; when no title is specified on the manuscript, but has been assigned by the modern editors, the title is given as they have it, but preceded with an asterisk (*) to indicate this difference.

The contents of individual volumes follow those of Huang Dekuan 黄德寬 ed.-in-chief, *Qinghua daxue cang Zhanguo zhujian jiaoshi* 清華大學藏戰國竹簡校釋 (Beijing: Shangwu yinshuguan, forthcoming), hereafter "*Jiaoshi*," and do not necessarily follow the contents of the individual volumes of *Qinghua daxue cang Zhanguo zhujian*. These volumes have been reorganized to reflect conceptual coherence. When there is evidence that two or more manuscripts were originally bound together, whether published in a single volume of *Qinghua daxue cang Zhanguo zhujian* or not, they are kept together.

Individual volumes of this series are the work of the individual author credited on the title page, who is solely responsible for the contents. Nevertheless, all authors would like to express their gratitude to colleagues at Tsinghua University's Research and Conservation Center for Unearthed Texts, who have been most helpful in sharing their scholarship with us, and also to the authors of the other volumes in the series, who have graciously read and criticized the volumes in draft.

Volumes begin with two General Prefaces by the general editors, followed by a Preface by the author of the individual volume. This is followed in turn by an introductory chapter or chapters discussing general questions concerning the manuscript or manuscripts included in the volume. Each individual manuscript is presented in separate chapters, with the following contents:

A. An introduction that discusses codicological features of the manuscript in question: material features of the manuscript, including its calligraphy and relevant paratextual features.

B. A slip-by-slip transcription and annotated translation. These transcriptions and translations are presented in four registers:

1. Images of the individual graphs on a single bamboo slip, presented horizontally. These have been scanned from high-resolution photographs of the slips, with the background removed, and hand-processed to produce a black-and-white image. These have been prepared for the volumes by colleagues at the Research and Conservation Center for Unearthed Texts of Tsinghua University, to whom we express our heartfelt gratitude for the clarity brought about by this process.

2. Strict or literal transcriptions (generally called *yanshi liding* 嚴式隸定 in Chinese) of the individual graphs, in which each individual component is rendered into its *kaishu* 楷書 equivalent, generally in the same position within the character. In almost all cases, these transcriptions follow those given in *Qinghua daxue*

cang Zhanguo zhujian. This transcription includes only punctuation that is explicit on the manuscript. Other conventions in it are as follows:

a) □ indicates a single missing graph

b) ▨ indicates an indeterminate number of missing graphs

c) punctuation seen on the manuscript is reflected with formal symbols

   (1) duplication marks, whether indicative of the standard ligature (*hewen hao* 合文號) or repetition (*chongwen hao* 重文號) marks, are given with subscript equals sign ($_=$)

   (2) heavy black squares or rectangles in the text, which seem to serve to indicate a break in the text or emphasis, are rendered formulaically as ■, ▬ or ▭ as appropriate

   (3) the 乙-shaped mark routinely used to mark the end of a section or end of a text is given as ⬧

3. Interpretive transcriptions (generally called *kuanshi liding* 寬式隸定 or *podu* 破讀 in Chinese), in which a graph of the manuscript is rendered with a corresponding modern Chinese character (written in standard Chinese characters [*fantizi* 繁體字]). In addition, this transcription includes modern punctuation (according to standard Chinese punctuation) indicating the author's understanding of the grammar. At the end of this line of transcription is given the number of the slip, in Chinese characters inside subscript square brackets ($_{[—]}$). Other conventions are as follows:

a) □ indicates a single missing graph

b) ▨ indicates an indeterminate number of missing graphs

24

c) 〔〕 indicates a missing graph or graphs that can be restored on the basis of context

d) , ; : ? ! are used as in English punctuation

e) 、 (called *dunhao* 頓號 in Chinese) separates items in lists

f) 。 represents a period (.)

g) " " indicates direct quotation (like quotation marks [" "] in English)

4. An annotated English translation. Note numbers are given to the English text whether the note concerns matters of transcription or of translation. At the end of this line of translation is given the number of the slip, in Arabic numerals inside subscript square brackets ($_{[1]}$). Some general comments concerning the translations seem warranted.

a) Every effort has been made to translate and not just to paraphrase the text, though without sacrificing intelligibility in English. Wording that is missing because of a break in the bamboo slip is indicated by two dots (..) for a single missing character (corresponding to □ in the Chinese transcription) or by three dots (…) for an indeterminate number of graphs (corresponding to ☑ in the Chinese transcription). Wording that is missing because of a break in the slip or that is otherwise illegible, but which can be restored on the basis of context is placed inside square brackets ([ ]). Wording that is added to make the meaning clear or to supply added information is placed inside parentheses (( )), though such additions are used only when essential.

b) The annotations are explanatory, but not exhaustive. In general, translations consistent with the explanation given in *Qinghua daxue cang Zhanguo zhujian* are not noted. Translations that differ and which draw on other scholarship, whether formally published or available on the internet, generally note either the earliest study to present the explanation or the most definitively argued study and explain why it has been adopted. Full bibliographic citations are provided at the first mention of any scholarship within a single chapter; thereafter, within that chapter citation is by author, an abbreviated title, and page number. For scholarship found on the internet, the url and date of posting, if available, is given; it is often not possible to provide page numbers for internet citations. Reconstructions of archaic pronunciation are generally given as in Axel Schuessler, *Minimal Old Chinese and Later Han Chinese: A Companion to* Grammata Serica Recensa (Honolulu: University of Hawai'i Press, 2009), with the addition of the rhyme group as typically given in Chinese scholarship.

C. The complete text, first in Chinese (according to the interpretive transcription) and then in English, presented in paragraph form to show the underlying structure of the text. These presentations include the slip numbers ($_{[–]}$ in the Chinese text, and $_{[1]}$ in the English text) so as to facilitate comparison with the annotated slip-by-slip transcription and translation. This is generally unannotated.

D. Any additional material that might bear on the understanding of the manuscript.

Introduction to Volume Three

The present book is a critical translation and study of six manuscripts published in three different volumes of the *Qinghua daxue cang Zhanguo zhujian* 清華大學藏戰國竹簡: *Chi jiu zhi ji Tang zhi wu* 赤鳩之集湯之屋 *A Red Pigeon's Alighting on Tang's Hut* (hereafter *Chi jiu*) in Volume 3, **Yin zhi* 尹至 **Yin's Arrival* and **Yin gao* 尹誥 **Yin's Announcement* in Volume 1, as well as **Tang zai Chimen* 湯在啻門 **Tang at the Gate of the Thearch* (hereafter **Chimen*), **Tang chu yu Tangqiu* 湯處於湯丘 **Tang Resided at Tang Hill* (hereafter **Tangqiu*), and *Yin Gaozong wen yu San Shou* 殷高宗問於三壽 *The High Ancestor of Yin Asked the Three Long-Lived Ones* (hereafter *Yin gaozong*) in Volume 5. All of these manuscripts are about legendary Shang kings and their ministers. Among them, the first five concern the exemplary relationship between Tang, the first king of Shang, and his minister Yi Yin. Since their publication, scholars have been accustomed to treating them as a single group known as the "Five Yi Yin Texts/Manuscripts." The last one, *Yin gaozong*, contains dialogues between the High Ancestor of Yin (namely, the much-admired King Wu Ding 武丁 of Shang) and the half-mythological Ancestor Peng (Pengzu 彭祖) known for his longevity. These texts were most likely composed during the Warring States period (403–221 BCE), a time when anecdotes about Xia, Shang, and Western Zhou kings and their ministers proliferated and diversified in the hands of philosophers and storytellers.

In addition to thematic similarity, some of these manuscripts were physically bound together. The Tsinghua editors already pointed out in the first publication that *Yin zhi* and *Yin gao* in Volume 1 constituted a single bundle of bamboo slips, and so did *Chimen* and *Tangqiu* in Volume 5. Later, it was found that *Chi jiu* was placed before *Yin zhi* and *Yin gao* in the same bundle (for more discussion, see Chapters 1 and 4). The order in which they appear in this book reflects the current consensus about their original arrangement, determined on the basis of physical and codicological features such as the length of bamboo slips, the number of notches cut for the binding straps, diagonal slash marks on the reverse sides of the slips, and so on. The table below summarizes the basic information of the manuscripts in this volume:

Title	Number of slips	Original title	Slips numbered	Slip length	No. of Notches
Chi jiu	15	Y	Y	45cm	3
Yin zhi	5	N	Y	45cm	3
Yin gao	4	N	Y	45cm	3
Chimen	21	N	N	44.5cm	3
Tangqiu	19	N	N	44.4cm	3
Yin gaozong	28	Y	Y	45cm	3

Close analysis of the calligraphy shows that the six manuscripts were copied by two scribes, who were also responsible for many other manuscripts in the Tsinghua corpus published to this day. In a series of articles, Li Songru 李松儒 gives a list of Tsinghua manuscripts copied by the two scribes:[1]

Scribe A:

- Manuscripts translated in this book: *Yin zhi*, *Yin gao*, *Chi jiu*, *Yin Gaozong*
- Other manuscripts in Tsinghua Volume 1: *Qi ye* 耆夜 *Toasting at

1 See Li Songru 李松儒, "Qinghua wu ziji yanjiu" 清華五字迹研究, *Jianbo* 簡帛 13 (2016): 79–89; "*Qinghua daxue cang Zhanguo zhujian* (liu) zhi *Guan Zhong* ziji yanjiu" 《清華大學藏戰國竹簡》(陸)之《管仲》字迹研究, *Shufa yanjiu* 書法研究 2016.4: 34–45; "Qinghua jian *Nai ming* de shuxie, zhizuo yu bianlian" 清華簡《廼命》的書寫、製作與編聯, *Chutu wenxian* 出土文獻 1 (2020): 75–81.

Qi, Zhou Wu Wang you ji Zhou Gong suo zi yi dai wang zhi zhi 周武王有疾周公所自以代王之志 *The Record of King Wu of Zhou Being Ill and the Duke of Zhou Using Himself to Substitute for the King*, and *Zhai Gong zhi gu ming* 祭公之顧命 *The Duke of Zhai's Retrospective Command*.

- Other manuscripts in Tsinghua Volume 3: *Fu Yue zhi ming* 傅敚之命 *The Command of Fu Yue, Zhou Gong zhi qinwu* 周公之琴舞 *The Duke of Zhou's Zither and Dance*, and *Rui Liangfu bi* 芮良夫毖 *Liangfu of Rui's Admonition*.

Scribe B
- Manuscripts translated in this book: *Chimen, *Tangqiu*
- Other manuscripts in Tsinghua Volume 6: *Guan Zhong* 管仲
- Other manuscripts in Tsinghua Volume 9: *Nai ming* 廼命 *Then Commanding* (1&2), and *Dao ci* 禱辭 *Prayers*.

This is an open-ended list subject to modification. Jia Lianxiang 賈連翔 has recently argued that *She ming* 攝命 *The Command to She* (originally Volume 8) and *Houfu* 厚父 (originally Volume 5) were also copied by scribe A. He divides scribe A's fourteen manuscripts into six sub-groups, claiming that the *Chi jiu* bundle and *Yin Gaozong* belong to the same group. Although *Yin Gaozong* is certainly not part of the *Chi jiu* bundle, some of their bamboo slips are similar in physical form.[2] If he is correct, then scribe A must have been very interested in classical documents concerning Shang and Western Zhou histories—all the manuscripts copied by him deal with such topics.

As can be expected, the publication of the Yi Yin manuscripts sparked a new round of interest in the Yi Yin lore.[3] To be sure, Yi Yin has always

---

2   See Jia Lianxiang, "Qinghua jian *Yin zhi* shushou ziji de kuoda ji xiangguan wenti tantao" 清華簡《尹至》書手字迹的擴大及相關問題探討, *Chutu wenxian zonghe yanjiu jikan* 出土文獻綜合研究輯刊 13 (2021): 79–100.

3   To give a few representative examples: Xia Dazhao 夏大兆 and Huang Dekuan 黃德寬, "Guanyu Qinghua jian *Yin zhi Yin gao* de xingcheng he xingzhi — cong Yi Yin chuanshuo

been of great interest to early China scholars. Prior to the discovery of the Tsinghua corpus, there were already numerous studies of Yi Yin's image in transmitted and excavated texts.[4] Here I shall briefly recapitulate the findings of these studies, plus a few observations of my own, as a background to the Yi Yin manuscripts translated in this book.[5] In oracle bone inscriptions, Yi Yin was highly respected and received sacrificial offerings together with the former Shang kings. His spirit was deemed extremely potent, for the Shang people beseeched him for rain and good harvests. However, he was never called by the official title "lesser servant" (*xiao chen* 小臣), even though there were plenty of other lesser servants doing all kinds of important or small jobs. The official duties of the lesser servants were diverse; they seem to have enjoyed a relatively high social status in the Shang but lost some of their status in the Western Zhou period.[6] In later times, *xiao chen* became almost a proper name for Yi Yin, as we shall see in *Chi jiu*, *Chimen, *Tangqiu, and many other Warring States texts, but it seems that Yi Yin's only official title in late Shang was Yin 尹 "Governor."

The earliest evidence that associates Yi Yin with the lesser servant is a set

---

zai xian Qin chuanshi he chutu wenxian zhong de liubian kaocha" 關於清華簡《尹至》《尹誥》的形成和性質——從伊尹傳説在先秦傳世和出土文獻中的流變考察, *Wenshi* 文史 2014.3: 213–239; Wen Haoyue 温皓月, "Chutu wenxian yu chuanshi wenxian zhi Yi Yin cailiao zhengli ji xiangguan wenti yanjiu" 出土文獻與傳世文獻之伊尹材料整理及相關問題研究 (M.A. thesis: Jilin University, 2016); Jing Lingling 荊鈴鈴, "Xian Qin shiqi Yi Yin xingxiang de yanbian" 先秦時期伊尹形象的演變, *Chutu wenxian* 出土文獻 11 (2017): 184–193; Xu Wenxian, *Qinghua jian Yi Yin wu pian yanjiu*, 3–18.

4 See, for example, Chen Mengjia 陳夢家, *Yinxu buci zongshu* 殷墟卜辭綜述 (Beijing: Zhonghua shuju, 1988), 362–364; Du Zhengsheng 杜正勝, *Gudai shehui yu guojia* 古代社會與國家 (Taipei: Yunchen wenhua, 1992), 258–269, 897–900; Mayvis L. Marubbio, "Yi Yin, Pious Rebel: A Study of the Founding Minister of the Shang in Early Chinese Texts" (Ph.D. dissertation, University of Minnesota, 2000); Chang Yuzhi 常玉芝, *Shangdai zongjiao jisi* 商代宗教祭祀 (Beijing: Zhongguo shehui kexue chubanshe, 2010), 399–406; Roel Sterckx, *Food, Sacrifice, and Sagehood in Early China* (Cambridge: Cambridge University Press, 2011), 65–75.

5 The *Yin gaozong* will not be addressed here but in the preface to Chapter 6.

6 Studies of the term "lesser servant" are too numerous to cite in all. For two important recent articles, see Wang Jinfeng 王進鋒, "Yin Shang shiqi de xiaochen" 殷商時期的小臣, *Gudai wenming* 古代文明 8.3 (2014): 35–53; Ondřej Škrabal 石安瑞, "Lun Xi Zhou jinwen zhong de xiaochen ji qi zhiwu yanbian" 論西周金文中的小臣及其職務演變, *Beida shixue* 北大史學 20 (2016): 1–23.

of Eastern Zhou bronze inscriptions discovered in 1123 and preserved in hand copies only. The patron of the bronze vessels was Shu Yi 叔夷, who said in the inscriptions that he moved from Song 宋 to Qi 齊 and served Duke Ling 靈 of Qi (r. 581–554 BCE). As a descendant of Duke Mu 穆 of Song (r. 728–720 BCE), he traced his ancestry back to Cheng Tang rather than the founding fathers of the Zhou and praised Yi Yin as Tang's assistant. This is the only mention of Yi Yin in bronze inscriptions of any period:

> 夷典其先舊及其高祖：赫赫成湯，有嚴在帝所，敷受天命，嗣伐夏后，敗厥靈師。伊小臣唯輔。咸有九州，處禹之土。
>
> I, Yi, model myself after the Former Old Ones and High Ancestor: Brilliant Cheng Tang, majestically dwelling upon the place of the Thearch, broadly received Heaven's Mandate and cut down and attacked the Lord of Xia, defeating his numinous army. Yi, the lesser servant, was his aide. (Tang) occupied the entire Nine Regions, residing in Yu's territories.[7]

Shu Yi called Yi Yin by his personal name Yi and regarded him as a lesser servant. It is not clear from his tone whether the lesser servant was still held to be respectable at the time. There is some evidence, however, that the status of this official position declined considerably in the Eastern Zhou. In a famous conspiracy that took place in 656 BCE, Duke Xian 獻 of Jin 晋 (r. 676–651 BCE) used a lesser servant to try poisonous food:

> 大子祭于曲沃，歸胙于公。公田，姬寘諸宮六日。公至，毒而獻之。公祭之地，地墳。與犬，犬斃。與小臣，小

---

7   These inscriptions are numbered from 272 to 285 in Zhongguo shehui kexue yuan kaogu yanjiusuo 中國社會科學院考古研究所 eds. *Yin Zhou jinwen jicheng (zengbu xiuding ben)* 殷周金文集成 (增補修訂本) (Beijing: Zhonghua shuju, 2007). For a translation of the whole inscription, see Constance A. Cook and Paul R. Goldin, *A Source Book of Ancient Chinese Bronze Inscriptions* (Berkeley: The Society for the Study of Early China, 2020), 258–264.

臣亦斃。

The heir apparent offered a sacrifice at Quwo and sent the sacrificial meat and wine back to the duke. The duke was hunting,
so Li Ji kept the offerings in the palace for six days. When the
duke arrived, she put poison in it and presented it to him. The
duke offered some of it to the ground and the earth boiled up.
He gave some to a dog, and the dog died. He gave some to a
lesser servant, and the lesser servant also died.[8]

My tentative observation is that two things happened in the period between
the Shang and Warring States: (1) Yi Yin came to be regarded as a lesser servant; (2) the social status of the lesser servant declined. Of course, we cannot reconstruct a historical process that spanned many centuries based on
a few textual references; however, if there is any truth to what I suggested,
then these developments paved the way for Yi Yin's new identities in Warring States theories of "exalting the worthy" (*shang xian* 尚賢), according
to which Yi Yin, as a lowly lesser servant, was discovered and promoted to
minister by Tang because of his worthiness alone.

As mentioned above, it was during the Warring States period that anecdotes about Yi Yin flourished and diversified. The main reason for this bur-
geoning interest was that newly emerged philosophers started to treat Yi Yin
as one of the stock examples of moral and political persuasion. When they
used Yi Yin to illustrate their arguments, they did not always feel obliged to
respect the historicity of the anecdotes, but freely modified or even fabricated them to suit their own purpose.[9] As a result, Yi Yin came to assume

---

8 Yang Bojun 楊伯峻, *Chunqiu Zuozhuan zhu (xiuding ben)* 春秋左傳注(修訂本) (Beijing: Zhonghua shuju, 1990), 296–297; Stephen Durrant, Wai-yee Li, and David Schaberg
   trans. *Zuo Tradition, Volume One* (Seattle: University of Washington Press, 2016), 268.
   Zuo zhuan 左傳 *Zuo Tradition* also mentions that Yi Yin exiled Tai Jia 太甲 but later
   still served as his minister (in the 21st year of Duke Xiang). See *Zuo Tradition, Volume
   Two*, 1086–1087.

9 For a collection of articles on the rhetorical function of anecdotes in early China, see Paul
   van Els and Sarah A. Queen eds. *Between History and Philosophy: Anecdotes in Early China*
   (Albany: SUNY Press, 2017). See also Paul van Els, "Tilting Vessels and Collapsing Walls:

several new identities as a spy, a cook, and a dowry escort. As a spy, he traveled back and forth between Xia and Shang to collect information for Tang. As a lowly cook or betrothal servant, he rose to prominence and proved that one's worthiness had nothing to do with birth or social rank. As a specialist in culinary arts, he used his expertise in blending flavors as an analogy for achieving political harmony. Some of these identities may have had earlier origins, but they became more elaborate, dramatic, and diversified in the Warring States period. All of them appear in the Five Yi Yin Texts: in *Yin zhi* he was a spy; in *Chi jiu* and *Tangqiu* he was a cook; in *Tangqiu* he was also a dowry escort. Notably, in the Tsinghua manuscripts, Yi Yin's new identities rarely have argumentative functions. He made a magical soup in *Chi jiu*, but rather than lecturing on the philosophy of cooking and its relevance to government, he angered Tang by stealing the soup on Tang's wife's orders. Likewise, in *Tangqiu*, he pleased Tang and the Shen girl with his culinary arts, but when Tang asked him whether such skills could be used to harmonize the people, he said nothing more than a "yes." In both cases, the Tsinghua manuscripts show no special interest in the philosophical analogy between cooking and statecraft.

In addition to fabricating Yi Yin anecdotes, Warring States philosophers also put words directly into his mouth and made him the putative author of their own doctrines. In such a case, Yi Yin was treated only as an impersonal voice of authority, and the teachings attributed to him need not have anything to do with the abovementioned identities. A case in point is the *Jiu zhu* 九主 *The Nine Lords* manuscript from Mawangdui tomb no. 3, in which Yi Yin instructed Tang how to wield power and control ministers.[10] The main part of *Jiu zhu* is a discussion of the nine ways of rulership,

---

On the Rhetorical Function of Anecdotes in Early Chinese Texts," *Extrême-Orient, Extrême-Occident* 34 (2012): 141–166.

10 Xu Baogui 徐寶貴 and Wu Kejing 鄔可晶 eds. *Jiu zhu* 九主, in Hunan sheng bowuguan 湖南省博物館 and Fudan daxue chutu wenxian yu guwenzi yanjiu zhongxin 復旦大學出土文獻與古文字研究中心 eds. *Changsha Mawangdui Hanmu jianbo jicheng* 長沙馬王堆漢墓簡帛集成 vol. 4 (Beijing: Zhonghua shuju, 2014), 97–106. For an English translation, see Robin D. S. Yates, *Five Lost Classics: Tao, Huanglao, and Yin-Yang in Han China* (New York: Ballantine Books, 1997), 180–191.

eight of which are bad examples to be avoided. The only successful example, known as the "model lord" (*fajun* 法君), follows the Way of Heaven and hides personal feelings and desires from the ministers, ruling over his ministers without being manipulated by them. *Jiu zhu* reads very much like a political treatise in the *Guanzi* 管子 or *Han Feizi* 韓非子 if we remove the two interlocutors Tang and Yi Yin.[11] Everything they say reflects the late Warring States political environment and mentality, and in principle could be put into the mouth of any other legendary king and minister. A similar example is the Tsinghua manuscript *Chimen*, which formulates a numerological cosmology through a dialogue between Tang and Yi Yin. The two figures are totally replaceable, for there is no narrative prelude that relates the dialogue to their personal background.

We have good reason to believe that Yi Yin's popularity in philosophical discourse started with Mohists. In the *Lun yu* 論語 *Analects*, Yi Yin appears only once (12.22) as a virtuous minister with no special significance, but *Mozi* 墨子 for the first time uses his anecdotes to illustrate the idea of "exalting the worthy." This brings us to an interesting but problematic hypothesis proposed by some scholars that the Tsinghua corpus reflects the influence of Mohism in the Warring States Chu cultural area.[12] According to this line of argument, the influence can be seen in the following respects: Mozi traveled to the state of Chu carrying many bamboo texts, and probably presented them to the Chu king (see Appendix C for more discussion). The prominence of Yi Yin in the corpus indicates a Mohist interest in historical examples of exalting the worthy. Many passages in the Tsinghua manuscripts have textual parallels in

---

11 Many scholars have pointed out that the doctrine of *Jiu zhu* is most similar to the "Qi chen qi zhu" 七臣七主 "The Seven Ministers and Seven Lords" chapter of *Guanzi*.

12 See Cheng Hao 程浩, "Gushu chengshu yanjiu zai fansi—yi Qinghua jian shu lei wenxian wei zhongxin" 古書成書研究再反思——以清華簡"書"類文獻為中心, *Lishi yanjiu* 歷史研究 2016.4: 132–143; Liu Chengqun 劉成群, "Qinghua jian yu Moxue guankui" 清華簡與墨學管窺, *Qinghua daxue xuebao (zhexue shehui kexue ban)* 清華大學學報(哲學社會科學版) 32.3 (2017): 131–138; Cheng Hao, "Cong 'mengfu' dao 'xingtan' xian-Qin shu lei wenxian de shengcheng, jieji yu liubian" 從"盟府"到"杏壇"：先秦"書"類文獻的生成、結集與流變, *Qinghua daxue xuebao (zhexue shehui kexue ban)* 清華大學學報(哲學社會科學版) 36.6 (2021): 85–106.

Mozi and *Lüshi chunqiu* 呂氏春秋 *The Annals of Lü Buwei*, and there is a demonstrable Mohist legacy in *Lüshi chunqiu* itself. Two manuscripts, **Zhi bang zhi dao* 治邦之道 **The Way of Governing the State* in Tsinghua Volume 8 and **Zhi zheng zhi dao* 治政之道 **The Way of Governance* in Tsinghua Volume 9, are even believed by the editors to be lost Mohist treatises.[13] Finally, the Tsinghua manuscripts that have been attributed to the *shu* 書 "scriptures" genre sometimes agree with quotations of *shu* in *Mozi* rather than in Confucian texts. Mozi was a serious student of *shu* and frequently quoted them, but his quotations were often different from the received *Shang shu* 尚書 *Exalted Scriptures* (also known as the *Classic of Documents*) as we have it. This seems to mean that there was a Mohist tradition of *shu* transmission independent of the Confucian one.[14] Both *Mozi* and the transmitted *Li ji* 禮記 *Records of Ritual* quote a line from the "Yue ming" 兌命 "The Command of Yue" chapter of *Shang shu*. The "Yue ming" chapter in the received canon is a forgery, but a self-titled manuscript *Fu Yue zhi ming* 傅說之命 *The Command of Fu Yue* published in Tsinghua Volume 3 is widely held to be the Warring States "Yue ming." Comparing the *Mozi* and *Li ji* quotations with the line in the *Fu Yue zhi ming* manuscript, scholars find that the *Mozi* quotation is much closer to the manuscript:

> *Fu Yue zhi ming*
>
> 且惟口起戎出好。惟干戈作疾。惟哀載病。惟干戈省厥身。
>
> And it is the mouth that gives rise to military conflict or brings forth good will. It is weapons that create illness. It is sadness that carries disease. It is weapons that cause one to inspect oneself.

---

13 The two manuscripts were published separately, but scholars later discovered that they were originally bound together. For a more detailed discussion of "Mohist doctrines" in the two manuscripts, see Ma Teng 馬騰, "Lun Qinghua jian *Zhi bang zhi dao* de Mojia sixiang" 論清華簡《治邦之道》的墨家思想, *Xiamen daxue xuebao (zhexue shehui kexue ban)* 廈門大學學報(哲學社會科學版) 2019.5: 63–73.

14 For a classic study of quotations of the classics in *Mozi*, see Luo Genze 羅根澤, "You *Mozi* yin jing tuice ru mo liang jia yu jingshu zhi guanxi" 由《墨子》引經推測儒墨兩家與經書之關係, in Luo Genze ed. *Gu shi bian* 古史辨, vol.4 (Shanghai: Shanghai guji chubanshe, 1982), 278–299.

Mozi, "Shang tong zhong" 尚同中 "Conforming Upwards B"
是以先王之書《術令》之道曰：「唯口出好興戎。」
Therefore, one of the Scriptures of the former kings, *Shu ling*,[15] says: "It is the mouth that brings forth good will or gives rise to military conflict."

Li ji, "Zi yi" 緇衣 "Black Jacket"
《兌命》曰：「惟口起羞。惟甲冑起兵。惟衣裳在笥。惟干戈省厥躬。」
Yue ming says: "It is the mouth that gives rise to insult. It is armor that gives rise to warfare. It is clothes in the chest. It is weapons that cause one to inspect oneself."

If the *Mozi* quotation matches *Fu Yue zhi ming* better, then the Tsinghua manuscript might have been a *shu* spread by Mohists to the state of Chu.

Interesting as it is, this argument is not backed up by any conclusive evidence. Most of the justifications offered above are tangential and controversial, not to mention the unwarranted assumption about the ideological uniformity of the entire Tsinghua corpus. Consider, for example, quotations of the four sentences in *Yue ming*. *Mozi* quotes only the first sentence, but *Li ji* quotes all of them. It is true that the *Mozi* quotation of the first sentence is closer to *Fu Yue zhi ming*; however, the same is true of the *Li ji* quotation of the last sentence. Had *Mozi* quoted all four sentences, the other three could also have been different. Moreover, the identification of *Zhi bang zhi dao* and *Zhi zheng zhi dao* as Mohist treatises is also highly controversial. Chen Minzhen 陳民鎮 has developed a strong argument against attributing them to Mohism, pointing out that the doctrines of the two manuscripts are more syncretic than homogenous.[16]

---

15 Sun Yirang 孫詒讓 (1848–1908) has pointed out that *Shu ling* 術令 (*Cə-lut–*riŋ-s) is nearly homophonous with *Yue ming* 兌命 (*l̥ot-s–*m-riŋ-s). See Sun Yirang, *Mozi jiangu* 墨子閒詁 (Beijing: Zhonghua shuju, 2001), 84.

16 Chen Minzhen, "Qinghua jian *Zhi zheng zhi dao Zhi bang zhi dao* sixiang xingzhi chutan" 清華簡《治政之道》《治邦之道》思想性質初探, *Qinghua daxue xuebao*

Development of the Yi Yin lore must have resulted in a large number of Yi Yin related texts. When Western Han scholars collected and edited them, they classified the varied Yi Yin texts into three general categories.[17] Two of them are found in the "Masters" (*zhuzi* 諸子) section of the "Yi wen zhi" 藝文志 "Records of Arts and Literature" chapter of *Han shu* 漢書 *Book of Han*: 51 chapters of *Yi Yin* 伊尹 in the "Daoism" subsection and 27 chapters of *Yi Yin shuo* 伊尹說 *Stories about Yi Yin* in the "Petty Stories" (*xiaoshuo* 小說) subsection. The last category does not appear as an independent entry in the "Yi wen zhi," but according to Sima Qian's 司馬遷 (145–c. 90 BCE) account in the "Yin benji" 殷本紀 "Basic Annals of the Yin" chapter of *Shi ji* 史記 *Records of the Scribe*, Yi Yin composed nine texts that came to be included in the *Shang shu* circulating in early Western Han. The titles of these *Shang shu* chapters given by Sima Qian are "Nü jiu" 女鳩, "Nü fang" 女房, "Xian you yi de" 咸有一德 "Both Had a Unifying Virtue," "Yi xun" 伊訓 "Yi's Instructions," "Si ming" 肆命 "Setting Out the Commands," "Cu hou" 徂后 "The Deceased Lord," and three chapters of "Tai Jia xun" 太甲訓 "Tai Jia's Instructions."[18] Combining these reports, we have a total of 87 texts either about Yi Yin or supposedly composed by him, but not a single one of them survived to this day through transmission.

Excavated manuscripts, on the other hand, tell us something about what these categories might have included. We do not know for sure whether the five Tsinghua manuscripts were seen by Liu Xiang 劉向 (77 BCE–6 BCE) when he edited the Yi Yin texts, but they certainly provide us with some clues as to the possible content of the lost anthologies of *Yi Yin* and *Stories about Yi Yin*.[19] The former must have included Yi Yin's philosophical

---

(zhexue shehui kexue ban) 清華大學學報 (哲學社會科學版) 35.1 (2020): 48–52.

17 For a more detailed analysis of these bibliographic categories, see Li Shoukui 李守奎, "Handai Yi Yin wenxian de fenlei yu Qinghua jian zhong Yi Yin zhupian de xingzhi" 漢代伊尹文獻的分類與清華簡中伊尹諸篇的性質, *Shenzhen daxue xuebao (renwen shehui kexue ban)* 深圳大學學報 (人文社會科學版) 32.3 (2015): 41–49.

18 Sima Qian, *Shi ji* (Beijing: Zhonghua shuju, 2014), 122–129.

19 Liu Xiang must have seen the **Jiu zhu* and included in it the *Yi Yin*, because his discussion of the "nine lords" is quoted in Pei Yin's 裴駰 (fl. 5th century) *Shi ji jijie* 史記集解. See Sima Qian, *Shi ji*, 122–124.

dialogues with Tang on the way of government, while the latter seems to have been miscellanies of Yi Yin stories featuring fantastic and occultist elements. Had Liu Xiang seen and classified the five Yi Yin manuscripts, he would have included *Chimen* as part of *Yi Yin* in "Daoism" and *Chi jiu* as part of *Stories about Yi Yin* in "Petty Stories," but found it difficult to find a place for *Tangqiu* in his taxonomy. As for *Yin zhi* and *Yin gao*, virtually everyone agrees that they originally belonged to the *shu* genre. *Yin gao* in particular has been identified as the "Xian you yi de" chapter mentioned by Sima Qian, because its first two sentences match ancient quotations of "Xian you yi de" in *Li ji* (see Chapter 3 for more discussion). Although four of the five Yi Yin Texts fall readily into the "Yi wen zhi" categories, we should bear in mind that these categories are Han inventions that may not do justice to the scope and complexity of pre-imperial texts. They reflect Han scholars' understanding of an earlier tradition, but are not necessarily intrinsic to that tradition itself. Ancient as they are, the Han categories should not be made our default methodological approach.

I hope this summary of the development of Yi Yin anecdotes and texts has provided at least the basic context for understanding the significance of the five Yi Yin manuscripts, which will be discussed in more detail in the individual prefaces to the following chapters. Many aspects of these manuscripts still remain puzzling, and will continue to remain so without further discoveries. I have tried my best to produce a readable translation that incorporates the most up-to-date paleographic scholarship and reflects the most widely accepted reading, or, in controversial cases, what I judge to be the most plausible reading. Since the primary purpose of this book is to make these mansucripts accessible to a wider academic community, I shall not provide detailed justification for my choice in every situation, unless I come up with a reading that has not been proposed before or deviates from the current consensus (which is rare). While technical discussions are still inevitable, I strive to be as concise and clear as possible.

Five of the six manuscripts in this book have been rendered into English before, and in the case of *Tang zai Chimen*, more than once. I have consulted and benefited from the following translations:

> Sarah Allan, "'When Red Pigeons Gathered on Tang's House': A Warring States Period Tale of Shamanic Possession and Building Construction set at the turn of the Xia and Shang Dynasties," *Journal of the Royal Asiatic Society* 25.3 (2015): 419–438.
>
> Dirk Meyer, "'Patterning Meaning': A Thick Description of the Tsinghua Manuscript '*Tāng zài Chì/Dì mén' (Tāng was at the Chì/Dì Gate) and What It Tells Us about Thought Production in Early China," *Bulletin of the Jao Tsung-I Academy of Sinology* 5 (2018): 139–167.
>
> Dirk Meyer, "'*Yǐn zhì' 尹至," in *Documentation and Argument in Early China* (Berlin: De Gruyter, 2021), 201–207.
>
> Joachim Gentz, "Literary Forms of Argument in the Tsinghua University Manuscript *Tang Zai Chimen*," in *Qinghua jian yanjiu* 3 (Shanghai: Zhong Xi shuju, 2019), 194–221.
>
> Paul Nicholas Vogt, "Consumption, Knowledge, and the Limits of the Body in the Xiaochen Texts," in *Qinghua jian yanjiu* 3 (Shanghai: Zhong Xi shuju, 2019), 237–260.
>
> Rudolf G. Wagner, "Out-put Driven Proposals in the Transcription, *shiwen* 釋文, of Chinese Excavated Texts: A Study of *Yin Gaozong wen yu san shou*," in *Qinghua jian yanjiu* 3 (Shanghai: Zhong Xi shuju, 2019), 298–327.

What sets this translation apart from the others is the degree to which it incorporates ongoing research into Chinese paleography, which frequently takes the form of piecemeal notes addressing individual characters or technical details. As these notes pile up, some scholars in China would compile them in handy volumes known as the "collected interpretations" (*jishi* 集釋). For the manuscripts translated in this book, there have been four such collections thus far (in chronological order):

Li Shuang 李爽, "Qinghua jian Yi Yin wu pian jishi" 清華簡 "伊尹"五篇集釋 (M.A. thesis: Jilin University, 2016).

Li Meichen 李美辰, "Qinghua jian Wuding lei wenxian jishi yu yanjiu" 清華簡武丁類文獻集釋與研究 (M.A. thesis: Jilin University, 2016).

Wang Jinfeng 王進鋒, "Qinghua jian (wu) *Yin Gaozong wen yu san shou, Tang chu yu Tangqiu, Tang zai Chimen* sanpian jishi" 清華簡(伍)《殷高宗問於三壽》《湯處於湯丘》《湯在啻門》三篇集釋, in Li Xueqin 李學勤, Sarah Allan, and Michael Lüdke eds. *Qinghua jian yanjiu* 清華簡研究 3 (Shanghai: Zhong Xi shuju, 2019), 392–497.

Xu Wenxian 許文獻, *Qinghua jian Yi Yin wu pian yanjiu* 清華簡伊尹五篇研究 (Taipei: Wanjuanlou, 2021).

All of them have been my sources of advice as I worked on this book. Although the compilers did a fantastic job and saved other scholars a great deal of time, some of these volumes are outdated, which is to be anticipated given the field's rapid progress. Every year, new manuscripts that could provide information on previously unidentified characters as well as new articles that improved solutions to long-standing problems are published. A case in point is the reading of a very difficult character on slip 1 of *Yin gao* (see note 120). Many scholars speculated and debated about its meaning, but the problem was not resolved until Shi Xiaoli's 石小力 2019 article that definitively closed the case. My major objective, however, is to extract the best information from the sea of (often laborious) philological studies, not to create yet another exhaustive *jishi* in English. Since the comprehensive *jishi* projects are non-selective and include random hypotheses in addition to sound arguments, even ardent readers may be put off by their enormous scope. I see it as my responsibility to sift through the multitude of ideas contained therein and present what I believe to be the most reasonable and insightful findings.

For Old Chinese reconstruction, I primarily rely on the 2014 version of the Baxter-Sagart system.[20] It is clearly outside the purview of this study to tackle disputes regarding their overall methodology and reconstructed items, and I am not equipped with the necessary expertise to do so. For the purpose of displaying rhyming patterns, however, the technical details of reconstruction are not essential as long as we know that word A and word B belong to the same rhyme category. Occasionally, I raise doubts about their reconstruction, particularly when phonology is crucial for identifying a phonetic loan (see, for example, note 195). Nevertheless, my discussion pertains only to individual cases and does not involve judgment of the system as a whole.

Many colleagues and friends have helped me tremendously with this project. I am deeply grateful to the Tsinghua manuscripts translation team: Edward L. Shaughnessy, Rens Krijgsman, Maddalena Poli, Jens Østergaard Petersen, Newell Ann Van Auken, Yegor Grebnev, Ondřej Škrabal, David Lebovitz, Adam Schwartz, Vincent Leung, Christopher Foster, Ethan Harkness, and Zhang Hanmo, from whose insightful comments I have learned enormously. I owe a debt of gratitude to members of the Research and Conservation Center for Unearthed Texts at Tsinghua, especially Huang Dekuan, Li Shoukui, Jia Lianxiang, Cheng Hao, and Ma Nan. I would also like to thank Huang Kuan-yun, Sam Goldstein, and David Hogue for reading and commenting on certain parts of my translation draft, as well as Yang Qiyu, Zhang Xinyu, and Zhang Ruixue for various kinds of help. This book could not have been completed without their generous support.

Finally, I wish to dedicate this book to my beloved grandparents, Cheng Xianyong 程顯庸 and Ji Fei 紀斐. I had always promised to dedicate my first book to them, but sadly, my grandpa passed away on October 6, 2021,

---

20 William H. Baxter and Laurent Sagart, *Old Chinese: A New Reconstruction* (Oxford: Oxford University Press, 2014). The list of reconstructed items is also available online at http://ocbaxtersagart.lsait.lsa.umich.edu/.

before its publication. On a brighter note, my grandma continues to be in good health, and she will be overjoyed to see my promise fulfilled.

Zhou Boqun 周博群
14 September, 2022
Hong Kong

Chapter One

Chi jiu zhi ji Tang zhi wu 赤鳩之集湯之屋
A Red Pigeon's Alighting on Tang's Hut

The Tsinghua manuscript of *Chi jiu zhi ji Tang zhi wu* (hereafter *Chi jiu*) was published in Volume 3 of *Qinghua daxue cang Zhanguo zhujian*. The manuscript was written on fifteen slips, which were originally bound with three binding straps. The slips are 45cm in length and well preserved, with only slips 1 and 2 each missing one character at the bottom. The number of characters on each slip ranges from 28 to 32. The slips are numbered on the backs, and the title *Chi jiu zhi ji Tang zhi wu* is written on the back of slip 15. There are thirteen in-text punctuation marks and a text-ending mark at the end of slip 15.

Physical properties of the slips show that the *Chi jiu* was originally bound together with *Yin zhi and *Yin gao, and the three manuscripts were also copied by the same scribe.[1] Evidence for this can be found on the back of the slips (see image below[2]):

---

1   For a classic study of their relationship, see Xiao Yunxiao 肖芸曉, "Shilun Qinghua zhushu Yi Yin san pian de guanlian" 試論清華竹書伊尹三篇的關聯, *Jianbo* 簡帛 8 (2013): 471–476.

2   Taken from Xiao Yunxiao, "Shilun Qinghua zhushu Yi Yin san pian de guanlian," 473. The diagonal line breaks between the right two slips of *Yin zhi that are adjacent to *Yin gao, but the numbers on the back (4 and 5) are consecutive. This may be due to the fact that a bamboo slip was lost after the line was cut but before text was copied on the front side.

Chi jiu   **Yin zhi*   **Yin gao*

Judging from the diagonal marks and the position of the nodes, we can tell that all slips of the *Chi jiu* and slips 1–3 of the **Yin zhi* come from the same bamboo culm, while slips 4 and 5 of the **Yin zhi* and all slips of the **Yin gao* come from a different one. If we were simply to consider the physical evidence alone, we might be tempted to treat them as one continuous text that bears the title *Chi jiu zhi ji Tang zhi wu*. Nevertheless, the manuscripts are clearly distinguished by the slip numbers written at the nodes, which confirm the order suggested by the diagonal marks. Text-ending marks and blank spaces on the last slips of each manuscript also serve to separate them from each other. The fact that different manuscripts were grouped in a bundle with only a single title sheds light on the structure of some "chapters" (*pian* 篇) in early Chinese transmitted texts. Many such chapters contain heterogeneous materials that obviously do not belong together. We could imagine that they might have been different manuscripts bound together with one written title but without slip numbers to distinguish them.

As Xiao Yunxiao points out, the physical order of the manuscripts corresponds with the chronological order of the narrative: Yi Yin's activities in the *Chi jiu* took place prior to the conquest of Xia, whereas **Yin zhi* and **Yin gao* are about the conquest itself and post-war policies respectively.[3] While **Yin zhi* and **Yin gao* are identified by most scholars as belonging to the textual tradition of *shu* 書 "scriptures," *Chi jiu* is markedly different in style. Compared to the realistic accounts of Tang and Yi Yin's campaign against Xia in the other two manuscripts, *Chi jiu* is a fantastic story about magic, exorcism, and numinous animals, written in more elaborate but less archaic language, with neither condemnation of the corrupt Xia nor approbation of the benevolent Tang. The grouping of *Chi jiu* with two *shu*-type texts raises interesting questions about the boundaries of *shu* in Warring States textual culture, questions not so much about whether these manuscripts are "chapters" of an established *Shang shu* canon as about how Warring States scholars recognize certain texts as *shu*.[4] That being said, we should also bear in mind that physical grouping does not necessarily mean proximity of textual genre. As Sarah Allan argues, the three manuscripts were probably placed in such an order simply because they all concerned Yi Yin.[5] Textual genre might not have played any role in the compilation.

The narrative of *Chi jiu* can be divided into two parts. In the first part (slips 1–6), Tang captured a magic bird, commanded his lesser servant Yi Yin, known for his culinary arts, to make a soup with it, and then left. When

---

3   Xiao Yunxiao, "Shilun Qinghua zhushu Yi Yin san pian de guanlian," 473.

4   For discussions of how to define the *shu* genre, see Sarah Allan, "On *Shu* 書 (Documents) and the Origin of the *Shang shu* 尚書 (Ancient Documents) in Light of Recently Discovered Bamboo Slip Manuscripts," *Bulletin of the School of Oriental and African Studies* 75.3 (2012): 547–557; Rens Krijgsman, "Cultural Memory and Excavated Anecdotes in 'Documentary' Narrative: Mediating Generic Tensions in the *Baoxun* Manuscript," in Paul van Els and Sarah A. Queen eds. *Between History and Philosophy: Anecdotes in Early China* (Albany: SUNY Press, 2017), 301–330; Dirk Meyer, *Documentation and Argument in Early China* (Berlin: De Gruyter, 2021); Cheng Hao 程浩, *You wei yan zhi: xian-Qin "shu" lei wenxian de yuan yu liu* 有為言之：先秦"書"類文獻的源與流 (Beijing: Zhonghua shuju, 2021).

5   Allan, "When Red Pigeons Gathered on Tang's House," 5.

the soup was ready, Tang's wife Ren Huang 紝冘 forced Yi Yin to give her the soup. They both tasted it and became clairvoyant. When Tang returned to the court, he was so angry that he put a spell on Yi Yin, causing him to be dumb and paralyzed on the road. In the second part (slips 6–15), a flock of crows found Yi Yin on the road and tried to eat him, but a magic crow among them recognized Yi Yin and stopped the other crows. To save Yi Yin, it told the other crows to go eat the Lord of Xia's sacrificial offerings, and explained that the point of sacrifice is to alleviate the lord's pain. When the other crows left, the magic crow possessed the paralyzed Yi Yin and took him to the lord's place. It spoke through Yi Yin's mouth to the lord about the cause of his illness and instructed him how to remove the haunting plants and animals. The lord then followed the crow's advice and captured the animals, but one white rabbit escaped. The text concludes abruptly by saying that the lord started covering huts with tiled roofs to defend against the white rabbit.

Such a story, together with its depiction of legendary king and minister, is quite unparalleled in early Chinese literature. The relationship between Tang and Yi Yin is not one of friendship but antagonism. Yi Yin fled to Xia not as a spy but because he had made Tang angry, and he did cure the Lord of Xia's illness in the end. Although the "Shen da" 慎大 "Being Careful When the State Is Large" chapter of *Lüshi chunqiu* says that Tang put on a show of shooting arrows at Yi Yin to deceive Xia (see Appendix A), in the *Chi jiu* the arrows are shot at the pigeon and there is no hint of espionage at all.

Many scholars argue that *Chi jiu* belongs to the genre of *xiaoshuo* 小説 "petty stories," a bibliographic category in the "Yi wen zhi" chapter of the *Han shu*.[6] While in modern Chinese the term is the equivalent of "fiction," the "Yi wen zhi" defines it disparagingly as "street talk and alley conversa-

---

6   See, for example, Huang Dekuan, "Qinghua jian *Chi hu zhi ji Tang zhi wu* yu xian-Qin 'xiaoshuo'—lüe shuo Qinghua jian dui xian-Qin wenxue yanjiu de jiazhi" 清華簡《赤鵠之集湯之屋》與先秦"小説"——略説清華簡對先秦文學研究的價值, *Fudan xuebao (shehui kexue ban)* 復旦學報（社會科學版）55.4 (2013): 81–86; Yao Xiaoou 姚小鷗, "Qinghua jian *Chi jiu* pian yu Zhongguo zaoqi xiaoshuo de wenti tezheng" 清華簡《赤鳩》篇與中國早期小説的文體特征, *Wenyi yanjiu* 文藝研究 2014.2: 43–58.

tions, created by those who heard and told them on the way" (街談巷語, 道聽途說者之所造也). The first title listed in this section is *Yi Yin shuo* 伊尹說 *Stories about Yi Yin*, described by Ban Gu 班固 himself as "shallow and thin" (*qianbo* 淺薄).[7] Since no text in this section survives to this day, studies of their content and style are mostly conjectural. According to Wang Zhizhong 王枝忠, although the term *xiaoshuo* appears in a number of pre-Qin texts, it is used there mostly in a derogatory, non-technical way. It was not until the time of Huan Tan 桓譚 (c. 23 BCE – 56 CE) that *xiaoshuo* became something like a bibliographic category. When Han scholars used the term, they usually meant miscellanies of short stories or sayings that had little or nothing to do with great matters concerning morality and politics but were often related to occult practices.[8] Defined as such, the term *xiaoshuo* does describe some features of *Chi jiu*, although it could not have been an established literary genre in the Warring States.

Sarah Allan, on the other hand, argues that *Chi jiu* can be taken as an *historiola*, a term borrowed from the study of magic and ritual in the ancient Near East, the Classical world of Greece and Rome, and Christian Europe. Instead of relating *Chi jiu* to traditional bibliographic classifications, she attempts to make sense of the text by focusing on its function and performative context. An *historiola* is "a form of narration in which a mythical paradigm is used to render power to magical rites, particularly healing rites." It often involves "performative transmission of power from a mythic realm articulated in the narrative to the human present."[9] From the perspective of *historiolae*, the disconnected last sentence, which Allan translates as "This is why they began to make parapets on houses; they were for keeping out the

---

7   Ban Gu, *Han shu* (Beijing: Zhonghua shuju, 1962), 1744–1745.

8   Wang Zhizhong, *Han Wei Liuchao xiaoshuo shi* 漢魏六朝小説史 (Hangzhou: Zhejiang guji chubanshe, 1997), 15–24. Huan Tan 桓譚 (c. 23 BCE – c. 56 CE) first uses the term *xiao shuo jia* 小説家 "the tradition of petty stories" in his *Xin lun* 新論 *New Treatise*. See Zhu Qianzhi 朱謙之, *Xin jiben Huan Tan Xin lun* 新輯本桓譚新論 (Beijing: Zhonghua shuju, 2009), 1–2. See also Judith T. Zeitlin, "*Xiaoshuo*," in Franco Moretti ed. *The Novel, Volume 1: History, Geography, and Culture* (Princeton: Princeton University Press, 2006), 249–261.

9   Allan, "When Red Pigeons Gathered on Tang's House," 8.

white rabbit," is where the mythic account of the past finds a connection to the living world. No matter how one reads the character translated by Allan as "parapet," it is certainly an architectural feature. The text tells the story not only to explain its origin, but also to give it defensive power against the haunting white rabbit or generally against illness of all kinds. The story might have been recited in a rite of exorcism when the construction of a house was completed. Allan's interpretation is plausible, although I find it hard to imagine that a story of such length and narrative detail was routinely recited in ritual. Compared to typical early Chinese incantations seen in excavated texts, *Chi jiu* seems too complicated for oral performance on the spot.[10]

The above two theories both make good sense, but neither is without problem. There are still many uncertainties concerning the nature and genre of *Chi jiu*, which is unlike any other surviving anecdote about Tang and Yi Yin. One thing, however, is certain: *Chi jiu* is a story about magic. Magical creatures and things—the red pigeon that alighted on the hut, the soup that gave Ren Huang and Yi Yin clairvoyance, the spell that caused Yi Yin to be dumb and paralyzed, the magic crow that possessed Yi Yin, the plants and animals sent by the Thearch to harm the Lord of Xia—surround the legendary political figures and intervene in (or sometimes directly manipulate) their actions. Whoever composed this story had no interest in how the virtue of Tang and Yi Yin prevailed over Xia. The real protagonists seem to be the magic birds—in the first part, a bird (or perhaps several birds) was eaten by Ren Huang and Yi Yin; in the second part, a flock of birds tried to eat Yi Yin but one of them saved him and possessed him. In the end, however, it was not the magic crow but the white rabbit that became the focus. All the birds disappear without a trace.

Chi jiu strikes one as a disconnected story. In the course of its narrative, subjects and figures appear and disappear abruptly without any appar-

---

10 For a discussion of these incantations, see Lü Yahu 呂亞虎, *Zhanguo Qin Han jianbo wenxian suo jian wushu yanjiu* 戰國秦漢簡帛文獻所見巫術研究 (Beijing: Kexue chubanshe, 2010), 254–263.

ent logic or causal relationship. Tang punishes Yi Yin for portioning out his soup but does nothing to Ren Huang who forced Yi Yin to do so. The clairvoyance that Yi Yin gains in the first part plays no role in the second part at all. The magic crow saves Yi Yin and cures the Lord of Xia for no reason, and the flock of crows persuaded by it never show up again. All of these narrative gaps make *Chi jiu* seem like a random collage of episodes. We are not yet sure about the purpose of such a story, but it shows that the image of Tang and Yi Yin in the Warring States period was extremely diverse.

Chi jiu zhi ji Tang zhi wu 赤鳩之集湯之屋
A Red Pigeon's Alighting on Tang's Hut

曰 故 又 赤 鶹 集 于 湯 之 廛 湯 羢 之 賸 之 乃 命 小 臣 曰
脂 猺 之 我 亓 言 之 ＿ 湯 遑 □

曰：古有赤鳩集于湯之屋。湯射之獲之，乃命小臣曰："旨羹之。我其享之。"湯往□。[一]

It is said: in ancient times, there was a red pigeon[11] that alighted on Tang's hut. Tang shot[12] at it and bagged it, and then commanded the Lesser Servant, saying: "Make a delicious soup[13] with it. I look forward to enjoying it." Tang went to .. [1]

---

11 Bird imagery plays an important part not only in Shang culture but also in early divination in general. In the "Gao zong rong ri" 高宗肜日 chapter of *Shang shu*, for example, a pheasant alighted on the handles of a tripod and cried out during Wu Ding's sacrifice to Tang. Also, in the "Ying tong" 應同 chapter of the *Lüshi chunqiu*, a fiery-red crow alighted on the altars of Zhou holding a cinnabar document in its beak.

12 The graphic form of *she* 射 "to shoot" here is unusual. It has three components: *gong* 弓 "bow," *shi* 矢 "arrow," and *guai* 夬 "jade ring," the third of which is usually absent. Zhao Ping'an 趙平安 argues cogently that *guai* is a pictograph of a hand wearing a jade ring for pulling the bow and is the original form of *jue* 玦 "jade ring." See Zhao Ping'an, "Guai de xingyi he ta zai chujian zhong de yongfa — jian shi qita guwenzi ziliao zhong de guai zi" 夬的形義和它在楚簡中的用法 ——兼釋其他古文字資料中的夬字, in *Xinchu jianbo yu guwenzi guwenxian yanjiu* 新出簡帛與古文字古文獻研究 (Beijing: Shangwu yinshuguan, 2009), 332–338.

13 For the reading of this character as *geng* 羹 "soup," see Chen Jian 陳劍, "Shi Shangbo zhushu he Chunqiu jinwen de 'geng' zi yiti" 釋上博竹書和春秋金文的"羹"字異體, at http://www.fdgwz.org.cn/Web/Show/295, posted 6 January 2008.

小 臣 既 彊 之 湯 句 妻 紝 冘 胃 小 臣 曰 嘗 我 於 而 彊 小
臣 弗 敢 嘗 曰 句 亓 □

小臣既羹之，湯后妻紝冘謂小臣曰："嘗我於爾羹。" 小臣弗敢嘗，曰："后其 [殺] [二]

When the Lesser Servant had made the soup, Ren Huang,[14] the wife of Lord Tang, said to the Lesser Servant: "Let me taste your soup." The Lesser Servant dared not let her taste, saying: "My lord will [kill] [2]

---

14 The name of Tang's wife is never mentioned elsewhere in ancient texts.

我 紝 宄 胃 小 臣 曰 尔 不 我 嘗 虐 不 亦 殺 尔 小 臣 自 堂
下 受 紝 宄 彊 紝 宄 受 小 臣 而

我。"紝宄謂小臣曰:"尔不我嘗,吾不亦殺尔?"小臣自堂下授紝宄羹。紝宄受小
臣而[三]

me." Ren Huang said to the Lesser Servant: "And if you don't let me taste it,
will I not also kill you?" The Lesser Servant handed the soup to Ren Huang
from below the hall. Ren Huang received it from the Lesser Servant, [3]

嘗之 ＿ 乃 卲 然 四 亢 之 外 亡 不 見 也 ＿ 小 臣 受 亓 余
而 嘗 之 亦 卲 然 四 晦 之 外 亡 不 見 也 ＿

嘗之，乃昭然。四荒之外，無不見也。小臣受其餘而嘗之，亦昭然。四海之外，
無不見也。 [四]

tasted it, and then became clairvoyant. Beyond the Four Remote Lands there was nothing she did not see. The Lesser Servant received what was left, tasted it, and also became clairvoyant. Beyond the Four Seas there was nothing he did not see. [4]

湯羿騜 小臣饋 湯悫曰笪 泅虘弜 小臣思 乃 逃 于 顕
湯 乃 袏 之 小臣 乃 痳 而 歸

湯返廷，小臣饋。湯怒曰：“孰偷吾羹？”小臣懼，乃逃于夏。湯乃袏之。小臣乃痿
而寢[五]

When Tang returned to the court, the Lesser Servant presented (the soup). Tang said angrily: "Who stole[15] my soup?" The Lesser Servant was terrified and then fled to Xia. Tang then put a spell[16] on him. The Lesser Servant was then paralyzed[17] and lay [5]

---

15 The character *zhou* 泅 appears in *Shuowen jiezi* 説文解字 *Explaining Simple Characters and Analyzing Compound Characters* as *chen* 彤, glossed as "to sail by boat" (*chuan xing ye* 船行也). It is also the archaic form of *yu* 俞, whose original meaning "to cross the river (in a boat)" is preserved in some characters that have 俞 as the phonophore, such as *yu* 逾 "to cross over," *shu* 輸 "to transport," and *yu* 喻 "to convey." Hou Naifeng 侯乃峰 reads it as *tou* 偷 "to steal." See Hou Naifeng 侯乃峰, "Ye shuo Qinghua jian *Chi jiu zhi ji Tang zhi wu* pian de 'zhou'" 也説清華簡《赤鳩之集湯之屋》篇的"泅", *Zhongguo wenzi yanjiu* 中國文字研究 24 (2016): 64–67. For a systematic analysis of this character, see Li Shoukui 李守奎, "'Yu' zi de chanshi ji kaoshi: *Shuowen* yilai de hanzi chanshi" "俞"字的闡釋及考釋：《説文》以來的漢字闡釋, in Jia Jinhua 賈晉華, Chen Wei 陳偉, Wang Xiaolin 王小林, and Lai Guolong 來國龍 eds. *Xin yuwenxue yu zaoqi Zhongguo yanjiu* 新語文學與早期中國研究 (Shanghai: Shanghai renmin chubanshe, 2018), 260–278.

16 The character transcribed as 袏 here is partially obscured, but there is a general consensus that Tang used some kind of ritual or incantation to curse the Lesser Servant. See, for example, Wang Ning 王寧, "Du Qinghua jian san *Chi hu zhi ji Tang zhi wu* sanzha" 讀清華簡三《赤鳩之集湯之屋》散札, at http://www.bsm.org.cn/?chujian/5995.html, posted 16 January 2013.

17 While the Tsinghua editors read the character 痳 as either *mei* 眜 "impaired eyesight" or *mei* 寐 "sleep," the next sentence says that the Lesser Servant was "able to see but unable to speak." What seems more plausible is Feng Shengjun's 馮勝君 reading *wei* 痿 "paralyzed," especially because the character has the "illness" signific (*ne* 疒). See Feng Shengjun, "Du Qinghua san *Chi hu zhi ji Tang zhi wu* zhaji" 讀清華三《赤鳩之集湯之屋》記, in Qinghua daxue chutu wenxian yanjiu yu baohu zhongxin 清華大學出土文獻研究與保護中心 eds. *Chutu wenxian yu Zhongguo gudai wenming* 出土文獻與中國古代文明 (Shanghai: Zhong Xi shuju, 2016), 254.

於迻見而不能言眾鶿牰飲之晉鶿曰是小臣也
不可飲也顕句又疾牰襥楚于飲

於路，視而不能言。眾鳥將食之。巫鳥曰："是小臣也，不可食也。夏后有疾，將撫楚。
于食 [六]

on the road, able to see but unable to speak. A flock of crows was about to
eat him. A magic crow said: "This is the Lesser Servant, who must not be
eaten. The Lord of Xia has an illness and is about to relieve his pain (with a
sacrifice).[18] Let's go eat [6]

---

18 *Fuchu* 襥楚 literally means "relieving pain." It must have involved some kind of sacrificial rite, because *fu* is written with the "sacrifice" signific *shi* 示. The crows later went to
eat the "sacrificial offerings."

亓 祭 ＿ 衆 鶩 乃 倃 晉 鶩 曰 頤 句 之 疾 女 可 晉 鶩 乃 言
曰 帝 命 二 黄 它 與 二 白 兔 居 句 之 帰 室

其祭。" 衆鳥乃訊巫鳥曰："夏后之疾如何？" 巫鳥乃言曰："帝命二黄蛇與二白兔居
后之寢室[七]

his sacrificial offerings." The flock of crows then questioned the magic
crow: "What is the Lord of Xia's illness like?" The magic crow said: "The
Thearch commanded two yellow snakes and two white rabbits to dwell on
the ridgepole of the lord's bedchamber [7]

之 棟 亓 下 舍 句 疾 是 凶 句 悲 疾 而 不 智 人 ＿ 帝 命 句
土 爲 二 茨 屯 共 居 句 之 牀 下 亓

之棟，其下予后疾。是使后心疾而不知人。帝命后土為二悲筍共居后之床下，其[八]

and send down[19] illness on the lord. This made the lord's mind[20] so ill that he did not recognize people. The Thearch also commanded the Lord of the Soil to produce two sprouting bamboo shoots[21] to dwell together under the lord's bed and [8]

---

19 The editors read the character composed of 余 and 口 as *she* 舍 "to release," but there is no other example of this character being read as *she* in Warring States manuscripts. Instead, I read *yu* 余 (*la) as *yu* 予 (*laʔ) "to give." The same character also appears in *Yin gao* (the fifth character on slip 4).

20 The editors take the phrase *jiji* 悲疾 as a verb modified by an adverb meaning "to fall ill quickly." Feng Shengjun, on the other hand, takes it as a scribal error. According to him, the manuscript was probably copied from a base text that had 悲= at the same place. The function of "=" is ambiguous in Warring States scribal convention. A symbol like 悲= can indicate one of the three following possibilities: (1) 悲 should be split into *xin ji* 心疾 or *ji xin* 疾心 "to be ill in heart/mind"; (2) 悲 should be read twice as *ji ji* 悲悲 "ill ill"; (3) only part of 悲 should be duplicated, resulting in either *ji ji* 悲疾 "to fall ill quickly" or *ji xin* 悲心 (same as #1). Feng argues that the base text would have intended the first of these possibilities, but the scribe of the *Chi jiu* mistook it for the third. Therefore, the *ji ji* in the manuscript should actually be *xin ji* 心疾 "to be ill in heart/mind." See Feng Shengjun, "Du Qinghua san *Chi hu zhi ji Tang zhi wu* zhaji," 251. Feng's reading works better with the following statement that the lord suffered from cognitive impairment. Moreover, by taking *ji ji* as "illness in heart/mind," we have a parallelism between animals making the heart/mind ill from above and plants making the body ill from below, although the parallelism disappears on slip 13 when the Lesser Servant repeats the cause of illness. In any case, it seems clear that the "heart" signific in 悲 is meaningful. For a classic analysis of the semantic function of the "heart" signific in Warring States excavated texts, see Pang Pu 龐樸, "Ying Yan shu shuo: Guodian Chu jian Zhongshan san qi xin pang wenzi shi shuo" 郢燕書說: 郭店楚簡中山三器心旁文字試說, in Wuhan daxue Zhongguo wenhua yanjiuyuan 武漢大學中國文化研究院 eds. *Guodian Chu jian guoji xueshu yantaohui lunwenji* 郭店楚簡國際學術研討會論文集 (Wuhan: Wuhan Renmin chubanshe, 2000), 37–42.

21 茨 is a variant of *ling* 蔆 attested in the Baoshan 包山 manuscripts (slip 154). I follow Chen Jian 陳劍 in reading *lingzhun* 蔆屯 as *taisun* 悲筍 "sprouting bamboo shoots." See Chen Jian, "Qinghua jian ziyi lingzha liangze" 清華簡字義零札兩則, in Fudan daxue chutu wenxian yu guwenzi yanjiu zhongxin 復旦大學出土文獻與古文字研究中心 eds. *Zhanguo wenzi yanjiu de huigu yu zhanwang* 戰國文字研究的回顧與展望 (Shanghai: Zhong Xi shuju, 2017), 197–200.

止 K 句 之 體 是 思 句 之 身 畫 蓍 不 可 壟 于 箬 _ 衆 鳶
乃 逞 晉 鳶 乃 歎 小 臣 之 胸 渭

上刺后之體。是使后之身苛蛪，不可及于席。"衆烏乃往。巫烏乃宅小臣之喉隈。 [九]

stab[22] the lord's body above. This made the lord's body itch and sting[23] so that he was unable to take his place at the mat." The flock of crows then went (to the sacrifice). The magic crow then took residence in a cavity[24] of the Lesser Servant's throat. [9]

---

22 The Tsinghua editors note that K is a variant of *xi* 析 "split," which is a common phonetic loan for *ci* 朿 "to stab." Additional evidence in support of this reading is that in the Wangshan 望山 slips the character *ce* 策, the lower half of which is 朿, is written as 札 (slip 2, character 48).

23 I here follow Feng Shengjun in reading 畫蓍 as *kehe* 苛蛪 "itch and sting," unpleasant feelings caused by the pointed ends of the bamboo shoots. See Feng Shengjun, "Du Qinghua san *Chi hu zhi ji Tang zhi wu* zhaji," 252.

24 The editors read 胸渭 as *houwei* 喉胃 "throat and stomach," but it does not make good sense to say that the magic crow took residence in both the throat and the stomach. I suspect that 渭 should instead be read as *wei* 隈 "bend/corner," for *wei* 胃 is an attested phonetic loan for *wei* 畏 in ancient texts. The magic crow took residence in a "cavity of the Lesser Servant's throat" in order to speak for him.

小臣乃起而行至于頤₌句₌曰尔隹晨＿ 小臣曰我天
晉夏句乃愻小臣曰女尔天晉

小臣乃起而行。至于夏后，夏后曰：“尔惟疇？”小臣曰：“我天巫。”夏后乃訊小臣曰：
“如尔天巫，[十]

Then the Lesser Servant got up and left. When he arrived at the Lord of
Xia's place, the Lord of Xia said: "Who[25] are you?" The Lesser Servant said:
"I am a heavenly magician." The Lord of Xia then questioned the Lesser
Servant: "If you are a heavenly magician, [10]

---

25 The interrogative pronoun "who" is expressed with the archaic word *chou* 疇, mostly
seen in the speeches of the Xia and Shang chapters of *Shang shu*.

而 智 朕 疾 小 臣 曰 我 智 之 顕 句 曰 朕 疾 女 可 ＿ 小 臣
曰 帝 命 二 黄 它 與 二 白 兔 居 句 之 帰

而知朕疾？ ”小臣曰：“我知之。”夏后曰：“朕疾如何？ ”小臣曰：“帝命二黄蛇與二白兔居后之寢 [十一]

do you know my illness?" The Lesser Servant said: "I know it." The Lord of Xia said: "What is my illness like?" The Lesser Servant said: "The Thearch commanded two yellow snakes and two white rabbits to dwell on the ridge-pole of my lord's [11]

室之棟亓下舍句疾是思句懋=恂=而不智人_帝命
句土爲二莢屯共居句之牀下

室之棟，其下予后疾。是使后薆薆恂恂而不知人。帝命后土為二蔥筍共居后之床下，[十二]

bedchamber and send down illness on my lord. This made my lord so muddled and confused that my lord did not recognize people. The Thearch also commanded the Lord of the Soil to produce two sprouting bamboo shoots to dwell together under my lord's bed [12]

亓 走 Ｋ 句 之 身 是 思 句 窜 疅 甘 心 句 女 敳 塵 殺 黄 它
與 白 兔 圭 墅 斬 茷 ＿ 句 之 疾 其 瘳

其上刺后之身。是使后混亂甘心。后如徹屋，殺黄蛇與白兔，坺地斬篸，后之疾其瘳。"[十三]

and stab my lord's body above. This made my lord's mind disturbed and painful.[26] If my lord demolishes the hut, kills the yellow snakes and white rabbits, digs[27] the ground, and chops the bamboo shoots, my lord will recover from the illness." [13]

---

26 As the editors have pointed out, the phrase *ganxin* 甘心 also appears in the "Bo xi" 伯兮 poem in *Shi jing* 詩經 *Book of Odes* in the context *ganxin shouji* 甘心首疾, where *shouji* means "headache." The parallelism between *ganxin* and *shouji* suggests that *ganxin* means something like "pain in the heart/mind."

27 *Shuowen* defines *chu* 坺 as "*qi* coming out from the soil" (*qi chu tu ye* 氣出土也). As Liu Lexian 劉樂賢 points out, in the Shuihudi 睡虎地 slips this character appears twice with the meaning "to dig." Here it seems that both meanings are intended, and to *chu* the ground is to dig a hole so as to aerate the soil. Liu's article is no longer available on the website where it was originally published, but his argument is quoted in Li Shuang 李爽, "Qinghua jian Yi Yin wu pian jishi" 清華簡"伊尹"五篇集釋 (M.A. thesis: Jilin University, 2016), 96–97.

颐 句 乃 從 小 臣 之 言 敚 塵 殺 二 黃 它 與 一 白 兔 ＿ 乃
坴 壄 又 二 萩 厲 乃 斬 之 亓 一 白 兔

夏后乃從小臣之言徹屋，殺二黃蛇與一白兔。乃垏地，有二慫筍，乃斬之。其一白
兔 [十四]

The Lord of Xia then followed the Lesser Servant's advice, demolished the
hut, and killed the two yellow snakes and one white rabbit. Then he dug the
ground, found the two sprouting bamboo shoots, and then chopped them.
The other white rabbit [14]

不曼是𠚕爲埤巾者麈以戋白兔

不得。是始為甈，覆諸屋以御白兔。[十五]

was not gotten. Thus began the practice of covering huts with tile[28] (roofs) to ward off white rabbits. [15]

---

28 This is the most contested phrase in the entire manuscript; each of the characters has been interpreted in so many ways that it is impossible to give an adequate account of them in a footnote. Briefly, my translation follows the most influential reading proposed by Guo Yongbing 郭永秉, who takes the second character ⛰ as an inverted *shan* 山 and reads it as *fu* 覆 "to overturn/to cover." The character also appears on slip 6 of *Rui Liangfu bi* 芮良夫毖 *Liangfu of Rui's Admonition* in Tsinghua Volume 3, slip 11 of *Shi fa* 筮法 *Stalk Divination* in Tsinghua Volume 4, as well as slip 7 of *Yin gaozong* (see p.189, n.9). See Guo Yongbing, "Shi Qinghua jian zhong daoshanxing de 'fu' zi" 釋清華簡中倒山形的"覆"字, in *Guwenzi yu guwenxian lunji xubian* 古文字與古文獻論集續編 (Shanghai: Shanghai guji chubanshe, 2015), 262–274. As for the first character *pi* 埤, while the transcription offers no problem, possible readings include *pi* 埤 "parapet," *bi* 蔽 "shelter," *bi* 畢 "net," and *pi* 甈 "tile." I here adopt Liu Jiao's 劉嬌 reading *pi* 甈 "tile," for it corresponds with the legend that "Jie made tile-covered chambers" (*Jie zuo wa wu* 桀作瓦屋) mentioned in several ancient texts. See Liu Jiao, "Qinghua jian *Chijiu zhi ji Tang zhi wu* 'shi shi wei pi' yu 'Jie zuo wawu' chuanshuo" 清華簡《赤鳩之集湯之屋》"是始為埤"與"桀作瓦屋"傳說, *Guwenzi yanjiu* 古文字研究 32 (2018): 378–383.

VERSO

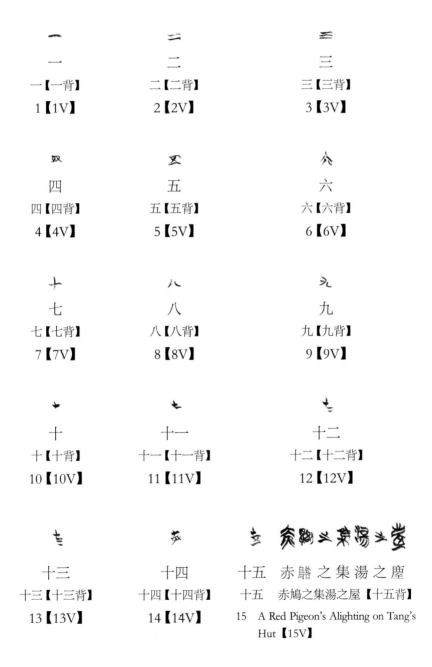

一【一背】
1【1V】

二【二背】
2【2V】

三【三背】
3【3V】

四【四背】
4【4V】

五【五背】
5【5V】

六【六背】
6【6V】

七【七背】
7【7V】

八【八背】
8【8V】

九【九背】
9【9V】

十【十背】
10【10V】

十一【十一背】
11【11V】

十二【十二背】
12【12V】

十三【十三背】
13【13V】

十四【十四背】
14【14V】

十五   赤鳩之集湯之屋【十五背】

15   A Red Pigeon's Alighting on Tang's Hut【15V】

赤鳩之集湯之屋

曰：古有赤鳩集于湯之屋。

湯射之獲之。乃命小臣曰："旨羹之。我其享之。"

湯往□。[一] 小臣既羹之，湯后妻紝宄謂小臣曰："嘗我於爾羹。"

小臣弗敢嘗，曰："后其 [殺][二] 我。"

紝宄謂小臣曰："尔不我嘗，吾不亦殺尔？"

小臣自堂下授紝宄羹。

紝宄受小臣而[三]嘗之，乃昭然。四荒之外，無不見也。

小臣受其餘而嘗之，亦昭然。四海之外，無不見也。[四]

湯返廷，小臣饋。湯怒曰："孰偷吾羹？"小臣懼，乃逃于夏。

湯乃袢之。小臣乃痿而寢[五]於路，視而不能言。

衆鳥將食之。巫鳥曰："是小臣也，不可食也。夏后有疾，將撫楚。于食[六]其祭。"

衆鳥乃訊巫鳥曰："夏后之疾如何？"

巫鳥乃曰："帝命二黃蛇與二白兔居后之寢室[七]之棟，其下予后疾。是使后心疾而不知人。帝命后土為二篸筍共居后之床下，其[八]上刺后之體。是使后之身苛蛰，不可及于席。"

衆鳥乃往。巫鳥乃宅小臣之喉隈。[九]小臣乃起而行。

至于夏后，夏后曰："尔惟疇？"

小臣曰："我天巫。"

夏后乃訊小臣曰："如尔天巫，[十]而知朕疾？"

小臣曰："我知之。"

夏后曰："朕疾如何？"

小臣曰："帝命二黃蛇與二白兔居后之寢[十一]室之棟，其下予后疾。是使后棼棼恂恂而不知人。帝命后土為二篸筍共居后之床下，[十二]其上刺后之身。是使后混亂甘心。后如徹屋，殺黃蛇與白兔，圿地斬篸，后之疾其瘳。"[十三]

夏后乃從小臣之言徹屋，殺二黃蛇與一白兔。乃圿地，有二篸筍，乃斬之。其一白兔[十四]不得。是始為毚，覆諸屋以御白兔。[十五]

A Red Pigeon's Alighting on Tang's Hut

It is said: in ancient times, there was a red pigeon that alighted on Tang's hut.

Tang shot at it and bagged it, and then commanded the Lesser Servant, saying: "Make a delicious soup with it. I look forward to enjoying it."

Tang went to .. [1] When the Lesser Servant had made the soup, Ren Huang, the wife of Lord Tang, said to the Lesser Servant: "Let me taste your soup."

The Lesser Servant dared not let her taste, saying: "My lord will [kill] [2] me."

Ren Huang said to the Lesser Servant: "And if you don't let me taste it, will I not also kill you?"

The Lesser Servant handed the soup to Ren Huang from below the hall.

Ren Huang received it from the Lesser Servant, [3] tasted it, and then became clairvoyant. Beyond the Four Remote Lands there was nothing she did not see.

The Lesser Servant received what was left, tasted it, and also became clairvoyant. Beyond the Four Seas there was nothing he did not see. [4]

When Tang returned to the court, the Lesser Servant presented (the soup). Tang said angrily: "Who stole my soup?" The Lesser Servant was terrified and then fled to Xia.

Tang then put a spell on him. The Lesser Servant was then paralyzed and lay [5] on the road, able to see but unable to speak.

A flock of crows was about to eat him. A magic crow said: "This is the Lesser Servant, who must not be eaten. The Lord of Xia has an illness and is about to relieve his pain (with a sacrifice). Let's go eat [6] his sacrificial offerings."

The flock of crows then questioned the magic crow: "What is the Lord of Xia's illness like?"

The magic crow said: "The Thearch commanded two yellow snakes and two white rabbits to dwell on the ridgepole of the lord's bedchamber [7] and send down illness on the lord. This made the lord's mind so ill that he did not recognize people. The Thearch also commanded the Lord of the Soil to produce two sprouting bamboo shoots to dwell together under the lord's bed and [8] stab the lord's body above. This made the lord's body itch and sting so that he was unable to take his place at the mat."

The flock of crows then went (to the sacrifice). The magic crow then took residence in a cavity of the Lesser Servant's throat. [9] Then the Lesser Servant got up and left.

When he arrived at the Lord of Xia's place, the Lord of Xia said: "Who are you?"

The Lesser Servant said: "I am a heavenly magician."

The Lord of Xia then questioned the Lesser Servant: "If you are a heavenly magician, [10] do you know my illness?"

The Lesser Servant said: "I know it."

The Lord of Xia said: "What is my illness like?"

The Lesser Servant said: "The Thearch commanded two yellow snakes and two white rabbits to dwell on the ridgepole of my lord's [11] bedchamber and send down illness on my lord. This made my lord so muddled and confused that my lord did not recognize people. The Thearch also commanded the Lord of the Soil to produce two sprouting bamboo shoots to dwell together under my lord's bed [12] and stab my lord's body above. This made my lord's mind disturbed and painful. If my lord demolishes the hut, kills the yellow snakes and white rabbits, digs the ground, and chops the bamboo shoots, my lord will recover from the illness." [13]

The Lord of Xia then followed the Lesser Servant's advice, demolished the hut, and killed the two yellow snakes and one white rabbit. Then he dug the ground, found the two sprouting bamboo shoots, and then chopped them. The other white rabbit [14] was not gotten. Thus began the practice of covering huts with tile (roofs) to ward off white rabbits. [15]

A Red Pigeon's Alighting on Tang's Hut [15V]

Chapter Two

*Yin zhi 尹至

*Yin's Arrival

The *Yin zhi manuscript, published in Volume 1 of *Qinghua daxue cang Zhanguo zhujian*, was written on five almost intact slips, originally bound with three binding straps. There is almost no loss of writing, except for one character at the top of slip 2. The slips are 45cm in length, numbered on the backs, each having 29 to 32 characters. There are 5 in-text punctuation marks and a text-ending mark at the end of slip 5. The manuscript originally had no title; the editors gave it the title *Yin zhi based on the opening sentence "So it was (Yi) Yin who went from Xia to Bo and arrived at Tang's place at night."

As mentioned in Chapter 1, *Chi jiu*, *Yin zhi, and *Yin gao were copied by the same scribe and originally bound together. Despite the physical grouping, *Yin zhi and *Yin gao are markedly different from *Chi jiu* in both content and style. Most scholars believe that these two manuscripts belong to the textual tradition of *shu* 書 "scriptures." More evidence for such an identification will be discussed in the next chapter about *Yin gao, which contains lines that match quotations of a lost *Shang shu* text in other ancient sources. As for *Yin zhi, although it cannot be matched with any such quotations, it so closely resembles *Yin gao that the two texts might have been composed together. The beginning of *Yin zhi, "So it was (Yi) Yin who went from Xia to Bo and arrived at Tang's place at night" (惟尹自夏徂亳彔至在湯), has almost the same format as the beginning of *Yin gao, "So it

69

was after (Yi) Yin had joined Tang that both had a unifying virtue" (惟尹既及湯咸有一德). Both texts are short and unembellished. Both call Yi Yin by the official title Yin "Governor" and his less common personal name Zhi 摯, as opposed to the "Lesser Servant" in *Chi jiu*, *Chimen*, and *Tangqiu*. Both use the term "Western City" for the Xia capital.[1] Both distinguish *min* 民 "people" from *zhong* 眾 "multitudes" (although the precise meaning of that distinction is still open to dispute). *Yin gao* reads very much like a sequel to *Yin zhi* written by the same hand. The two texts seem to belong to an earlier period than all other manuscripts translated in this volume, but there is no decisive evidence for an exact date.[2]

The narrative of *Yin zhi* begins with Yi Yin's arrival at Tang's place at night from Xia. He reported the corruption of the Xia lord, the rebellious sentiments of the people, and bad omens in the sky. The topics mentioned by him—the ruler's virtue, the people's will, and heavenly omens—constitute almost a full list of the essential components of the Mandate of Heaven, the ideological legitimacy of rulership in early China. Encouraged by Yi Yin's words, Tang won his support and decided to attack Xia. Together they defeated Xia and drove the remaining Xia troops to a place called Shui 水, where they fought the last battle and Tang gave the command to kill every single Xia soldier. What is interesting about this story is that it implies, though does not directly say, that Yi Yin spied on Xia for Tang. The nocturnal setting of the arrival was probably a sign of secrecy; the following conversation was all about the information Yi Yin collected at Xia; Tang "swore a covenant with Yin" and thereby "secured a great support" (slip 4) because he was unsure about Yi Yin's loyalty. Yet Yi Yin's report of Xia's decadence gave Tang enough confidence to launch a campaign, and they finally formed an alliance.

---

1   For a discussion of the term "Western City" in oracle bones, see Cai Zhemao 蔡哲茂, "Xia wangchao cunzai xinzheng — shuo Yin buci de 'xiyi'" 夏王朝存在新證——說殷卜辭的"西邑," *Zhongguo wenhua* 中國文化 44 (2016): 47–51.

2   One influential dating offered by Xia Dazhao and Huang Dekuan is the early Warring States. See Xia Dazhao and Huang Dekuan, "Guanyu Qinghua jian *Yin zhi Yin gao* de xingcheng he xingzhi," 213–239.

In fact, this is not the first time that Yi Yin appears as a spy; legends of his espionage are well attested in Warring States sources.[3] According to the "Yong jian" 用間 "Using Spies" chapter of *Sunzi* 孫子:

> 昔殷之興也，伊摯在夏。周之興也，呂牙在殷。
>
> Of old, the rise of Yin (was due to) Yi Zhi's being at Xia. The rise of Zhou (was due to) Lü Ya's being at Yin.[4]

Here Yi Yin is called by the name "Yi Zhi," a combination of his two personal names Yi and Zhi. *Sunzi* is obviously appropriating famous king-minister paradigms for its own purpose when it draws the analogy between Yi Yin's role in Tang's conquest of Xia and Lü Ya's (namely, Jiang Ziya 姜子牙, also known as Grand Duke Wang 太公望) role in King Wu's conquest of Yin/Shang. I suspect that such legends originated with military thinkers, but they are by no means limited to military texts. In chapter 6B6 of *Mengzi*, Yi Yin is reported to have "five times sought out Tang and five times sought out Jie" (五就湯五就桀).[5] The "ancient text" (*guben* 古本) of *Zhushu jinian* 竹書紀年 *Bamboo Annals* further specifies that he approached Jie through Jie's wife Mo Xi 末喜:

> 后桀伐岷山，岷山女于桀二人，曰琬，曰琰。桀愛二女，無子。刻其名于苕華之玉，苕是琬，華是琰。而棄其元妃于洛，曰末喜氏。末喜氏以與伊尹交，遂以間夏。
>
> Lord Jie attacked (the people from) Mount Min, and (the people from) Mount Min sent Jie two girls (as concubines), one called Wan and the other called Yan. Jie loved the two girls, but had no children with them. He carved their names on the "panicle" and "flower" jades, Wan's name on the "panicle"

---

3   For a discussion of these legends, see Li Ling 李零, Sunzi *shisan pian zonghe yanjiu*《孫子》十三篇綜合研究 (Beijing: Zhonghua shuju, 2006), 438–440.

4   Li Ling, Sunzi *shisan pian zonghe yanjiu*, 89.

5   Jiao Xun 焦循 (1763–1820), *Mengzi zhengyi* 孟子正義 (Beijing: Zhonghua shuju, 1987), 829.

jade and Yan's name on the "flower" jade, and abandoned his primary wife Mo Xi near the Luo river. Mo Xi then had intercourse with Yi Yin, who thereby spied on Xia.[6]

However, this version of the story is contradicted by an account in *Guo yu* 國語 :

> 昔夏桀伐有施，有施人以妹喜女焉。妹喜有寵，于是乎
> 與伊尹比而亡夏。
>
> Of old, Jie of Xia attacked the Shi clan, and the people of the Shi clan sent him a girl named Mo Xi. Mo Xi was in favor (with Jie) and thereby sided up with Yi Yin and destroyed Xia.[7]

In *Zhushu jinian*, Mo Xi cooperated with Yi Yin because she was abandoned by Jie, but in *Guo yu*, she was Jie's favorite and probably took advantage of his trust. *Guo yu* does not mention the other two concubines. Finally, in the "Shen da" 慎大 "Being Careful When the State Is Large" chapter of *Lüshi chunqiu*, we see a developed version of the story:

> 湯乃惕懼。憂天下之不寧，欲令伊尹往視曠夏。恐其不信，
> 湯由親自射伊尹。伊尹奔夏三年，反報于亳，曰：“桀迷
> 惑於末嬉，好彼琬、琰。不恤其衆，衆志不堪。上下相疾，
> 民心積怨，皆曰‘上天弗恤，夏命其卒’。”湯謂伊尹曰：
> “若告我曠夏盡如詩。”湯與伊尹盟，以示必滅夏。伊尹
> 又復往視曠夏，聽於末嬉。末嬉言曰：“今昔天子夢西方
> 有日，東方有日。兩日相與鬥，西方日勝，東方日不勝。”

---

6   Fang Shiming 方詩銘 and Wang Xiuling 王修齡, *Guben* Zhushu jinian *jizheng* 古本竹
    書紀年輯證 (Shanghai: Shanghai guji chubanshe, 1981), 16–18. This text is quoted in
    a few places with some variations. I adopt the quotation in volume 135 of the *Taiping
    yulan* 太平御覽. The names of the two girls also appear in the Shanghai Museum manu-
    script *Rongcheng shi* 容成氏, but the *Rongcheng shi* does not depict Yi Yin as a spy. See
    Shan Yuchen 單育辰, *Xinchu Chujian* Rongcheng shi *yanjiu* 新出楚簡《容成氏》研究
    (Beijing: Zhonghua shuju, 2016), 202–206.
7   Xu Yuangao 徐元誥, *Guoyu jijie* 國語集解 (Beijing: Zhonghua shuju, 2002), 250.

伊尹以告湯。

Tang then grew vigilant and terrified. Worrying about the unrest in the world, he wanted to send Yi Yin to observe the ferocious Xia. Fearing (that Yi Yin would) not be trusted (by Xia), Tang himself shot arrows at Yi Yin. Three years after Yi Yin had fled to Xia, he returned to the Shang capital at Bo and reported: "Jie is entranced by Mo Xi and favors the women Wan and Yan. He shows no pity for his multitudes, who are no longer willing to tolerate (such treatment). Superiors and subordinates hate each other, and the people accumulate ever greater resentment in their hearts, all saying, 'Heaven on high shows no pity. May the mandate of Xia expire.'" Tang said to Yi Yin: "You are telling me that the ferocious Xia is all like this." Tang and Yi Yin swore a covenant to demonstrate their determination to annihilate Xia. Yi Yin once again went to observe the ferocious Xia, and he heeded the words of Mo Xi. Mo Xi said: "Just last evening the Son of Heaven dreamt that there was a sun in the west and a sun in the east and that these two suns fought. The sun in the west was victorious and the sun in the east did not win." Yi Yin reported this to Tang.[8]

The *Lüshi chunqiu* story seems to have combined these other accounts (especially the one from *Yin zhi*), but it also differs from them. Jie did not abandon Mo Xi but loved all three women. The two omens in Yi Yin's report were not real astrological signs but suns in Jie's dream, and the two suns even fought with each other. Yi Yin did not hear it from the Xia people but from Mo Xi. These differences demonstrate just how variable the figure Yi Yin can be in Warring States texts — not only his identities, but also anecdotes about a single identity of his are diverse and unstable.

---

8   Xu Weiyu 許維遹, *Lüshi chunqiu jishi* 呂氏春秋集釋 (Beijing: Zhonghua shuju, 2009), 354–356. For a full translation of the *Lüshi chunqiu* chapter, see Appendix A.

There is an interesting puzzle about how the terms "east" and "west" are used in different versions of this story. The puzzle concerns the meaning of the "sun/omen in the east/west" in *Yin zhi* and *Lüshi chunqiu*, as well as the "Western City Xia" in *Yin zhi* and *Yin gao*. I am not here concerned about the actual geographic location of these place names or whether there was a "Xia dynasty," but only how their spatial relationship is represented in the three texts, and particularly a potential contradiction in the representation. According to *Yin zhi* and *Lüshi chunqiu*, the "sun/omen in the west" prevailed over the "sun/omen in the east," which seems to indicate that the "sun/omen in the west" refers to Shang, the historical winner. However, both *Yin zhi* and *Yin gao* use the term "Western City" for Xia. If Xia was to the west of Shang, then how could Shang be the "sun/omen in the west"? The problem is complicated by the description of the route of Tang's attack. *Yin zhi* says that Tang "attacked the Western City from the west" (自西翦西邑), and *Lüshi chunqiu* says (immediately following the passage quoted above):

> 商涸旱，湯猶發師，以信伊尹之盟。故令師從東方出於國，西以進。
>
> Shang was suffering from a drought, but Tang still sent out an army to stand by his covenant with Yi Yin. Accordingly, he ordered the army to leave the state from the east and advance from the west.

If Tang attacked Xia from the west, then it seems that his own city should have been to the west of the "western city" Xia. How do we reconcile the discrepancy between these accounts?

In fact, if we consider the overall context of the *Lüshi chunqiu* story carefully, we would find that the "sun in the west" refers to Xia, not Shang.[9]

---

9   The point is made in Cai Zhemao, "Xia wangchao cunzai xinzheng — shuo Yin buci de 'xiyi'," 49.

In other words, it was an omen in favor of Jie. This is clear from the sentence "Shang was suffering from a drought, but Tang still sent out an army to stand by his covenant with Yi Yin." The drought was a verification of the omen, and Tang acted *despite* the natural disaster to keep his promise (which is strongly suggested by the word "still"). This is why the text specifies the route of Tang's army: he took a detour (leaving from the east, but attacking from the west of Xia) to avoid being the inauspicious "sun in the east."

This interpretation, however, cannot be applied to *Yin zhi* so easily. In Yi Yin's report to Tang in *Yin zhi*, the omen seems to be a sign of Jie's losing Heaven's favor, a piece of good news that gave Tang enough reason to launch the attack. There is no mention of a drought and no use of a word like "still." And yet the meaning of the sign itself is ambiguous. That the "omen in the east is not clear" does not necessarily mean that the side coming from the east will lose the battle. It can also mean that there will be a threat from the east, or that Xia will suffer from those coming from the east. If that is the case, then the attacking route in *Yin zhi* does not have any hemerological significance. Despite the superficial similarity, the omens in *Lüshi chunqiu* and *Yin zhi* may have very different meanings.

Finally, Tang's ruthless command at the end reminds one of the famous chapter 7B3 in *Mengzi* about not trusting *Shang shu*. Mengzi says:

> "盡信《書》，則不如無《書》。吾於《武成》，取二三策
> 而已矣。仁人無敵於天下。以至仁伐至不仁，而何其血
> 之流杵也？"
>
> "It would be better not to have the *Scriptures* than to believe everything in them. I accept only two or three bamboo slips in the 'Completion of the War.' A benevolent person has no enemies in the world. When the one who was supremely benevolent attacked the one who was supremely unbenevolent, how could it be that 'the blood flowed till it floated the pestles?'"[10]

---

10 Jiao Xun, *Mengzi zhengyi*, 959. Translation modified from Bryan W. Van Norden trans.

Mengzi dismisses records of massive bloodshed in *Shang shu* for moral and philosophical reasons. He would probably have said the same thing about *Yin zhi* had he seen it. For him, the ancient sage kings were paragons of benevolence. Their conquests would be more than welcomed by the people. How could they carry out appalling massacres like these?

Mengzi: With Selections from Traditional Commentaries (Indianapolis, IN: Hackett Publishing Company, 2008), 185.

*Yin zhi 尹至
*Yin's Arrival

佳 尹 自 頣 蔗 白 彔 至 才 湯₌ 曰 各 女 亓 又 吉 志 尹 曰 句
我 逨 越 今 昀₌ 余 屵 亓 又 頣 眔

惟尹自夏徂亳，彔至在湯。湯曰："格。汝其有吉志。"尹曰："后，我來越今旬日。
余蔑其有夏眾[一]

So it was (Yi) Yin who went[11] from Xia to Bo[12] and arrived at Tang's place
at night.[13] Tang said: "Come forth! You ought to have auspicious inten-

---

11 The editors read 蔗 as *cu* 徂 "to go." The reading is based on the definition of 徂 in
   Shuowen jiezi, which says that the archaic form (or more accurately the *zhouwen* 籀文
   form) of 徂 is 遳 . Obviously, 遳 in *Shuowen* and 蔗 in the manuscript share the same
   phonophore *cuo* 虘.

12 Bo was the capital city of Shang.

13 The editors read 彔 , consisting of a 彔 and a 夕, as *lu* 逯 "to travel." Most scholars now
   accept Guo Yongbing's 郭永秉 argument, which relates the character to 🉂 (also consisting of 彔 and 夕) in oracle bone inscriptions. The character in oracle bone inscriptions
   means "nighttime" (the signific *xi* 夕 "night" being actually significant here), and the
   phrase *zhonglu* 中彔 means "midnight." See Guo Yongbing, "Qinghua jian *Yin zhi* 'lu
   zhi zai Tang' jie" 清華簡《尹至》"彔至在湯"解, in *Guwenzi yu guwenxian lunji xubian*
   古文字與古文獻論集續編 (Shanghai: Shanghai guji chubanshe, 2015), 248–253. For
   the meaning of *zhonglu* in oracle bone inscriptions, see Huang Tianshu 黃天樹, "Yinxu
   jiaguwen suojian yejian shicheng kao" 殷墟甲骨文所見夜間時稱考, in *Huang Tianshu
   guwenzi lunji* 黃天樹古文字論集 (Beijing: Xueyuan chubanshe, 2006), 178–193. With
   the publication of the Anhui University manuscript of *Shi jing*, Guo's reading gains additional support. In the "Qiang you ci" 墙有茨 poem, where the received *Shi jing* reads
   中冓之言, the manuscript reads 宀彔之言, replacing the *zhonggou* 中冓 with *zhonglu*
   宀彔. Early imperial commentators struggled with the meaning of the phrase *zhonggou* in the received *Shi jing*. While the Mao commentary interprets it as a spatial term
   meaning "inner palace" (*neigou* 內冓), the Han 韓 commentary glosses it as "midnight"
   (*zhongye* 中夜). For the manuscript version of the "Qiang you ci," see Anhui daxue

tions."[14] (Yi) Yin said: "My lord, till now it has been ten days since I came. I spied on[15] the multitudes[16] of Xia, [1]

不 吉 好 亓 又 句 乓 志 亓 倉 ＿ 龍 二 玉 弗 叧 亓 又 衆 民
沇 曰 余 返 女 皆 芒 隹 戝 盧 悳 癋 悚

不吉好。其有后厥志其喪。寵二玉，弗虞其有衆。民允曰：'余及汝皆喪。'惟茲虐德、暴動、[二]

(whose situation was) not auspicious and well. Their lord will lose his will.[17]

---

hanzi fazhan yu yingyong yanjiu zhongxin 安徽大學漢字發展與應用研究中心 eds. *Anhui daxue cang zhanguo zhujian* 安徽大學藏戰國竹簡 (Shanghai: Zhong Xi shuju, 2019), 128–129. For the Han commentary on the "Qiang you ci," see Wang Xianqian 王先謙, *Shi sanjia yi jishu* 詩三家義集疏 (Beijing: Zhonghua shuju, 1987), 220. For a phonological analysis of the variants *gou* 篝 and *lu* 彔, see Adam Smith and Maddalena Poli, "Establishing the text of the *Odes*: the Anhui University bamboo manuscript," *Bulletin of the School of Oriental and African Studies* 84.3 (2022): 541–544.

14 "Auspicious intentions" (*jizhi* 吉志) can also be rendered as "good intentions" or "a good report." See Adam Schwartz, *The Oracle Bone Inscriptions from Huayuanzhuang East* (Berlin: De Gruyter, 2019), 80, n. 16.

15 The Fudan Reading Group reads *wei* 微 as *wei* 職 "to watch secretly, to spy on" citing the following sentence from the "Lu wen" 魯問 chapter of *Mozi*: "When the ruler makes a mistake, watch him secretly in order to remonstrate" (上有過則微之以諫). See Fudan daxue chutu wenxian yu guwenzi yanjiu zhongxin yanjiusheng dushuhui 復旦大學出土文獻與古文字研究中心研究生讀書會, "Qinghua jian *Yin zhi Yin gao* yandu zhaji" 清華簡《尹至》《尹誥》研讀札記, at http://www.fdgwz.org.cn/Web/Show/1352, posted 5 January 2011.

16 In both *Yin zhi* and *Yin gao*, *zhong* 衆 "multitude" and *min* 民 "people" are strictly distinguished, but the nature of the distinction is not immediately clear from the context. Although there are numerous studies of the two terms in ancient Chinese texts, the findings of those studies cannot be easily mapped onto *Yin zhi* and *Yin gao*, mostly because the meaning of the two terms changed over time, and we cannot be sure about the historical stage to which the meaning in *Yin zhi* and *Yin gao* belongs. I shall simply maintain the distinction in my translation without explaining it. For a recent discussion of the meaning of *min* in Western Zhou political thought, see Joern Peter Grundmann, "The Term min 民 as a Political Concept in Western Zhou Thought," *Bulletin of the Jao Tsung-I Academy of Sinology* 4 (2017): 111–135.

17 The editors read *cang* 倉 as *shuang* 爽 "mistaken." Shen Pei 沈培 and Chen Minzhen 陳民鎮 read it as *sang* 喪 "to lose." They cite two pieces of evidence. First, the Mao

He dotes on the two jades[18] and has no pity for his multitudes. The people indeed[19] said: 'I and you will both expire.'[20] It is this[21] (Jie) who abuses the virtuous, engages in violence,[22]
[2]

commentary on the "Sang rou" 桑柔 poem in *Shi jing* reads *cang* 倉 as *sang* 喪 "loss" (in the line *cang xiong tian xi* 倉兄填兮, which literally means "loss has been increasing for a long time" according to Mao). The gloss itself has been questioned by most later commentators, but it at least shows that such a reading was possible in the Han. Second, in the Shanghai Museum manuscript *Rongcheng shi* 容成氏, the place name Cangwu 蒼 梧 is written as Sanghu 桑虍 (slip 41), and *sang* 桑 (*sˤaŋ) is a common phonetic loan for *sang* 喪 (*s-mˤaŋs). Shen Pei's reading is published in an online reply to Fudan daxue chutu wenxian yu guwenzi yanjiu zhongxin yanjiusheng dushuhui, "Qinghua jian *Yin zhi Yin gao* yandu zhaji." See also Chen Minzhen, "Qinghua jian *Yin zhi* jishi" 清華簡《尹 至》集釋, at http://www.fdgwz.org.cn/Web/Show/1647, posted 12 September 2011. The *Rongcheng shi* example can be found in Shan Yuchen, *Xinchu Chujian* Rongcheng shi *yanjiu*, 219–220.

18   The "two jades" are a metaphor for Jie's favorite concubines Wan 琬 and Yan琰. The two characters themselves are jade names.

19   I follow Sun Feiyan 孫飛燕 in reading 沇 as *yun* 允 is "truly, indeed, sincerely." See Sun Feiyan, "Du *Yin zhi Yin gao* zhaji" 讀《尹至》《尹誥》札記, in Zhongguo wenhua yichan yanjiuyuan 中國文化遺產研究院 eds. *Chutu wenxian yanjiu* 出土文獻研究 10 (Beijing: Zhonghua shuju, 2011), 38–41.

20   Nothing in the manuscript indicates that the quotation stops here, but this line also appears in the transmitted "Tang shi" 湯誓 "Tang's Declaration" chapter of *Shang shu* as "When will this sun expire? I and you will both perish" (時日曷喪? 予及汝皆亡). It is also quoted in *Mengzi* 1A2.

21   I follow Wang Ning 王寧 in reading 佳䣈 as *weizi* 惟茲 "it is this," a common phrase in *Shang shu*. His reading is published in an online reply to Liu Bo 劉波, "Qinghua jian *Yin zhi* 'tong wang dian' bushuo" 清華簡《尹至》"僮亡典"補説, at http://www.fdgwz.org. cn/Web/Show/1421, posted 4 March 2011.

22   The character 憧 (with a 心 on the left) was originally transcribed as 膧 (with a 身 on the left) by the editors. It has been read variously as *zhong* 腫 "ulcer," *tong* 僮 "boy" (especially slave boy), *dong* 動 "to move," and even "being pregnant." See Wu Kejing 鄔可晶, "*Yin Zhi* 'wei zi nue de bao chong wu dian' ju shi jie"《尹至》"惟䣈虐德暴 膧亡典"句試解, *Chutu wenxian* 出土文獻 9 (2016): 166–172. In a recent article, Jia Lianxiang demonstrates convincingly that the editors' transcription is mistaken, because the 心 component of the character is partly damaged by the notch so that it looks like 身. I follow him in reading 憧 as *dong* 動 "to move, to act." See Jia Lianxiang, "Qiantan zhushu xingzhi xianxiang dui wenzi shidu de yingxiang — yi Qinghua jian ji chu wenzi bushi weili" 淺談竹書形制現象對文字釋讀的影響——以清華簡幾處文字補釋為 例, *Chutu wenxian* 出土文獻 1 (2020): 82–90.

亡 箕 頭 又 恙 才 西 才 東 見 章 于 天 亓 又 民 衒 曰 隹 我
棘 褐 咸 曰 矗 今 東 恙 不 章 _ 今

無典。夏有祥在西在東，見章于天。其有民率曰：'惟我速禍。'咸曰：'曷今東祥不
章？今 [三]

and has no canons. Xia had omens in the west and east, appearing clearly
in the heavens. The people all said: 'We will soon suffer disasters' (They) all
said: 'How come now the omen in the east is not clear? Now [3]

亓女台_ 湯曰女告我顕睡衕若寺_ 尹曰若寺_
湯禜憇返尹莩乃柔大絭湯逞

其如台？'" 湯曰："汝告我夏隱率若時？" 尹曰："若時。" 湯盟質及尹，兹乃柔大援。
湯往 [四]

what should we do?'" Tang said: "Are you telling me that the distress[23] of
Xia is all like this?" (Yi) Yin said: "It is like this." Tang swore a covenant
with (Yi) Yin, thereby securing great support.[24] Tang went to [4]

---

23 I follow the editors in glossing 隱 as *tong* 痛 "pain, distress."

24 Feng Shengjun reads *ying* 絭 as *yuan* 援 "help, support," arguing that the phrase *da yuan* 大援 "great support" appears many times in the political speeches of the *Zuo zhuan*
and *Guo yu*. While there is no direct textual evidence for *ying* and *yuan* being used as
phonetic loans for each other, Feng gives circumstantial evidence based on the phonetic
series of *ying* 絭 (no Baxter and Sagart reconstruction available for this character), *ying*
營 (*ɢweŋ), and *rong* 榮 (*N-qwreŋ) on the one hand and *yuan* 爰 (*ɢwan), *yuan* 袁
(*ɢwan), and *qiong* 睘/嬛 (*ɢwˤren) on the other. Both *ying* 營 and *rong* 榮 are common
loans for *qiong* 睘/嬛, which has *yuan* 袁 as its phonophore. See Feng Shengjun, "Qinghua jian *Yin zhi* 'zi nai rou da ying' jie" 清華簡《尹至》"兹乃柔大絭"解, in Zhongguo
wenhua yichan yanjiuyuan 中國文化遺產研究院 eds. *Chutu wenxian yanjiu* 出土文獻
研究13 (Shanghai: Zhong Xi shuju, 2014), 310–317. In contrast, Ziju 子居 reads *rou* 柔
as *wu* 務 "to work on" and *ying* 絭 as *ying* 禜, a sacrificial rite for warding off natural
disasters such as flood, drought, and plague. He further notes that many ancient texts,
including the "Shen da," mention that the world was suffering from a drought at the time
of the conquest. His article is no longer available on the website where it was originally
published, but his argument is quoted in Chen Minzhen, "Qinghua jian *Yin zhi* jishi,"
72–73. Ziju's reading is phonologically tenable, while Feng Shengjun's reading makes better sense in context (for *Yin zhi* makes no mention of a drought). I am inclined toward
Feng's reading, but his phonological argument relies on a circuitous methodology that is
open to criticism. For a critique of this approach, see Lai Guolong 來國龍, "Shi 'e' yu 'xie':
jianlun 'yi xing wei zhu' yu 'yin xing yi zonghe' liangzhong butong de guwengzi kaoshi
fangfa" 釋"乤"與"离"：兼論"以形為主"與"音形義綜合"兩種不同的古文字考釋
方法, *Bulletin of the Jao Tsung-I Academy of Sinology* 6 (2019): 187–224.

征弗附，摯度摯德不僭。自西翦西邑，戠其有夏。夏播民入于水曰："戰！"帝曰："一勿遺！" [五]

conquer those who would not rally around,[25] and Zhi[26] deemed his own virtue flawless.[27] (They) attacked the Western City from the west and quelled Xia. The escaped[28] Xia people entered Shui[29] and said, "Fight!" The

---

25 The Fudan Reading Group takes 𩰥 as a variant of *fu* 鳧 and reads it as *fu* 附 "to rally around." See Fudan daxue chutu wenxian yu guwenzi yanjiu zhongxin yanjiusheng dushuhui, "Qinghua jian *Yin zhi Yin gao* yandu zhaji."

26 Zhi is also Yi Yin's personal name, but less common than Yi.

27 It is also possible to translate the second part of this sentence as "Zhi's standards and virtue are flawless." See Yao Sujie 姚蘇傑, "Qinghua jian *Yin gao* 'yi de' lunxi" 清華簡《尹誥》"一德"論析, *Zhonghua wenshi luncong* 中華文史論叢 2013.1: 375.

28 The transcription of the character 𤯓 is very controversial. The editors transcribe it as 㪚, the archaic form of *bo* 播 "to scatter, to escape, to abandon" in *Shuowen jiezi*, rendering the sentence as "The escaped Xia people entered Shui." The Fudan Reading Group, on the other hand, points out that 播 appears as 𢽳 in the Shanghai Museum *Zi yi* 緇衣 *Black Jacket* manuscript (slip 15, character 22), which is slightly different from the graph here. Strictly speaking, 𤯓 should be analyzed into 𣬛 (*mi* 米) and 𣁡 (*dou* 斗) and therefore transcribed as *liao* 料 "to count." The phrase *liaomin* 料民 "to count the number of people" appears in the "Zhou yu shang" 周語上 chapter of the *Guo yu* 國語. See Fudan daxue chutu wenxian yu guwenzi yanjiu zhongxin yanjiusheng dushuhui, "Qinghua jian *Yin zhi Yin gao* yandu zhaji." This reading is further contested by Shi Xiaoli 石小力, who supports the editors' original reading but modifies their transcription. According to him, the same character appears twice in the Tsinghua manuscript *Yue Gong qi shi* 越公其事 *May the Lord of Yue Attend*, as 𤯓 (slip 4, the 20th character) and 𤯓 (slip 23, the 21st character). In both cases, the character is combined with *qi* 棄 "to abandon" to form a compound. This shows that the original 播 transcription is correct, because *boqi* 播棄 "to abandon, to give up" is a synonymous compound attested in the "Ming gui xia" 明鬼下 chapter of *Mozi* and the "Wu yu" 吳語 chapter of the *Guo yu*. See Shi Xiaoli, "Ju Qinghua jian (qi) buzheng jiushuo si ze" 據清華簡(柒)補證舊說四則, at https://www.ctwx.tsinghua.edu.cn/info/1081/2232.htm, posted 23 April 2017.

29 According to the Tsinghua editors, the place name Shui 水 "Water" appears in the "San bian" 三辯 chapter of *Mozi* as Daben 大本, but the Daozang 道藏 recension of *Mozi*

Thearch[30] said: "Leave no one!" [5]

---

has Dashui 大水 instead of Daben. This shows that 本 might be a graphic error for Shui 水. In the "Shen da," Jie fled to a place called Dasha 大沙, and 沙 might also be a graph-ic error for 水.

30   There is some controversy over whether *di* 帝 "Thearch" refers to "God on High" or Tang himself. In the latter case, "Thearch" would be a new title that Tang received after he had defeated Xia. In the *Chi jiu*, the Thearch appears to be God on High, but in the next manuscript *Yin gao*, it is Heaven that defeated Xia, not God on High. Given that the *Yin zhi* is much more similar to *Yin gao*, the "Thearch" here probably refers to Tang.

VERSO

一

一【一背】

1【1V】

二

二【二背】

2【2V】

三

三【三背】

3【3V】

四

四【四背】

4【4V】

五

五【五背】

5【5V】

* 尹至

惟尹自夏徂亳，录至在湯。

湯曰：“格。汝其有吉志。”

尹曰：“后，我來越今旬日。余瞂其有夏眔[一]不吉好。其有后厥志其喪。寵二玉，弗虞其有眔。民允曰：‘余及汝皆喪。’惟茲虐德、暴動、[二]無典。夏有祥在西在東，見章于天。其有民率曰：‘惟我速禍。’咸曰：‘曷今東祥不章？今[三]其如台？’”

湯曰：“汝告我夏隱率若時？”

尹曰：“若時。”

湯盟質及尹，茲乃柔大援。

湯往[四]征弗附，摯度摯德不僭。自西翦西邑，戡其有夏。

夏播民入于水曰：“戰！”帝曰：“一勿遺！”[五]

*Yin's Arrival

So it was (Yi) Yin who went from Xia to Bo and arrived at Tang's place at night.

Tang said: "Come forth! You ought to have auspicious intentions."

(Yi) Yin said: "My lord, till now it has been ten days since I came. I spied on the multitudes of Xia, [1] (whose situation was) not auspicious and well. Their lord will lose his will. He dotes on the two jades and has no pity for his multitudes. The people indeed said: 'I and you will both expire.' It is this (Jie) who abuses the virtuous, engages in violence, [2] and has no canons. Xia had omens in the west and east, appearing clearly in the heavens. The people all said: 'We will soon suffer disasters' (They) all said: 'How come now the omen in the east is not clear? Now [3] what should we do?'"

Tang said: "Are you telling me that the distress of Xia is all like this?"

(Yi) Yin said: "It is like this."

Tang swore a covenant with (Yi) Yin, thereby securing great support.

Tang went to [4] conquer those who would not rally around, and Zhi deemed his own virtue flawless. (They) attacked the Western City from the west and quelled Xia.

The escaped Xia people entered Shui and said, "Fight!" The Thearch said: "Leave no one!" [5]

Chapter Three

Yin gao 尹誥

Yin's Announcement

The Tsinghua manuscript *Yin gao* was published in Volume 1 of *Qing-hua daxue cang Zhanguo zhujian*. The manuscript was written on four slips, which are well preserved with only slip 4 missing part of its first character because the top has broken off. The slips, originally bound with three binding straps, are 45cm in length and numbered on the backs. The number of characters on each slip ranges from 31 to 34, except for slip 4, which has only 15 characters. There is a text-ending punctuation mark on slip 4, and the remainder of the slip is left blank. As mentioned in Chapters 1 and 2, physical and codicological features of the bamboo slips show that the *Chi jiu*, *Yin zhi*, and *Yin gao* were originally copied by the same scribe and bound together.

Yin gao is a short conversation between Tang and Yi Yin right after they had conquered Xia. If, as suggested in Chapter 2, *Yin gao* was indeed meant to be a sequel to *Yin zhi*, then the first sentence "So it was after (Yi) Yin had joined Tang that both had a unifying virtue" might allude to a once uneasy alliance. Remember that toward the end of *Yin zhi*, Tang felt unsure about Yi Yin's allegiance. He "swore a covenant with Yin" and thereby "secured great support" (slip 4). Now that they had defeated Xia, their alliance, stronger than ever before, was manifested in their "unifying virtue." The next important thing was how to make peace with the former Xia people and win their loyalty. Yi Yin advised Tang to share the spoils with them and send them good words. Following his advice, Tang gathered the Xia people in the capital city of Shang.

The *Yin gao* manuscript originally had no title. Its current title, *Yin's Announcement,* is given by the Tsinghua editors in the belief that it is the lost "Xian you yi de" 咸有一德 "Both Had a Unifying Virtue" chapter of *Shang shu.* Such an identification involves a complicated argument based on ancient quotations. According to the "Yin benji" chapter of *Shi ji,* Yi Yin composed a text entitled "Xian you yi de," which was included in *Shang shu* as a chapter.[1] However, this chapter has not always been part of *Shang shu* due to the existence of different texts. While the *jinwen* 今文 or "modern script" *Shang shu* preserved by Fu Sheng 伏生 (fl. 200 BCE) does not have a chapter with this title, the *guwen* 古文 or "ancient script" *Shang shu,* adopted in the canonical *Wujing zhengyi* 五經正義 *Correct Meaning of the Five Classics* edited by Kong Yingda 孔穎達 (574–648) and his assistants, not only has the title but also a complete text, which has been transmitted to this day. Long before the discovery of the Tsinghua manuscripts, scholars had already doubted the authenticity of the "ancient script" *Shang shu,* and that it was a forgery had been almost universally accepted since the 18th century. Thanks to the efforts of generations of philologists and textual critics, the once canonical ancient-script text, including the transmitted "Xian you yi de," is now widely considered to be the "pseudo-ancient script" (*wei guwen* 偽古文) *Shang shu.* The original ancient-script text was still existent when Mei Ze 梅賾 (fl. 4th century CE) presented the pseudo-ancient-script text to the Eastern Jin (317–420) court. It had been completely lost by the early 7th century, according to the "Jing ji zhi" 經籍志 "Records of Classics and Documents" chapter of *Sui shu* 隋書 *Book of Sui* completed in 636.[2]

The original "Xian you yi de" mentioned by Sima Qian, the author of *Shi ji,* seems hopelessly lost except for two ancient quotations in the "Zi yi" 緇衣

---

1   Sima Qian, *Shi ji,* 126.
2   See Jiang Shanguo 蔣善國, *Shang shu zongshu* 尚書綜述 (Shanghai: Shanghai guji chubanshe, 1988), 52–53, for a discussion of the transmission of different ancient-script *Shang shu* texts.

"Black Jacket" chapter of the transmitted *Li ji*. The transmitted "Zi yi" quotes a *Shang shu* chapter entitled "Yin ji" 尹吉 (literally "Yin's Auspiciousness") twice. The first commentator to relate the title "Yin ji" to "Xian you yi de" was the Eastern Han scholar Zheng Xuan 鄭玄 (127–200). The meaning of these quotations is obscure because of numerous textual corruptions, some of which were already noted by Zheng Xuan. Since we are dealing with Zheng Xuan's commentary here, my translation of Q1 and Q2 is strictly based on his interpretation regardless of whether it is correct or not:[3]

Quotation 1 (Q1):

《尹吉》曰：“惟尹躬及湯咸有一德。”

"Yin ji" says: "So it was both (Yi) Yin himself and Tang who had a unifying virtue."

【鄭注】吉當為告。告，古文誥。字之誤也。《尹告》，伊尹之誥也。《書序》以為《咸有一德》，今亡。咸，皆也。君臣皆有一德不貳，則無疑惑也。

[Zheng's commentary] The character *ji* 吉 should be *gao* 告, and the character 告 is the ancient form of *gao* 誥 "announcement." This is a graphic error. "Yin gao" is the announcement of Yi Yin. (This text is what) *Prefaces to the Scriptures* take as the "Xian you yi de." It is now lost. *Xian* 咸 means "both/all." If the lord and the servant both had a unifying virtue and were not double-minded, then there was no doubt or confusion.[4]

---

3   It is worth noting that the two quotations of "Yin gao" appear in different chapters in the transmitted pseudo-ancient script *Shang shu*, Q1 in "Xian you yi de" and Q2 in the "Tai Jia shang" 太甲上 chapter of the "pseudo-ancient script" *Shang shu*. This is seen by many as one piece of evidence that the ancient script *Shang shu* is a forgery. See Ruan Yuan 阮元 ed. *Shangshu zhengyi* 尚書正義, in *Shisan jing zhushu*, vol. 1 (Taipei: Yiwen, 2001), 8.18b, 116; 8.25b, 120.

4   Ruan Yuan ed. *Li ji zhushu* 禮記注疏, in *Shisan jing zhushu*, vol. 5 (Taipei: Yiwen, 2001), 6b–7a, 929–930.

Quotation 2 (Q2):

《尹吉》曰: "惟尹躬天見于西邑夏, 自周有終, 相亦惟終。"

"Yin ji" says: "So it was (Yi) Yin's own ancestors who saw that the Western City Xia was able to remain loyal and trustworthy until the end (of their days), and the servants were also (able to do the same) till the end."

【鄭注】《尹吉》, 亦《尹告》也。天當為先。字之誤。忠信為周。相, 助也, 謂臣也。伊尹言尹之先祖, 見夏之先君臣皆忠信以自終。今天絕桀者, 以其自作孽。伊尹始仕於夏, 此時就湯矣。夏之邑在亳西。見或為敗。邑或為予。

[Zheng's commentary] This "Yin ji" is also "Yin gao." The character *tian* 天 should be *xian* 先 "ancestor." This is a graphic error. "Loyal and trustworthy" is what *zhou* 周 means. *Xiang* 相 means "to assist" and refers to the servants. Yi Yin said that his ancestors had seen that the former rulers and servants of Xia had all been all loyal and trustworthy till the end (of their days). That Heaven was terminating Jie now was because he brought disasters on himself. Originally Yi Yin had served as an official in Xia, but at this time he joined Tang. The city of Xia was to the west of Bo. *Jian* 見 "to see" is also written as *bai* 敗 "to ruin" (in another manuscript). *Yi* 邑 "city" is also written as *yu* 予 "to give" (in another manuscript).[5]

In his commentary Zheng Xuan provides (1) glosses of difficult words, (2) emendations of graphic errors, (3) textual variants in other manuscripts, (4) identification of the title "Yin ji," and (5) an explanation of the meaning of entire sentences. Combining his report and the *Shi ji* account, we know at least the following things:

a)   Zheng Xuan had seen the *title* "Xian you yi de" in *Shu xu* 書序 *Prefaces to the Scriptures,* a text circulating in the Han

---

5   Ruan Yuan ed. *Li ji zhushu*, 55.11b–12a, 932.

and preserved in *Wujing zhengyi.* Originally the *Prefaces* was an independent text, but in *Wujing zhengyi* it was divided up and attached to the individual *Shang shu* chapters. Many of these prefaces also appear in the *Shi ji.*[6]

b) He had not seen the *text* of "Xian you yi de," which had been lost by his time.

c) He identified "Yin gao" as the lost "Xian you yi de" based on the four characters *xian you yi de* 咸有一德 "both had a unifying virtue" in Q1.[7] The identification could not have been made otherwise due to the loss of the text.

d) He had seen other manuscript copies of "Zi yi" (but not of "Yin gao" or "Xian you yi de") and noted the textual variants. In Zheng Xuan's technical terminology, *huowei* 或為 (or sometimes *huozuo* 或作) "also written as" is distinguished from *dangwei* 當為 "should be." The former marks a textual variant (as in "見 is also written as 敗"), whereas the latter marks an emendation (as in "天 should be 先").[8] Interestingly, many of the variants noted by him are graphic errors. Take the two variants at the end of Q1 for example. While in modern orthography, *yi* 邑 does not look like *yu* 予, in clerical script they are very similar (邑

---

6   The dating of these prefaces, a long-standing thorny problem in the history of *Shang shu* scholarship, is extremely controversial. Some scholars believe that Sima Qian was quoting from an established text of the prefaces, while others argue that the late Western Han scholar Zhang Ba 張霸 (fl. 1st century BCE) concocted the prefaces from Sima Qian's accounts. For two sides of the debate, see Jin Dejian 金德建, *Sima Qian suo jian shu kao* 司馬遷所見書考 (Shanghai: Shanghai renmin chubanshe, 1963), 57–60; Chen Mengjia 陳夢家, *Shang shu tonglun* 尚書通論 (Beijing: Zhonghua shuju, 1985), 94–102; Jiang Shanguo 蔣善國, *Shang shu zongshu* 尚書綜述 (Shanghai: Shanghai guji chubanshe, 1988), 61–74.

7   This is suggested in Yu Wanli 虞萬里, *Shanghai bowuguan cang Chu zhushu Zi yi zonghe yanjiu* 上海博物館藏楚竹書《緇衣》綜合研究 (Wuhan: Wuhan daxue chubanshe, 2009), 362.

8   For a comprehensive analysis of Zheng Xuan's use of *huowei* or *huozuo* in his *Li ji* commentary, see Yang Tianyu 楊天宇, *Zheng Xuan san Li zhu yanjiu* 鄭玄三禮注研究 (Tianjin: Tianjin renmin chubanshe), 524–587.

己 and 予 予). As for *jian* 見 and *bai* 敗, if we omit the 攵 on the right side of 敗, then its left part 貝 is very similar to 見.

The intertextuality of these quotations is further complicated by two Warring States Chu manuscripts of "Zi yi" published before the Tsinghua manuscripts. The first one was excavated in Guodian, Jingmen, Hubei in 1993 and published in 1998. The second one was unearthed by grave robbers, purchased by the Shanghai Museum in 1994, and published in 2001.[9] Neither the Guodian *Zi yi* nor the Shanghai Museum *Zi yi* bear a title, but they are recognizably the same text despite some differences in chapter order and a number of textual variants. Both have Q1 (attributed to *Yin Gao*), but neither has Q2. Q1 in the two *Zi yi* manuscripts, however, is not significantly different from the received "Zi yi."

Now the Tsinghua manuscript of *Yin gao* begins with Q1, which is followed immediately by Q2. The co-occurrence of Q1 and Q2 suggests strongly that this text is simply the "Yin gao" that "Zi yi" quoted from, hence its current title.[10] The Tsinghua *Yin gao* is completely different from the pseudo-ancient script "Xian you yi de" and seems to set the seal on its being a forgery.[11] Moreover, the variants it provides help to resolve a number of problems in the transmitted Q1 and Q2. With the publication of the Tsinghua *Yin gao*, we now have a total of seven occurrences of Q1 and Q2

---

9   Jingmen shi bowuguan 荊門市博物館 eds. *Guodian Chu mu zhujian* 郭店楚墓竹簡 (Beijing: Wenwu chubanshe, 1998), 129; Ma Chengyuan 馬承源 ed. -in-chief *Shanghai Bowuguan cang zhanguo Chu zhushu (yi)* 上海博物館藏戰國楚竹書（一）(Shanghai, Shanghai guji chubanshe, 2001), 117.

10 While most scholars in China agree on this, there are still some voices of dissent. One major objection is that the Tsinghua *Yin gao* records a private conversation rather than a public announcement. As such, it is unlike almost all other *Shang shu* chapters traditionally labelled *gao* 誥 "announcement." See Lu Puping 魯普平, "Qinghua jian *Yin gao* pianming niding zhi shangque" 清華簡《尹誥》篇名擬定之商榷, *Ha'erbin xueyuan yuanbao* 哈爾濱學院院報 35.2 (2014): 72–74.

11 For a discussion of *Yin gao*'s significance in the history of *Shang shu* scholarship, see Du Yong 杜勇, "Qinghua jian *Yin gao* yu wanshu *Xian you yi de* bianwei" 清華簡《尹誥》與晚書《咸有一德》辨偽, *Tianjin shifan daxue xuebao (shehui kexue ban)* 天津師範大學學報（社會科學版）2012.3: 20–28.

in either transmitted or unearthed sources:

(1) Q1 and Q2 in the Tsinghua *Yin gao,

(2) Q1 in the Guodian *Zi yi,

(3) Q1 in the Shanghai Museum *Zi yi,

(4) Q1 in the transmitted "Zi yi,"

(5) Q2 in the transmitted "Zi yi,"

(6) Q1 in the transmitted pseudo-Ancient Script Text of "Xian you yi de," and finally

(7) Q2 in the transmitted pseudo-Ancient Script Text of "Tai Jia shang"

For the sake of clarity, I compare these quotations with *Yin gao by aligning significant variants in vertical columns (marked with letters at the bottom):

	Q1			Q2									
1	佳尹	既	汲湯咸 又一憙	尹	念	天	歝	西邑顋 曰顋自	憶	亓 又	民	亦佳乓	衆
2	尹隹員 佳尹	允	及湯咸 又一憙										
3	尹隹員 佳尹	允	及康咸 又一憙										
4	惟尹	躬	及湯咸 有一德										
5	惟			尹	躬	天	見	于西邑 夏　自	周	有	終	相亦惟	終
6	惟尹	躬	暨湯咸 有一德										
7	惟			尹	躬	先	見	于西邑 夏　自	周	有	終	相亦惟	終
	a			b		c		d		e			f

Let us consider the variants. In each case, I shall start from the transmitted (4) and (5) and compare them with the unearthed (2), (3), and especially (1). The pseudo-ancient script (6) and (7) will only be considered when necessary. As we shall see, in almost every case (1) makes better sense than the other versions.

    a.   For the *gong* 躬 "self" in (4), (2) and (3) read *yun* 允 "indeed," while (1) reads *ji* 既 "already" (an aspect marker). These variants are probably graphic confusions.[12] In (1), given that the *ji* 既 is an aspect marker, the character *ji* 及 after it is better taken as a verb "to join, to reach" (note that it is written with the "walk" signific 辶). In (2) and (3), the sentence seems to mean "Indeed Yin and Tang both had a unifying virtue," where *ji* 及 now occurs without the "walk" signific and is taken as the conjunction "and." In (3), the sentence could mean either "Yin himself and Tang both had a unifying virtue" or "Yin himself joined Tang and both had a unifying virtue." Although all of them make some sense, (1) seems to make better sense than the others.

    b.   For the *gong* 躬 "self" in (5), (1) reads *nian* 念 "to think, to consider." The two characters might be phonetic loans.[13] It is interesting that the transmitted "Zi yi" has the

---

12 In the Guodian and Shanghai Museum *Zi yi*, the character 允 appears as 𨌤, with a 允 on top and a 身 on the bottom. This unusual structure makes it look more like 躬. For a comparative analysis of these variants, see Yu Wanli, *Shanghai bowuguan cang Chu zhushu* Zi yi *zonghe yanjiu*, 43–44.

13 For an analysis of this variant, see Liao Mingchun 廖名春, "Qinghua jian *Yin gao* yanjiu" 清華簡《尹誥》研究, *Shixueshi yanjiu* 史學史研究 2011.2: 111. See also Ma Nan 馬楠, "Zhou Qin liang Han *Shu jing* kao" 周秦兩漢書經考 (Ph.D. dissertation, Tsinghua University, 2012), 217. It should be noted that *nian* 念 (*nˤims) and its phonophore *jin* 今 (*krəm) have very different OC reconstructions. According to Zhang Fuhai 張富海, this is because the archaic form of 念 does not have 今 as its phonophore. In oracle bone script, 念 appears as 𠘧, with an inverted "mouth" on top and a "heart" underneath. The inverted "mouth" gradually became confused with 今, but the character 念 still preserved its original sound. See Zhang Fuhai, "Li yong xiesheng gouni shanggu yin yinggai zhuyi de jige wenti" 利用諧聲構擬上古音應該注意的幾個問題, *Chutu wenxian* 出土文獻 2021.1: 134. *Gong* 躬 (*kruŋ) and *jin* 今 (*krəm) are attested loans in ancient texts. The "Biao ji" 表記 chapter of *Li ji* quotes the *wo gong bu yue* 我躬不閱 line in the "Gu feng" 谷風 poem of *Shi jing* as *wo jin bu yue* 我今不閱. Also, in the "Jian" 蹇 hexagram of *Zhou yi* 周易 *Book of Changes*, the sentence *fei gong zhi gu* 匪躬

same *gong* 躬 for two completely different characters in (1), namely *ji* 既 and *nian* 念.

c.　For the *jian* 見 "to see" in (3), (1) reads *bai* 敗 (a variant form of *bai* 敗 "to ruin, to defeat"). In his commentary on Q2 in the transmitted "Zi yi," Zheng Xuan noted but did not adopt the variant *bai* 敗, because his version of Q2 was corrupted by a number of other mistakes that render this variant meaningless in context. Had he adopted the variant, his Q2 would have meant something like "Yi Yin was defeated by Xia," but he knew well that Yi Yin was on the winner's side.

d.　For the *zhou* 周 in (5), glossed by Zheng Xuan as "loyal and trustworthy," the manuscript has a difficult character 愒 (for a discussion of its transcription, see p.98, n.16 below), the phonetic part of which is *gai* 匃 (*qˤat). This character can be read as either *e* 遏 (*qˤat) "to repress" or *hai* 害 (*N-kˤat-s) "to harm." The transmitted 周 is certainly a graphic error, because in ancient script 周 𦥑 and 害 𡊅 look very similar. This shows that the Q2 in the transmitted "Zi yi" must have come from a manuscript that had 害 in place of 愒.

e.　For the *zhong* 終 "end" in (5), (1) reads *min* 民 "people." There is no obvious connection between the two characters, but column (f) provides a clue as to the cause of this variant. In (f), (5) also reads *zhong* 終, but (1) reads *zhong* 眾 (*tuŋ-s) "multitudes," which is not only a phonetic loan for *zhong* 終 (*tuŋ) but also a synonym for *min* 民.[14] In

之故 appears in the Shanghai Museum manuscript of *Zhou yi* as *fei jin zhi gu* 非今之古. See Ma Ruichen 馬瑞辰, *Maoshi zhuanjian tongshi* 毛詩傳箋通釋 (Beijing: Zhonghua shuju 1989), 135; Edward L. Shaughnessy, *Unearthing the Changes: Recently Discovered Manuscripts of the* Yi Jing (I Ching) *and Related Texts* (New York: Columbia University Press, 2014), 108–109.

14　For an analysis of this variant, see Ma Nan, "Zhou Qin liang Han *Shu jing* kao," 217.

other words, Q2 in the transmitted "Zi yi" must have come from a manuscript that had *zhong* 衆 at both (e) and (f).

The comparison shows that the Tsinghua *Yin gao* makes the best sense among these versions, while Q1 and Q2 in the transmitted "Zi yi" contain numerous textual errors. To be sure, we should never assume that an ancient manuscript is by default closer to a pristine *urtext* (if there ever was such a thing) simply due to its early date, but in this case it is quite obvious that the transmitted quotations are heavily corrupted. The Tsinghua *Yin gao* gives us an opportunity to detect these errors and evaluate the high standards of Zheng Xuan's philological work.

*Yin gao 尹誥
*Yin's Announcement

隹 田 ... （古文字）

佳 尹 旣 迓 湯 咸 又 一 惪 尹 念 天 之 敗 西 邑 顕 曰 顕 自
愄 亓 又 民 亦 佳 㢓 衆 非 民 亡 與 戰 邑

惟尹旣及湯，咸有一德。尹念天之敗西邑夏曰：「夏自遏其有民，亦惟厥衆。非民無
與守邑。[一]

So it was after (Yi) Yin had joined Tang that both had a unifying virtue.[15] (Yi)
Yin considered Heaven's ruining the Western City Xia and said: "The (ruler

---

15 The "unifying virtue" of Tang and Yi Yin may be an emphasis on their solidarity after
the reunion. In *Yin zhi, Yi Yin appears as someone who needs to be "secured" by a
covenant (slip 4). The wording implies potential betrayal. Zheng Xuan's commentary on
Q1 in the transmitted "Zi yi" also takes this to be a remark about solidarity. See Zhang
Chongli 張崇禮, "Qinghua jian Yin gao kaoshi" 清華簡《尹誥》考釋, at http://www.
fdgwz.org.cn/Web/Show/2400, posted 17 December 2014. On the other hand, Xiong
Xianpin 熊賢品 has recently argued that Tang Xian 湯咸 should be taken as Tang's
name because Tang is also called Xian 咸 in oracle bone inscriptions. He reads the sentence as 惟尹旣及湯咸，有懿德 "So it was after (Yi) Yin had reached Tang Xian that he
[i.e. Yi Yin] had a beautiful virtue." Nevertheless, as Xiong himself notes, whether Xian
is really Tang's name in the oracle bones is still open to dispute. See Xiong Xianpin, "Cong
jiagu wen 'xian wei Cheng Tang' tan Qinghua jian Yin gao 'Yin ji ji Tang xian you yi de'"
從甲骨文"咸為成湯"談清華簡《尹誥》"尹既及湯咸有一德," Jianbo yanjiu 簡帛研
究 2021 Fall and Winter: 1–9.

of) Xia himself repressed[16] his people, as well as his multitudes.[17] Without the people, he will not be able to defend his city. [1]

乑 辟 复 悄 于 民= 叠 之 甬 麗 心 我 戠 滅 頤 今 句 叀 不 藍
執 告 湯 曰 我 克 叕 我 咨 今

厥辟作怨于民，民復之用離心，我剪滅夏。今后曷不監？" 摯告湯曰："我克協我友，
今 [二]

Their ruler aroused resentment among the people, and the people repaid him with the intent to defect. (This was how) we attacked and destroyed Xia. Now why doesn't my lord reflect (on the failure of Xia)?" Zhi reported to Tang, saying: "We are able to maintain harmony with our friends. Now [2]

---

16 The transcription of this character 絕, a *hapax legomenon* in early Chinese texts, is controversial. Everyone agrees that the top component is *cao* 艸 "grass" and the bottom component *xin* 心 "heart." The middle part, however, has been transcribed by the editors as 弦 (弓 on the left and a variant form of 絲 or 絶 on the right) and by Su Jianzhou 蘇建洲 as 弦. See Su Jianzhou, "*Qinghua jian (yi)* kaoshi shiyi ze"《清華簡(壹)》考釋十一則, in *Chuwenzi lunji* 楚文字論集 (Taipei: Wanjuanlou, 2011), 343–396. The crucial question is what the right component of the middle part 絕 is. While both the editor and Su Jianzhou see a 幺 "silk" in it, the standard form of 幺 in Chu script is 幺, which looks very different. In a recent article, Shi Xiaoli 石小力 argues convincingly that 絕 is in fact 勾. The standard form of 勾 in bronze inscriptions is 勾, consisting of a 亡 on the left and a 刀 on the right. In Chu script, 亡 is sometimes written as 匕 and 刀 as 刁. The reason why 絕 is so difficult to identify is because the right half of its 刀 component is missing. The complete graph should look like 絕. If the phonophore is *gai* 勾 (*qˤat), then the character can be read as either *e* 遏 (*qˤat) "to repress" or *hai* 害 (*N-kˤat-s) "to harm." Moreover, the 怨 transcription makes it possible to account for a textual variant in the "Zi yi" chapter of the transmitted *Li ji*. As mentioned in the introduction to this chapter, the "Zi yi" quotation of this sentence has 周 in place of 怨, and the ancient form of 周 can be easily confused with 害. See Shi Xiaoli, "Qinghua jian *Yin Gao* 'gai' zi xin shi" 清華簡《尹誥》"怨"字新釋, *Kaogu yu wenwu* 考古與文物 2019.1: 110–113.

17 Like *Yin zhi*, this manuscript makes a distinction between *zhong* 眾 "multitudes" and *min* 民 "people" (slips 1 and 3), but the nature of the distinction is not clear.

佳 民 遠 邦 逗 志 湯 曰 於 虘₌ 可 复 于 民 卑 我 衆 勿 韋 朕
言 埶 曰 句 亓 李 之 亓 又 顕 之

雖民遠邦歸志。"湯曰："嗚呼！吾何作于民，俾我衆勿違朕言？" 摯曰："后其賚之
其有夏之 ₍三₎

even the people from faraway countries have the intention to join us."[18]
Tang said: "Aha! What should I do for the people so that our multitudes
don't defy my words?" Zhi said: "My lord should reward them with Xia's [3]

---

18 Most scholars take *yuanbang* 遠邦 as a phrase that modifies *min* 民 "people," but it can
mean either "people from faraway countries" (referring to the people who are not Shang)
or "people who had travelled far away from their country" (referring to the Shang people). The second meaning works better with the following verb "return," whereas the
first meaning works better with the previous remark about maintaining harmony with
friend states. See Wang Tingbin 王挺斌, "Qinghua jian *Yin gao* 'yuan bang gui zhi' kao"
清華簡《尹誥》"遠邦歸志"考, at http://www.fdgwz.org.cn/Web/Show/2082, posted
30 June 2013.

𩵋玉田邑舍之吉言乃至眔于白宀邑乚

[金]玉 田 邑 舍 之 吉 言 乃 至 眔 于 白 宀 邑 乚

[金]、玉、田、邑，予之吉言。"乃致眔于亳中邑。[四]

[metal], jades, fields,[19] and cities and send them auspicious words." So (Tang) gathered the multitudes in Bo, the Central City.[20] [4]

---

19   The editors transcribe this character as *ri* 日 "sun," but as Chen Jian points out, it is in fact *tian* 田 "field." See Chen Jian's argument published in an online reply to Fudan daxue chutu wenxian yu guwenzi yanjiu zhongxin yanjiusheng dushuhui, "Qinghua jian *Yin zhi Yin gao* yandu zhaji."

20   This indicates that the capital city Bo acquired its new name "the central city" after the conquest. This change seems to echo the new title of Tang at the end of *Yin zhi*.

VERSO

一

一【一背】

1【1V】

二

二【二背】

2【2V】

三

三【三背】

3【3V】

四

四【四背】

4【4V】

* 尹誥

惟尹既及湯，咸有一德。

尹念天之敗西邑夏曰："夏自遏其有民，亦惟厥衆。非民無與守邑。[一] 厥辟作怨于民，民復之用離心，我翦滅夏。今后曷不監？"

摯告湯曰："我克協我友，今[二] 雖民遠邦歸志。"

湯曰："嗚呼！吾何作于民，俾我衆勿違朕言？"

摯曰："后其賚之其有夏之[三] [金]、玉、田、邑，予之吉言。"

乃致衆于亳中邑。[四]

*Yin's Announcement

So it was after (Yi) Yin had joined Tang that both had a unifying virtue.

(Yi) Yin considered Heaven's ruining the Western City Xia and said: "The (ruler of) Xia himself repressed his people, as well as his multitudes. Without the people, he will not be able to defend his city. [1] Their ruler aroused resentment among the people, and the people repaid him with the intent to defect. (This was how) we attacked and destroyed Xia. Now why doesn't my lord reflect (on the failure of Xia)?"

Zhi reported to Tang, saying: "We are able to maintain harmony with our friends. Now [2] even the people from faraway countries have the intention to join us."

Tang said: "Aha! What should I do for the people so that our multitudes don't defy my words?"

Zhi said: "My lord should reward them with Xia's [3] [metal], jades, fields, and cities and send them auspicious words."

So (Tang) gathered the multitudes in Bo, the Central City. [4]

Chapter Four

Tang zai Chimen 湯在啻門

Tang at the Gate of the Thearch

The Tsinghua manuscript of *Tang zai Chimen* (hereafter *Chimen*) was published in Volume 5 of *Qinghua daxue cang Zhanguo zhujian*. The manuscript was written on 21 slips, which were originally bound with three binding straps. The slips are about 44.5cm in length and well preserved with no loss of writing. The slips are not numbered on the backs, but there are numerous in-text punctuation marks that are helpful for interpretation. The manuscript originally had no title; the editors gave it the title *Tang zai Chimen* based on the opening sentence "In the first month, on *jihai* (day 36), Tang asked the Lesser Servant at the Gate of the Thearch." The manuscript shows signs of proofreading, as some characters appear much smaller in the space between regular characters (see slips 6, 7, and 20). They must have been inserted after the text had been copied. Jia Lianxiang 賈連翔 argues that these characters were added by the same scribe who copied *Chimen* and *Tangqiu* because of their similar calligraphic style.[1]

Physical and codicological features of the slips show that *Chimen* and *Tang chu yu Tangqiu* (hereafter *Tangqiu*) were originally bound together and copied by the same scribe. The image below shows the bottom part of the back of their slips:

---

1   Jia Lianxiang, "Tan Qinghua jian suo jian shushou ziji he wenzi xiugai xianxiang" 談清華簡所見書手字迹和文字修改現象, *Jianbo yanjiu* 簡帛研究 2015 Fall and Winter: 38–52.

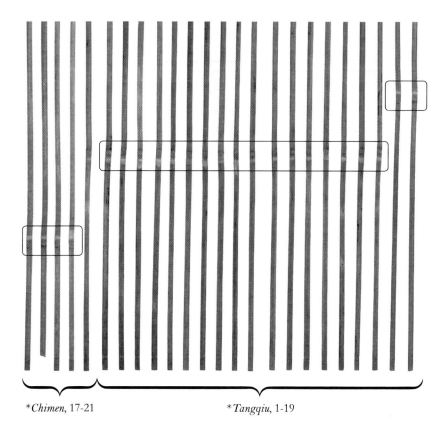

*Chimen, 17-21   *Tangqiu, 1-19

The slips of *Chimen and *Tangqiu can be divided into three physical groups. Slips 1–20 of *Chimen come from one bamboo culm; slip 21 of *Chimen and slips 1–17 of *Tangqiu are from another culm; slips 18–19 of *Tangqiu are from a third one. The textual content of the manuscripts is also similar, but not as similar as that of *Yin zhi and *Yin gao. Both consist of a series of questions and answers between Tang and Yi Yin, and yet *Chimen has nothing but the discussion, while the first part of *Tangqiu is a background story. The discussion itself is also notably different in style — the numerical lists that run through *Chimen are not seen in *Tangqiu at all.

*Chimen opens with Tang's question to Yi Yin about the "good words" of the ancient kings. In Yi Yin's answer, the ancient teachings turn out to be a series of words that are said to "complete" and "assist" the four domains of the cosmic order, namely heaven, earth, state, and person.[2] He goes through these words one after another, giving a highly structured catalogue of terms:

	Completed by	Assisted by
Person	Five flavors (5)	Virtue (1)
State	Four gods (4)	Virtue, service, employment, regulation, punishment (5)
Earth	Nine gods (9)	Metal, wood, water, fire, soil (5)
Heaven	Nine gods (9)	Day, night, spring, summer, autumn, winter (6)

Among these terms, some require no explanation. Ancient and modern readers should be able to understand the five things that assist earth and the six things that assist heaven. Some are given brief explanations in the text, such as the five things that assist the state. Others, such as the "four gods" of the state, the "nine gods" of earth, and the "nine gods" of heaven, are not explained at all. The text seems to expect its target audience to know the meaning of these terms already. In general, Yi Yin's answer does not read like a treatise, but more like a checklist of things that heaven does to maintain order in the world and the ruler does to maintain order in the state.

The most salient feature of *Chimen* is how the text is organized, or, to use the title of a recent collection of essays, its "literary form of argument."[3] Not surprisingly, Joachim Gentz and Dirk Meyer, the editors of that volume, each produced an English translation of *Chimen* and thoroughly analyzed its rhetorical structure. For Gentz and Meyer, the text seeks to convey its meaning not just on the semantic or lexical level, but also through carefully crafted rhymes, parallels, and interlocked patterns, which are combined with the dialogical form.[4] What seems to matter is not whether each individual

---

2   The four domains are reminiscent of the "four great matters" in chapter 25 of the *Laozi*, namely Way, heaven, earth, and the king.

3   See Joachim Gentz and Dirk Meyer eds. *Literary Forms of Argument in Early China* (Leiden: Brill, 2015), especially Gentz's chapter "Defining Boundaries and Relations of Textual Units: Examples from the Literary Tool-Kit of Early Chinese Argumentation," 112–157. See also Dirk Meyer, *Philosophy on Bamboo: Text and the Production of Meaning in Early China* (Leiden: Brill, 2012) for an analysis of the argumentative structure of manuscripts in the Guodian corpus.

4   See Meyer, "'Patterning Meaning': A Thick Description of the Tsinghua Manuscript

term has any profound philosophical meaning, but whether the entire catalogue is organized in a way that mirrors the cosmic order. The text does not
merely talk about order. It embodies the very order it advocates.

As such, *Chimen* belongs to a distinctive textual genre in the Warring
States period that usually features a scene of a new king receiving political
instructions from his minister, who is supposed to possess the time-hon-
ored wisdom of ancient sages. The instructions are often highly formulaic
and rhymed, including either enumeration of undefined (or briefly defined)
didactic items or schematic aphorisms.[5] As examples, one can name the
famous "Hong fan" 洪範 "Great Plan" chapter of *Shang shu*, many chapters of *Yi Zhou shu* 逸周書 *Leftover Zhou Scriptures*, the "Wu Wang jian
zuo" 武王踐阼 chapter of *Da Dai Li ji* 大戴禮記 *Record of Ritual of
the Elder Dai*, and so on. Two other manuscripts in the Tsinghua corpus
may also be included in this category: *Yin Gaozong* (see chapter six of this
volume) and the grand *Wu ji* 五紀 *The Five Cords* in Tsinghua Volume
11.[6] I should mention that this so-called "genre," which has received much
attention in recent scholarship, does not have clearly defined boundaries, but
is more of a "family resemblance" of overlapping similarities. Some texts,

---

'*Tāng zài Chì/Dì mén' (Tāng was at the Chì/Dì Gate) and What It Tells Us about
Thought Production in Early China," 139–167; Gentz, "Literary Forms of Argument in
the Tsinghua University Manuscript Tang Zai Chimen," 194–221.

5   Cao Feng 曹峰 calls them the "Teachers of the Thearchs" type of texts (帝師類文
    獻) and identifies them as "Daoist." The examples he includes in his category are much
    broader than what I am referring to here. He basically tries to give a comprehensive list
    of all such conversations between the legendary kings and their ministers, regardless of
    whether they have formulaic structures or not. See Cao Feng, "Daojia 'di shi' lei wenxian
    chutan" 道家"帝師"類文獻初探, *Zhexue lunji* 哲學論集 49 (2018): 33–60. For discus-
    sions of the significance of numerical lists, especially their place in the "Hong fan" and
    the *Yi Zhou shu*, see Zhao Boxiong 趙伯雄, "Lun xian Qin wenxian zhong de 'yi shu
    wen ji'" 論先秦文獻中的"以數為紀," *Wenxian* 文獻 1999.4: 25–32; Zhang Huaitong
    張懷通, "You 'yi shu wei ji' kan 'Hong fan' de xingzhi yu niandai" 由"以數為紀"看
    《洪范》的性質與年代, *Dongnan wenhua* 東南文化 2006.3: 51–57; Gentz, "Defining
    Boundaries and Relations of Textual Units," 128–129; Yegor Grebnev, "Numerical lists
    of foundational knowledge in early Chinese and early Buddhist traditions," *Asiatische
    Studien/Études Asiatiques* 74.4 (2020): 453–484.

6   See Qinghua daxue chutu wenxian yanjiu yu baohu zhongxin 清華大學出土文獻研究
    與保護中心 eds. *Qinghua daxue cang Zhanguo zhujian (shiyi)* 清華大學藏戰國竹簡(拾
    壹) (Shanghai: Zhong Xi shuju, 2021): 89–132.

such as the "Wen zhuo" 文酌 "Wen's Toast" chapter and the "Da wu" 大武 "Greater Military" chapter of *Yi Zhou shu*, make extensive use of numerical lists but do not situate them in a dialogical context. Others have the dialogical context, but replace the numerical lists with patterned sayings, such as *Yin Gaozong* and the "Wu Wang jian zuo."

What is unique about *Chimen* is that the cosmological framework constructed by Yi Yin features a long physiological description of human life (slips 5–10). The description, which has attracted special attention from scholars, can be divided into two parts, one about human embryonic development and the other about the growth and decay of *qi* after birth. The overall meaning of the passage is clear despite some difficult characters:

唯彼五味之氣，是始以為人。其末氣，是謂玉種。一月始揚。二月乃裹。三月乃形。四月乃固。五月或收。六月生肉。七月乃肌。八月乃正。九月解章。十月乃成，民乃時生。其氣潛濁發始，是其為長且好哉。其氣奮昌，是其為當壯。氣融交以備，是其為力。氣蹙乃老，氣徐乃搖。氣逆亂以妨，是其為疾殃。氣屈乃終，百志皆窮。

It is just the *qi* of the five flavors that starts to make up a person. The seminal *qi* is called the jade seed. In the first month, it starts to rise. In the second month, it is then surrounded (by a sac). In the third month, it then takes shape. In the fourth month, it then becomes firm. In the fifth month, some parts come together. In the sixth month, it grows flesh. In the seventh month, muscles then appear. In the eighth month, it is then properly formed. In the ninth month, separation becomes apparent. In the tenth month, (the fetus) is then complete, and then people are born at the proper time. Their *qi*, sunken in the mire, starts to issue forth; such is (how) they grow and become fair. Their *qi* bursts out and flourishes; such is (how) they are in their prime. The *qi* intermingles so that it is complete; such is (how) they have strength. When the *qi* shrinks, they grow old;

when the *qi* slackens, they falter. The *qi* becomes perverted and disturbed so that it is harmful; this is what makes illness and misfortune. When the *qi* retracts, (life) ends, and the hundred aspirations will all be exhausted."

The first thing to observe is that Yi Yin's response in this section is written in a significantly different style than his responses in the other sections. Recall that each of the four cosmic domains is said to be "completed" and "assisted" by several things. In the other sections, Yi Yin never elaborates upon the things in the "completion" part. The "four gods," "nine gods," and another set of "nine gods" that respectively complete the state, earth, and heaven are never defined, but the things that assist them are enumerated and sometimes explained in detail. In the case of "person," however, Yi Yin makes no mention of how virtue (which is said to "illuminate" personhood) encourages self-cultivation, but gives a long account of how *qi* completes the human body.[7]

Yi Yin's description of the ten-month fetal development has many parallels in early Chinese texts, such as in the "Shui di" 水地 "Water and Earth" chapter of *Guanzi* 管子, the Mawangdui manuscript *Taichan shu* 胎産

---

7 For studies of this passage, see Cao Feng 曹峰, "Qinghua jian *Tang zai Chimen* yu qi xiangguan neirong yanjiu" 清華簡《湯在啻門》與氣相關內容研究, *Zhexue yanjiu* 哲學研究 2016.12, 35–41;Huang Rener 黃人二, "Qinghua daxue cang Zhanguo zhujian (wu) *Tang zai Chimen* tongjie — jianlun ren huaitai shiyue ge jieduan mingcheng" 清華大學藏戰國竹簡（五）《湯在啻門》通解——兼論人懷胎十月各階段名稱, in Paul Fischer and Lin Zhipeng 林志鵬 eds. *Zhiqi yangxin zhi shu: Zhongguo zaoqi de xiushen fangfa* 治氣養心之術：中國早期的修身方法 (Shanghai: Fudan daxue chubanshe 2017), 106–112; Chen Ligui 陳麗桂, "*Tang zai Chimen* de qihua taichan shuo yu tian ren lunshu"《湯在啻門》的氣化胎産説與天人論述, in Fudan Daxue chutu wenxian yu guwenzi yanjiu zhongxin 復旦大學出土文獻與古文字研究中心 eds. *Chutu wenxian yu chuanshi dianji de quanshi* 出土文獻與傳世典籍的詮釋 (Shanghai: Zhong Xi shuju, 2019), 97–112; Huang Kuan-yun 黃冠雲, "Shuo *Tang zai Chimen* lun qi yi jie wenzi" 説《湯在啻門》論氣一節文字, in *Qinghua jian yanjiu* 3 (Shanghai: Zhong Xi shuju, 2019), 159–170; Shirley Chan 陳慧, "Shenti yu zhiguo — shidu Qinghua jian *Tang zai Chimen* jianlun 'ji'" 身體與治國——試讀清華簡《湯在啻門》兼論"疾," in *Qinghua jian yanjiu* 3, 171–182; Constance A. Cook, "Contextualizing 'Becoming a Complete Person' in the *Tang zai Chimen*," in *Qinghua jian yanjiu* 3, 183–193; Kuo Li-hua 郭梨華, "Qinghua jian (wu) guanyu wei zhi zhexue tanjiu" 清華簡（伍）關於味之哲學探究, in *Qinghua jian yanjiu* 3, 222–236.

書 *Book of the Generation of the Fetus, and the "Jing shen" 精神 "Quint-essential Spirit" chapter of the *Huainanzi* 淮南子. Let me quote some of these alternative accounts as examples for comparison:[8]

人，水也。男女精氣合而水流形。三月如咀。咀者何？曰五味。五味者何，曰五藏。酸主脾，鹹主肺，辛主腎，苦主肝，甘主心。五藏已具，而後生肉。脾生膈，肺生骨，腎生腦，肝生革，心生肉。五肉已具，而後發為九竅。脾發為鼻，肝發為目，腎發為耳，肺發為竅。五月而成，十月而生。

People are water. When the quintessential *qi* of males and females are joined together, water flows into form. In the third month, it develops the sense of taste. What does it taste? It tastes the five flavors. What are the five flavors? They are the five viscera. Sour governs the spleen; salty governs the lungs; spicy governs the kidneys; bitter governs the liver; sweet governs the heart. Once the five viscera are established, they produce the fleshy parts. The spleen produces membranes; the lungs produce the bones; the kidneys produce the brain; the liver produces the skin; and the heart produces the flesh. Once the five fleshy parts are established, they give rise to the nine orifices. The spleen gives rise to the nose; the liver gives rise to the eyes; the kidneys give rise to the ears; the lungs give rise to the orifices. In the fifth month (the fetus) is complete; in the tenth month it is born.[9]

---

8   For two comprehensive comparisons of these passages, see Gil Raz, "Birthing the Self: Metaphor and Transformation in Medieval Daoism," in Jinhua Jia, Xiaofei Kang, and Ping Yao eds. *Gendering Chinese Religion: Subject, Identity, and Body* (Albany: SUNY Press, 2014), 183–200; Zhang Hanmo 張翰墨, "*Tang zai Chimen*, shi yue huaitai yu zao-qi Zhongguo shushu shijieguan"《湯在啻門》、十月懷胎與早期中國術數世界觀, *Bulletin of the Jao Tsung-I Academy of Sinology* 4 (2017.5): 173–212.

9   Li Xiangfeng 黎翔鳳, *Guanzi jiaozhu* 管子校注 (Beijing: Zhonghua shuju, 2004), 815–816.

夫精神者，所受於天也；而形體者，所禀於地也。故曰：
"一生二，二生三，三生萬物。萬物背陰而抱陽，沖氣以
為和。"故曰："一月而膏，二月而胅，三月而胎，四月
而肌，五月而筋，六月而骨，七月而成，八月而動，九
月而躁，十月而生。"形體以成，五臟乃形。是故肺主目，
腎主鼻，膽主口，肝主耳 [，脾主舌]。

The quintessential spirit is what we receive from Heaven;
the physical body is what we are given by Earth. Therefore it
is said: "One begets two; two begets three; three begets the
myriad things. The myriad things carry on their backs the yin
and embrace in their arms the yang and, through the blending
of *qi*, become harmonious." Therefore it is said: "In the first
month, it becomes lard. In the second month, a corporeal mass
develops. In the third month, an embryo forms. In the fourth
month, the muscles develop. In the fifth month, the sinews
form. In the sixth month, the bones develop. In the seventh
month, (the fetus) is complete. In the eighth month, the fetus
moves. In the ninth month, it becomes restless. In the tenth
month, it is born." The physical body is thereby completed and
the five viscera are formed. Therefore, the lungs govern the
eyes; the kidneys govern the nose; the gallbladder governs the
mouth; the liver governs the ears [; and the spleen governs the
tongue].[10]

故人之產也，入於冥冥，出於冥冥，乃始為人。一月名
曰流形……二月始膏……三月始脂……[四月] 而水授
之，乃始成血。……五月而火授之，乃始成氣。……六
月而金授之，乃始成筋。……七 [月而] 木授 [之，乃始
成骨]。……八月而土授 [之，乃始成膚革。] ……[九
月而石授之，乃始成] 毫毛。……伺之十月。

---

10 He Ning 何寧, *Huainanzi jishi* 淮南子集釋 (Beijing: Zhonghua shuju, 1998), 505–506.

Therefore, as for the birth of human beings, they enter obscure darkness and exit from obscure darkness, and then start to become humans. In the first month it is called "flowing into the form." ... In the second month it first becomes lard. ... In the third month it first becomes suet. ... [In the fourth month] water is bestowed on it, and blood first forms. ... In the fifth month fire is bestowed on it, and *qi* first forms. ... In the sixth month metal is bestowed on it, and sinew first forms. ... In the seventh [month] wood is bestowed on [it, and bone first forms.] ... In the eighth month earth is bestowed on [it, and skin and hide first form.] ... [In the ninth month stone is bestowed on it, and] filament hairs [first form.] ... wait until the tenth month ... [11]

These accounts bear witness to competing models of integrating human embryogenesis and correlative cosmology. There are, on the one hand, various versions of a month-by-month description of fetal development and, on the other hand, different correlations between the five agents, five flavors, five viscera, five fleshy parts, and so on. The *Guanzi* passage highlights the third and fifth months as pivotal moments but does not detail the development month by month. In the third month, the fetus starts to taste the five flavors (that is, ingestion), which in turn gives rise to the five viscera, five fleshy parts, and nine orifices. The process is already completed in the fifth month, but the fetus is not born until the tenth month. The *Huainanzi* quotes a month-by-month description from an unknown source, which locates the completion of the fetus in the seventh month. Like the *Guanzi*, it mentions the formation of the five viscera, but the members of the five

---

11 Liu Zhao 劉釗 ed. "Taichan shu" 胎產書, in Hunan sheng bowuguan 湖南省博物館 and Fudan daxue chutu wenxian yu guwenzi yanjiu zhongxin 復旦大學出土文獻與古文字研究中心 eds. *Changsha Mawangdui Hanmu jianbo jicheng* 長沙馬王堆漢墓簡帛集成 vol. 6 (Beijing: Zhonghua shuju, 2014), 93–94; Donald Harper, *Early Chinese Medical Literature: The Mawangdui Medical Manuscripts* (New York: Kegan Paul International, 1997), 378–381.

viscera, the surface orifices that they govern, as well as the time when they are formed, are all different. The *Taichan shu also provides a month-by-month description, but it combines fetal development with the five-agent theory in a temporal fashion. From the fourth to the eighth month, the five agents in turn are "bestowed" (shou 受) on the fetus in their conquest order. With the bestowal of each agent, one essential element of the human body (but not the five viscera) is correspondingly completed.

Compared with these accounts, the passage from *Chimen appears to indicate an earlier stage of embryogenetic understanding, in which the five flavors are not yet part of a full-blown five-agent theory. This lack of interest in correlative cosmology sets it apart from the other passages that all seek to map the five agents/viscera onto human embryogenesis. The table below shows their differences:

	*Chimen	*Taichan shu	Huainanzi	Guanzi
Month-by-month description	Y	Y	Y	N
Five-agent/ viscera correlations	N	Y	Y	Y

The comparison demonstrates the fluid state of medical knowledge in early China, for there is simply no standard theory of human embryogenesis. Nevertheless, we see an increasing tendency to reconceptualize fetal development in terms of five agents/viscera correlations. The most obvious indicator of this is the shifting role of qi. While in *Chimen, qi is the driving force that governs the whole process, in *Taichan shu it is relegated to but one of the essential components bestowed upon the fetus by fire in the fifth month. The Guanzi and Huainanzi accounts sit in the middle between the two extremes by having both qi/water as the underlying force and a correlative framework.

113

*Tang zai Chimen 湯在啻門
*Tang at the Gate of the Thearch[12]

貞月己亥湯才啻門霹於小臣古之先帝亦有良言
青至於今虎小臣會

正月己亥，湯在帝門問於小臣：「古之先帝，亦有良言情至於今乎？」小臣答 [一]

In the first month, on *jihai* (day 36), Tang asked the Lesser Servant at the Gate of the Thearch:[13] "As for the former thearchs in ancient times, are there still good words (from them) that have truly come down to this day?" The Lesser Servant answered, [1]

---

12 In my translation of slip 1 below, I choose to read 啻 as *di* 帝 "thearch" (see p.114, n.13), but in the chinese title I have 啻 instead of 帝. This is because 湯在啻門 has become the widely known title of this manuscript.

13 I read *chi* 啻 as *di* 帝 "Thearch." The "Gate of the Thearch" might have been a fictitious location used only to evoke Tang's question about the teachings of the former Thearchs. At the end of the *Yin zhi* Tang himself received the title of "Thearch." For a discussion of this gate and its possible relationship to the *di* 禘 sacrifice, see Scott Cook, "Qinghua zhujian wu *Tang zai Chimen* zhaji" 清華竹簡（伍）《湯在啻門》札記, in *Qinghua jian yanjiu* 3 (Shanghai: Zhong Xi shuju, 2019), 144–145.

曰 又 才 ＿ 女 亡 又 良 言 清 至 於 今 則 可 目 成 人 可 以
成 邦 ＿ 可 目 成 墬 ＿ 可 目 成

曰：“有哉！如無有良言情至於今，則何以成人？何以成邦？何以成地？何以成 [二]

saying: "There are! If no good words (from them) have truly come down to this day, then how would a person be completed? How would a state be completed? How would earth be completed? How would [2]

天＿ 湯 或 𩰊 於 小 臣 曰 幾 言 成 人 ＿ 幾 言 成 邦 ＿ 幾
言 成 埊 ＿ 幾 言 成 天 ＿ 小 臣 會 曰

天？ ” 湯 又 問 於 小 臣 曰：“幾 言 成 人？ 幾 言 成 邦？ 幾 言 成 地？ 幾 言 成 天？ ” 小 臣 答 曰：

[三]

heaven be completed?" Tang again asked the Lesser Servant, saying: "How many words does it take to complete a person? How many words does it take to complete a state? How many words does it take to complete earth? How many words does it take to complete heaven?" The Lesser Servant answered, saying: [3]

五目成人悳目光之＿四目成邦五目槻之＿九目
成坓五目塑＿九目成天六

"五以成人，德以光之。四以成邦，五以相之。九以成地，五以將。九以成天，六 [四]

"It takes five to complete a person and virtue to illuminate him. It takes four to complete a state and five to assist it. It takes nine to complete earth and five to support (it).[14] It takes nine to complete heaven and six [4]

14　A pronoun *zhi* 之 "it" is missing here, but it appears later in slip 18 when the question is repeated.

目 行 之 ＿ 湯 或 霽 於 小 臣 曰 人 可 昃 目 生 ＿ 可 多 目
長 箁 少 而 老 ＿ 耆 猷 是 人 而

以行之。" 湯又問於小臣曰: "人何得以生? 何多以長? 孰少而老? 胡猶是人而 [五]

to set it in motion." Tang again asked the Lesser Servant, saying: "As for a
person, how does he come to be born? What does he have more of so that
he grows? What[15] does he have less of so that he ages? Why is it that this
same person is [5]

---

15 The manuscript uses *shu* 孰 "who/which/what" here instead of the *he* 何 "what" in the
other questions.

罷 亞 罷 好 ＿ 小 臣 倉 曰 唯 皮 五 味 之 燹 是 哉 以 為 人
亓 末 燹 是 胃 玉 穜 ⟨⟩- 月 台

一惡一好 [16]？ "小臣答曰："唯彼五味之氣，是始以為人。其末氣，是謂玉種。一月始 [六]

sometimes foul and sometimes fair?[17]" The Lesser Servant answered, saying: "It is just the *qi* of the five flavors[18] that starts to make up a person. The seminal *qi* is called the jade seed.[19] In the first month, it starts [6]

---

16 The character 好 is inserted in the space between 一 and 小.

17 Tang was not asking about moral goodness when he used the word *hao* 好 "good, fair," and the Lesser Servant's answer was all about physical growth and well-being. As Chen Jian 陳劍 points out, Tang's question is similar to the fourth question from the Mawang-dui manuscript *Shi wen* 十問 *Ten Questions*:

> 民始蒲淳溜刑，何得而生？溜刑成體，何失而死？何奂之人也，有惡有好，有夭有壽？
>
> When people first dispense the purity that flows into the form, what is obtained so that life occurs? When flowing into the form produces a body, what is lost so that death occurs? All being man alike, why are some foul while others are fair; why do some die young while others are long-lived?

See Chen Jian, "*Qinghua jian (wu) yu jiushuo huzheng liangze*"《清華簡（伍）》與舊 説互證兩則, at http://www.fdgwz.org.cn/Web/Show/2494, posted 14 April 2015. See also Donald Harper, *Early Chinese Medical Literature: The Mawangdui Medical Manuscripts* (New York: Kegan Paul International, 1997), 393.

18 In standard correlative cosmology, the five flavors are sour, salty, spicy, bitter, and sweet.

19 The editors gloss *mo* 末 as *zhong* 終 "the end," but the *moqi* 末氣 is certainly not the end but the "seed" (i.e. the sperm) and the beginning of growth. They also suggest that *mo* (*mˤat) might be a loan word for *mie* 蔑 (*mˤet) "none" or "little." Zhang Hanmo argues that there is no need to take *mo* as a loan word. Literally, *mo* refers to the tip of thin objects such a twig or hair. From this it derives the meanings of "end," "small," or "powder." The *moqi* is the seminal *qi* produced at one end of the male body. It seems to be just a different name for *jingqi* 精氣 "quintessential *qi*." See Zhang Hanmo, "*Tang zai Chimen*, shi yue huaitai yu zaoqi Zhongguo shushu shijieguan," 192.

匐 二 月 乃 裹 三 月 乃 刑 ＿ 四 月 乃 胠 ＿ 五 月 或 收 六
月 生 肉 七 月 乃 縢 ＿ 八 月 乃 正

揚。二月乃裹。三月乃 [20] 形。四月乃固。五月或收。六月生肉。七月乃肌。八月乃正。[七]

to rise.[21] In the second month, it is then surrounded (by a sac). In the third month, it then takes shape. In the fourth month, it then becomes firm. In the fifth month, some parts come together.[22] In the sixth month, it grows flesh. In the seventh month, muscles then appear. In the eighth month, it is then properly formed. [7]

---

20 The character 乃 is inserted in the space between 月 and 形.

21 The verb *yang* 揚 can mean either "to rise" or "to winnow." Since this is still the earliest stage of embryogenesis, the "winnow" meaning, which continues the seed metaphor, may also be implied. As Ma Nan notes, this verb is written with the (probably not meaningless) signific *bao* 勹, which is a variant of *bao* 包 "wrap" or *bao* 胞 "sac." Her reading can be found in Qinghua daxue chutu wenxian dushuhui 清華大學出土文獻讀書會, "Qinghua jian diwu ce zhengli baogao buzheng" 清華簡第五冊整理報告補正, at https://www.ctwx.tsinghua.edu.cn/info/1081/2214.htm, posted 8 April 2015.

22 The editors read *shou* 收 as *xiu* 褎 "flourishing." Wang Ning 王寧 reads it as *jiu* 糾 "twisted, intertwined" and relates it to the development of tendons. See Wang Ning, "Du *Tang zai Chimen* sanzha" 讀《湯在啻門》散札, at http://www.fdgwz.org.cn/Web/Show/2513, posted 6 May 2015. However, the original word *shou*, which literally means "to gather," seems to make good sense already.

九 月 緣 章 _ 十 月 乃 成 _ 民 乃 時 生 _ 亓 燹 䵞 緣 發
絀 _ 是 亓 為 長 虘 好 才 _ 亓 燹 奮

九月解章。十月乃成，民乃時生。其氣潛濁發始，是其為長且好哉。其氣奮 [八]

In the ninth month, separation becomes apparent.[23] In the tenth month, (the fetus) is then complete, and then people are born at the proper time. Their *qi*, sunken in the mire,[24] starts to issue forth; such is (how) they grow and become fair. Their *qi* bursts out and [8]

23　The character 緣 (consisting of 解 and 絲) is similar to another character 緣 (consisting of 角, 牛, and 糸) on the same slip. The editors take the 絲 (or what they transcribe as 絲) underneath to be the phonophore and read it as *xian* 顯 "clear, manifest." However, it seems more natural to take 解 as the phonophore and 絲 as the signific. I therefore follow Wang Ning in reading the character as *jie* 解 "separation" and rendering the phrase *jiezhang* 解章 as "separation becomes apparent." Wang Ning further takes this as referring to the differentiation of gender. See Wang Ning, "Du *Tang zai Chimen* sanzha."

24　As mentioned in note 23, the character 緣 is similar to 緣 in the ninth month of fetal development. Whether they should have the same reading is controversial. Strictly speaking, the phonophore of 緣 is 睾 rather than 解. The character 解 in Chu script has a fairly standard form that almost always has the 刀 component (see, for example, the second character on slip 17 of this manuscript). On the other hand, 睾 , according to the 6th century dictionary *Yu pian* 玉篇, is the archaic form of *chu* 觸 "knock against, touch, encounter, defy." This character also appears on slip 20 of the Shanghai Museum manuscript *Kongzi Shilun* 孔子詩論 *Confucius on the Odes* as 睾 . The phrase *qianchu* 潛觸, which literally means "to be submerged and to knock against," is very difficult and has provoked considerable discussion, but no agreement has been reached yet. Huang Kuan-yun 黃冠雲 relates the phrase to *chenzhuo* 沈濁 "sunken in the mire" in the *Zhuangzi*, arguing that *qian* 潛 is a synonym for *chen* 沈 and *chu* 觸 is a phonetic loan for *zhuo* 濁. See Huang Kuan-yun, "Shuo *Tang zai Chimen* lun qi yi jie wenzi," 160. This is not a perfect solution, but it makes better sense than the editors' *chongchu* 崇歔 "filled with anger."

昌 是 亓 為 壺 楒 熨 燹 交 以 備 是 亓 為 力 ＿ 熨 戚 乃 老
熨 纔 乃 猷 熨 逆 躝 昌 方

昌，是其為當壯。氣融交以備，是其為力。氣戚乃老，氣徐乃搖。氣逆亂以妨，[九]

flourishes; such is (how) they are in their prime.[25] The *qi* intermingles so that it is complete; such is (how) they have strength. When the *qi* shrinks, they grow old; when the *qi* slackens, they falter.[26] The *qi* becomes perverted and disturbed so that it is harmful; [9]

---

25 I follow the editors in reading 楒 as *zhuang* 壯 "strong, robust." The character is differentiated from 楒 (read as *xiang* 相 "assist") on slips 4 and 10 by having a *li* 力 "strength" signific. The phrase *dangzhuang* 當壯 "to be in one's prime" is usually contrasted with *lao* 老 "old," such as in the following sentence from the "Shang xing" 賞刑 "Rewards and Punishments" chapter of *Shang jun shu* 商君書 *Book of Lord Shang*: "Therefore, those who are in their prime devote themselves to battle, and those who are old and weak devote themselves to defense" (故當壯者務於戰，老弱者務於守).

26 I follow the editors in reading 纔 as *xu* 徐 "slacken." Shan Yuchen 單育辰 reads *you* 猷 as *yao* 搖 "to falter." See Shan Yuchen, "Qinghua daxue cang zhanguo zhujian (wu) shiwen dingbu"《清華大學藏戰國竹簡（伍）》釋文訂補, in Fudan daxue chutu wenxian yu guwenzi yanjiu zhongxin 復旦大學出土文獻與古文字研究中心 eds. *Zhanguo wenzi yanjiu de huigu yu zhanwang* 戰國文字研究的回顧與展望 (Shanghai: Zhong Xi shuju, 2017), 207.

是亓為疾央燹屈乃夂百志皆窮 ＿ 湯或霝於小臣
夫四目成邦五目楜之

是其為疾殃。氣屈乃終, 百志皆窮。" 湯又問於小臣:"夫 '四以成邦, 五以相之', [十]

this is what makes illness and misfortune. When the *qi* retracts, (life) ends, and the hundred aspirations will all be exhausted." Tang again asked the Lesser Servant: "As for 'It takes four to complete a state and five to assist it,' [10]

可 也 _ 小 臣 會 曰 唯 皮 四 神 是 胃 四 正 五 目 相 之 悳
事 设 正 型 _ 湯 或 䎽 於

何也？" 小臣答曰："唯彼四神，是謂四正。五以相之：德、事、役、政、刑。" 湯
又問於 [十一]

what does it mean?" The Lesser Servant answered: "It is the four gods that
are called the four governors.[27] 'It takes five to assist it,' this refers to virtue,
service, conscription, regulation, and punishment."[28] Tang again asked [11]

---

[27] The four gods are probably the gods of the four seasons. As for the *sizheng* 四正, the
editors point out that in the "Jun chen xia" 君臣下 chapter of the *Guanzi*, the term is an
official title: "The four governors and the five officers are the body of the state" (四正五
官，國之體也).

[28] The five terms can be divided into three groups: (1) virtue, (2) service and conscription,
and (3) regulation and punishment. While virtue is the ruler's personal merit, the other
four are public affairs of the state. The parallel between regulation and punishment is
very common in early texts, such as in *Analects* 2.3: "If you guide them with regulations
and keep them in line with punishments, the people will become evasive without any
sense of shame." (道之以政，齊之以刑，民免而無耻.)

小 臣 娓 悳 奚 若 亞 悳 奚 若 ＿ 岂 事 奚 若 亞 事 奚 若 ＿
岂 设 奚 若 亞 设 奚 若 ＿ 岂

小臣："美德奚若，惡德奚若？ 美事奚若，惡事奚若？ 美役奚若，惡役奚若？ 美 [十二]

the Lesser Servant: "What is fine[29] virtue like? What is foul virtue like? What is fine service like? What is foul service like? What is fine conscription like? What is foul conscription like? What is fine [12]

29　When the character 娓 (*mei* 美 "fine, good, beautiful") appears for the first time, it has the 女 signific, but in all later cases it is just written as 岂 without the signific.

125

正 奚 若 亞 正 奚 若 ＿ 屶 型 奚 若 亞 型 奚 若 ＿ 小 臣 會
悳 濬 明 執 訐 㠯 義 成 此 胃

政奚若，惡政奚若？美刑奚若，惡刑奚若？ ” 小臣答： “德濬明，執信以義成，此謂

[十三]

regulation like? What is foul regulation like? What is fine punishment like?
What is foul punishment like?" The Lesser Servant answered: "When virtue
is wise and bright, it holds fast to trustworthiness and is completed with
propriety, and this is called [13]

岜 悳 可 目 葆 成 ＿ 悳 宧 亟 執 譌 目 亡 成 此 胃 亞 悳 唯
成 或 澀 ＿ 记 事 又 穋 民 長

美德，可以保成；德褊急，執偽以亡成，此謂惡德，雖成或瀆。起事有穋，民長 [十四]

fine virtue, which is able to guarantee completion. When virtue is petty and
hasty,[30] it holds fast to falsehood and is completed with dissipation,[31] and
this is called foul virtue, which is profane even if it brings things to completion. When by initiating a service one reaps benefits, and the people for a
long time [14]

---

30 For the reading of 宧亟 as *bianji* 褊急 "petty and hasty," see Zhang Fuhai 張富海, "Shi
Qinghua jian *Tang zai Chimen* de bianji" 釋清華簡《湯在啻門》的褊急, *Chutu wenxian* 出土文獻 12 (2018): 130–134.

31 The editors point out that this meaning of *wang* 亡 "dissipated" can be found in *Mengzi*
1B5: "To delight in alcohol without satiation is what is meant by 'dissipated'" (樂酒無厭
謂之亡).

127

萬 之 此 胃 岂 事 ＿ 设 事 亡 穫 疒 民 亡 古 此 胃 亞 事 ＿
记 设 時 訓 民 備 不 甬 此 胃

賴之，此謂美事；起事無穫，病民無故，此謂惡事。起役時順，民備不用，此謂 [十五]

rely on it, it is called fine service. When by initiating a service one reaps no benefit but makes the people ill for no reason, it is called foul service. When one initiates conscription at the proper time so that the people are prepared but not deployed, it is called [15]

美役；起役不時，大費於邦，此謂惡役。政簡以成，此謂美政；政禍亂以無常，民 [十六]

fine conscription. When one initiates conscription at the improper time at great cost to the state, it is called foul conscription. When regulation is simple and[32] complete, it is called fine regulation. When regulation is disastrous,[33] chaotic, and inconstant, making the people [16]

32　All occurences of *yi* 以 (*ləʔ) on slips 16 and 17 should be taken as *er* 而 (*nə) "and" rather than "with." Therefore, *jian yi chang* 簡以成 means "simple and complete" rather than "completed with simplicity."

33　The Tsinghua editors read the character constituted by two 化 as *huo* 禍 "disastrous." It is also possible to read it as *hua* 嘩 "clamorous," because the same character also appears on slip 16 of *Tang Chu yu Tangqiu*, where it should certainly be read as *hua* 華 "florid." For a detailed argument for this alternative reading, see Wang Tingbin 王挺斌, "Tantan guwenzi ziliao zhong cong er hua de zi" 談談古文字資料中從二化的字, *Chutu wenxian* 出土文獻 10 (2017): 79–84.

咸 解 體 自 卹 此 胃 亞 正 ＿ 型 情 目 不 方 此 胃 屵 型= 簷
目 亡 棠 此 胃 亞 型 ＿ 湯 或

咸解體自卹, 此謂惡政。刑情以不妨, 此謂美刑; 刑滯以無常, 此謂惡刑。" 湯又 [十七]

all split apart[34] and care only about themselves, it is called foul regulation.
When punishment fits the reality (of crimes) and is not harmful, it is called
fine punishment. When punishment is heavy[35] and inconstant, it is called
foul punishment." Tang again [17]

---

34 According to the editors, the phrase *jieti* 解體 "to split apart" corresponds to the same
expression in the *Zuo zhuan* (the 8th year of Duke Cheng): "If trust cannot be ascer-
tained and propriety has no basis to be established, who among the territorial lords from
the four directions would not split apart?" (信不可知, 義無所立, 四方諸侯, 其誰不解
體?)

35 I follow Shan Yuchen in reading this character as *zhi* 滯, which usually means "congealed"
or "stagnant." Both the editors and Shan Yuchen gloss it as *zhong* 重 "heavy." See Shan
Yuchen, "Qinghua daxue cang zhanguo zhujian (wu) shiwen dingbu," 206–207.

（竹簡文字圖）

羣 於 小 臣 九 目 成 墜 五 目 塑 之 可 也 ＿ 小 臣 會 曰 唯
皮 九 神 是 胃 墜 真 五 目 塑 之

問於小臣：“九以成地，五以將之，何也？” 小臣答曰：“唯彼九神，是謂地真。五
以將之：[十八]

asked the Lesser Servant: "As for 'It takes nine to complete earth and five
to support it,' what does it mean?" The Lesser Servant answered, saying: "It
is the nine gods that are called the deities of earth.[36] 'It takes five to support it,' [18]

---

36 The editors suspect that *zhen* 真 is *qi* 祇 "deity." Huang Jie 黃傑 (a.k.a. Musilang 暮
四郎) further points out that 真 羣 is a graphic error for 祇, which is written as 羣 in
Yin gaozong. See Huang Jie (Musilang), "Qinghua wu *Tang zai Chimen* chudu" 清華
五《湯在啻門》初讀 #2, at http://www.bsm.org.cn/forum/forum.php?mod=view-
thread&tid=3248, posted 11 April 2015.

水火金木土目成五凵目穠五穀 _ 湯或羴於小臣
夫九目成天六目行之可也 _ 小

水、火、金、木、土，以成五曲，以植五穀。"湯又問於小臣："夫九以成天，六以行之，
何也？"小 [十九]

this refers to water, fire, metal, wood, and soil,[37] by which we complete the
five regions[38] and plant the five grains." Tang again asked the Lesser Servant:
"As for 'It takes nine to complete heaven and six to set it in motion,' what
does it mean?" The Lesser [19]

---

37 The five agents or elements here appear in the order of mutual conquest.
38 The editors gloss *qu* 曲 as *yu* 隅 "corner" and take *wuqu* 五曲 as a synonym of *wufang*
五方 "five regions." In standard correlative cosmology, the five regions are north, south,
east, west, and center. Ethan Harkness, in an online discussion, suggested that the five
regions might also be five concentric circles/squares. For a discussion of the concentric
model, see Huang Ruxuan 黃儒宣, "Zuozhong qiju ji bosai youxi xiangguan wenti yanjiu" 左冢棋局及博塞游戲相關問題探究, *Zhongyang yanjiuyuan lishi yuyan yanjiusuo
jikan* "中央研究院"歷史語言研究所集刊 93.2 (2022): 273–330.

臣 酓 曰 唯 皮 九 神 是 胃 九 宏 六 目 行 之 畫 麦 芚 顕 䉤
各 各 時 不 解 此 隹 事 首 亦

臣答曰:"唯 [39] 彼九神,是謂九宏。六以行之:晝、夜、春、夏、秋、冬,各司不懈。
此惟事首,亦 [二十]

Servant answered, saying: "It is the nine gods that are called the nine expanses.[40] 'It takes six to set it in motion,' this refers to day, night, spring, summer, autumn, and winter, each of which governs tirelessly. These are the beginning of (all) affairs, as well as [20]

39　The character 唯 is inserted in the space between 曰 and 彼.
40　The editors suggest that the "nine gods" probably refers to the gods of the "Nine Heavens" (*jiutian* 九天). The term *jiuhong* 九宏 "nine expanses," on the other hand, is never seen in ancient texts.

隹 天 道 ＿ 湯 曰 天 尹 唯 古 先᷂帝 之 良 言 則 可 目 改 之 ＿

惟天道。"湯曰："天尹！唯古之先帝之良言，則何以改之？"[二十一]

the Way of Heaven." Tang said: "Heavenly minister! These being the good words from the former thearchs in ancient times, how could I change them?"[21]

＊湯在啻門

正月己亥，

湯在帝門問於小臣：

　　　　“古之先帝，亦有良言情至於今乎？”

小臣答[一]曰：

　　　　“有哉！如無有良言情至於今，則

　　　　何以成人？

　　　　何以成邦？

　　　　何以成地？

　　　　何以成[二]天？”

湯又問於小臣曰：

　　　　“幾言成人？

　　　　幾言成邦？

　　　　幾言成地？

　　　　幾言成天？”

小臣答曰：[三]

　　　　“五以成人，德以光（＊kʷˤaŋ）之。

　　　　四以成邦，五以相（＊[s]aŋ）之。

　　　　九以成地，五以將（＊[ts]aŋ-s）。

　　　　九以成天，六[四]以行（＊Cə.[g]ˤraŋ）之。”

湯又問於小臣曰：

　　　　“人何得以生（＊sreŋ）？

　　　　何多以長（＊traŋʔ）？

　　　　孰少而老（＊C.rˤuʔ）？

　　　　胡猶是人而[五]一惡一好（＊qʰˤuʔ）？”

小臣答曰：

　　　　“唯彼五味之氣，是始以為人。

135

其末氣，是謂玉種。

一月始 [六] 揚。二月乃裏。三月乃形。四月乃固。五月或收。六月生肉。七月乃肌。八月乃正。[七] 九月解章。十月乃成，民乃時生。

其氣潛濁發始（ *l̩ə́ʔ），是其為長且好哉（ *[ts]ˤə ）。

其氣奮 [八] 昌（ *mə-tʰaŋ-s），是其為當壯（ *[ts]aŋ-s ）。

氣融交以備（ *[b]rək-s），是其為力（ *k.rək ）。

氣蹙乃老（ *C.rˤuʔ），氣徐乃搖（ *ɢ(r)u ）。

氣逆亂以妨（ *pʰaŋ），[九] 是其為疾殃（ *ʔaŋ ）。

氣屈乃終（ *tuŋ），百志皆窮（ *m-[g](r)uŋ ）。"

湯又問於小臣：

"夫'四以成邦，五以相之'，[十] 何也？"

小臣答曰：

"唯彼四神，是謂四正（ *C.teŋ ）。

五以相之：德、事、役、政、刑（ *[ɢ]ˤeŋ ）。"

湯又問於 [十一] 小臣：

"美德奚若，惡德奚若？

美事奚若，惡事奚若？

美役奚若，惡役奚若？

美 [十二] 政奚若，惡政奚若？

美刑奚若，惡刑奚若？"

小臣答：

"德濬明，執信以義成，此謂 [十三] 美德，可以保成；

德禍急，執偽以亡成，此謂惡德，雖成或潰。

起事有穫，民長 [十四] 賴之，此謂美事；

起事無穫，病民無故，此謂惡事。

起役時順，民備不用，此謂 [十五] 美役；

起役不時，大費於邦，此謂惡役。

政簡以成，此謂美政；

政禍亂以無常，民 [十六] 咸解體自恤，此謂惡政。

刑情以不妨，此謂美刑；

刑滯以無常，此謂惡刑。"

湯又[十七]問於小臣：
"九以成地，五以將之，何也？"
小臣答曰：
"唯彼九神（*Cə.li[n]），是謂地真（*ti[n]）。
五以將之：[十八]水、火、金、木、土，
以成五曲（*kʰ(r)ok），以植五穀（*[k]ˤok）。"

湯又問於小臣：
"夫九以成天，六以行之，何也？"
小[十九]臣答曰：
"唯彼九神，是謂九宏。
六以行之：晝、夜、春、夏、秋、冬，各司不懈。
此惟事首（*l̥uʔ），亦[二十]惟天道（*[kə.l]ˤuʔ）。"
湯曰：
"天尹！唯古之先帝之良言，則何以改之？"[二十一]

137

*Tang at the Gate of the Thearch

In the first month, on *jihai* (day 36), Tang asked the Lesser Servant at the Gate of the Thearch:

"As for the former thearchs in ancient times, are there still good words (from them) that have truly come down to this day?"

The Lesser Servant answered, [1] saying:

> "There are! If no good words (from them) have truly come down to this day, then
>
> How would a person be completed?
>
> How would a state be completed?
>
> How would earth be completed?
>
> How would [2] heaven be completed?"

Tang again asked the Lesser Servant, saying:

> "How many words does it take to complete a person?
>
> How many words does it take to complete a state?
>
> How many words does it take to complete earth?
>
> How many words does it take to complete heaven?"

The Lesser Servant answered, saying: [3]

> "It takes five to complete a person and virtue to illuminate him.
>
> It takes four to complete a state and five to assist it.
>
> It takes nine to complete earth and five to support (it).
>
> It takes nine to complete heaven and six [4] to set it in motion."

Tang again asked the Lesser Servant, saying:

> "As for a person,
>
> How does he come to be born?
>
> What does he have more of so that he grows?
>
> What does he have less of so that he ages?

Why is it that this same person is [5] sometimes foul and sometimes fair?"

The Lesser Servant answered, saying:

"It is just the *qi* of the five flavors that starts to make up a person.

The seminal *qi* is called the jade seed.

In the first month, it starts [6] to rise. In the second month, it is then surrounded (by a sac). In the third month, it then takes shape. In the fourth month, it then becomes firm. In the fifth month, some parts come together. In the sixth month, it grows flesh. In the seventh month, muscles then appear. In the eighth month, it is then properly formed. [7] In the ninth month, separation becomes apparent. In the tenth month, (the fetus) is then complete, and then people are born at the proper time.

Their *qi*, sunken in the mire, starts to issue forth; such is (how) they grow and become fair.

Their *qi* bursts out and [8] flourishes; such is (how) they are in their prime.

The *qi* intermingles so that it is complete; such is (how) they have strength.

When the *qi* shrinks, they grow old; when the *qi* slackens, they falter.

The *qi* becomes perverted and disturbed so that it is harmful; [9] this is what makes illness and misfortune.

When the *qi* retracts, (life) ends, and the hundred aspirations will all be exhausted."

Tang again asked the Lesser Servant:

"As for 'It takes four to complete a state and five to assist it,' [10] what does it mean?"

The Lesser Servant answered:

"It is the four gods that are called the four governors.

'It takes five to assist it,' this refers to virtue, service, conscription, regulation, and punishment."

139

Tang again asked [11] the Lesser Servant:

"What is fine virtue like? What is foul virtue like? What is fine service like? What is foul service like? What is fine conscription like? What is foul conscription like? What is fine [12] regulation like? What is foul regulation like? What is fine punishment like? What is foul punishment like?"

The Lesser Servant answered:

"When virtue is wise and bright, it holds fast to trustworthiness and is completed with propriety, and this is called [13] fine virtue, which is able to guarantee completion.

When virtue is petty and hasty, it holds fast to falsehood and is completed with dissipation, and this is called foul virtue, which is profane even if it brings things to completion.

When by initiating a service one reaps benefits, and the people for a long time [14] rely on it, it is called fine service.

When by initiating a service one reaps no benefit but makes the people ill for no reason, it is called foul service.

When one initiates conscription at the proper time so that the people are prepared but not deployed, it is called [15] fine conscription.

When one initiates conscription at the improper time at great cost to the state, it is called foul conscription.

When regulation is simple and complete, it is called fine regulation.

When regulation is disastrous, chaotic, and inconstant, making the people [16] all split apart and care only about themselves, it is called foul regulation.

When punishment fits the reality (of crimes) and is not harmful, it is called fine punishment.

When punishment is heavy and inconstant, it is called foul punishment."

Tang again [17] asked the Lesser Servant:

"As for 'It takes nine to complete earth and five to support it,' what does it mean?"

The Lesser Servant answered, saying:

"It is the nine gods that are called the deities of earth.

'It takes five to support it,' [18] this refers to water, fire, metal, wood, and soil, by which we complete the five regions and plant the five grains."

Tang again asked the Lesser Servant:

"As for 'It takes nine to complete heaven and six to set it in motion,' what does it mean?"

The Lesser [19] Servant answered, saying:

"It is the nine gods that are called the nine expanses.

'It takes six to set it in motion,' this refers to day, night, spring, summer, autumn, and winter, each of which governs tirelessly.

These are the beginning of (all) affairs, as well as [20] the Way of Heaven."

Tang said:

"Heavenly minister! These being the good words from the former thearchs in ancient times, how could I change them?" [21]

Chapter Five
*Tang chu yu Tangqiu 湯處於湯丘
*Tang Resided at Tang Hill

The Tsinghua manuscript *Tang chu yu Tangqiu* was published in Volume 5 of *Qinghua daxue cang Zhanguo zhujian*. The manuscript was written on nineteen slips, which were originally bound with 3 binding straps. The slips are about 44.4cm in length and well preserved with no loss of writing. There are no numbers on the backs of the slips. The manuscript originally had no title; the editors gave it the current title based on the opening sentence "Tang resided at Tang Hill." As mentioned in Chapter 4, scholars believe that *Tangqiu* and *Chimen* were originally bound together and copied by the same scribe. Like *Chimen*, *Tangqiu* also shows signs of proofreading. A few smaller characters are inserted in the space between regular characters on slips 8, 9, 16, and 19.

Tangqiu can be divided into two sections. The first section (slips 1–11) tells a story about Tang, Yi Yin, and another minister Fang Wei 方惟. The story itself can be further divided into two parts. In the first part (slips 1–3), Tang took a wife from the Shen clan 有莘, and Yi Yin went as the girl's dowry escort. He prepared delectable cuisine and conversed with Tang about harmony in governance and the culinary arts. In the second part of the story (slips 3–11), Tang suddenly started to conspire with Yi Yin against Xia. Before they completed the plan, Yi Yin fell ill and stayed home for three months. Tang went back and forth to see him and always stayed until night. When Fang Wei heard this, he showed disapproval of Tang's improper conduct, saying that Tang should summon Yi Yin to the court instead of going to him in person. Nevertheless, Tang disagreed and insisted on treating a talented minister such as Yi Yin with great respect. In the end, they reached a consensus and praised each other. Following the story, the second section (slips 10–19) is a series of questions and answers between Tang and Yi Yin, probably during those visits. Tang asks Yi Yin about a variety of things, such as whether they should attack Xia, how to be good rulers and ministers, how to care for oneself and for the people, and finally, how to worship the Mandate of Heaven. Yi Yin encourages Tang to take over Xia and gives him commonplace moral lectures.

The story in the first section might have combined materials from different sources, because the two parts of the story seem unrelated, and variations of their themes appear in other Warring States texts separately. The first theme about Tang's marriage and Yi Yin's identity as a dowry escort appears also in the "Ben wei" 本味 "Root of Flavors" chapter of *Lüshi chunqiu*. "Ben wei" offers a mythological account of Yi Yin's birth and how he came to live with the Shen clan before narrating the episodes about Tang's marriage:

有侁氏女子採桑，得嬰兒于空桑之中，獻之其君。其君令烰人養之。察其所以然，曰：“其母居伊水之上，孕，夢有神告之曰：‘臼出水而東走，毋顧。’明日，視臼出水，告其鄰，東走十里，而顧其邑盡為水。身因化為空桑。故命之曰伊尹。”此伊尹生空桑之故也。長而賢。湯聞伊尹，使人請之有侁氏。有侁氏不可。伊尹亦欲歸湯，湯於是請取婦為婚。有侁氏喜，以伊尹為媵送女。

While picking mulberry leaves, a woman of the Shen clan found a baby in the hollow trunk of a mulberry tree and presented it to her lord. Her lord ordered a cook to raise it. Having investigated how it came to be so, (the cook) said, "Its mother lived on the banks of the Yi river, became pregnant, and dreamt that a spirit announced to her, 'When your mortar produces water, move to the east and do not look back.' The next day, seeing that her mortar did produce water, she told her neighbor about it, went east ten li and, looking back, saw that her town was completely inundated. For that reason, she was changed into a hollow mulberry. Hence they called him 'Yi Yin.'" This is how Yi Yin came to be born in a hollow mulberry. Yi Yin grew to be a worthy man. When Tang heard about him, he sent a messenger to request him from the Shen clan. The Shen clan would not agree. Yi Yin also wished to join Tang, so Tang asked the family to grant him a wife in marriage. The Shen clan was overjoyed and sent Yi Yin as the girl's dowry escort.[1]

According to "Ben wei," Tang married the Shen girl *in order to* employ Yi Yin, whereas in *Tangqiu* Yi Yin joined Tang simply as a result of the marriage. The "Ben wei" passage does not elaborate on Yi Yin's cooking skills. Although the title "Ben wei" includes the word "flavor," the main argument of this chapter is the old Warring States theme of "exalting the worthy" rather than the philosophy of food.[2]

The second theme about Tang's visits to Yi Yin appears also in the "Gui yi" 貴義 "Valuing Propriety" chapter of *Mozi*. "Gui yi" is a collection of Mozi's sayings and dialogues, and the story is part of a relatively long dialogue between Mozi and Mu He 穆賀, a minister of King Xianhui 獻惠 of Chu (r. 489–432 BCE). Mu He was deeply impressed by Mozi's ideas, but worried that King Xianhui would refuse to listen to a lowborn person. Mozi then told a story about Tang and Yi Yin to suggest that a king would disregard a person's social status if his ideas were effective:

---

1   Xu Weiyu, *Lüshi chunqiu jishi*, 310. for a full translation of this chapter, see Appendix B.

2   The last story in "Ben wei," which includes a long and tedious digression on the whereabouts of the finest raw materials, is indeed about the philosophy of culinary arts. Still, the main point of "Ben wei" is articulated at the beginning of the chapter as exalting the worthy. The story serves as a demonstration of Yi Yin's worthiness.

昔者，湯將往見伊尹，令彭氏之子御。彭氏之子半道而
問曰：“君將何之？”湯曰：“將往見伊尹。”彭氏之子曰：
“伊尹，天下之賤人也。若君欲見之，亦令召問焉。彼受
賜矣。”湯曰：“非女所知也。今有藥此，食之則耳加聰，
目加明，則吾必說而強食之。今夫伊尹之於我國也，譬
之良醫善藥也。而子不欲我見伊尹，是子不欲吾善也。”
因下彭氏之子，不使御。

Of old, when Tang was about to go to see Yi Yin, he ordered
the son of the Peng family to drive the chariot. Halfway along
the road, the son of the Peng family asked, "Where is my lord
going?" Tang said, "I am going to see Yi Yin." The son of the
Peng family said, "Yi Yin is a low-born man under heaven. If
my lord wishes to see him, just summon him here and ask him
questions. (In that way) he will still receive a great favor (from
you)." Tang said, "This is not something you know about.
Now there was this medicine which, if I took it, would make
my hearing more acute and my vision sharper. Then I would
certainly be happy to make myself take it. Now to my state, Yi
Yin is just like a good doctor or an excellent medicine. If you
do not wish me to see Yi Yin, this amounts to your not wishing me to become good." As a result, he dismissed the son of
the Peng family and did not allow him to drive the chariot.[3]

In a typically Mohist style, Tang drew an analogy between Yi Yin and medicine to dismiss the relevance of social status. The *Mozi* story replaces Fang
Wei with the son of the Peng family, who served as Tang's driver.[4] The dia-

---

3   Wu Yujiang 吳毓江, *Mozi jiaozhu* 墨子校注 (Beijing: Zhonghua shuju, 2006), 686. For
a full translation of the dialogue, see Appendix C.

4   This, however, may not be a real difference. As Shen Jianhua 沈建華 points out, *fang*
方 (*C-paŋ) and *peng* 彭 (*C.[b]ˤraŋ) are very close in sound. Fang Wei may simply be
another name for the son of the Peng family. See Shen Jianhua, "Qinghua jian *Tang chu
yu Tangqiu* yu *Mozi Guiyi* wenben" 清華簡《唐(湯)處於唐丘》與《墨子·貴義》文本,
Zhongguo shi yanjiu 中國史研究 2016.1: 19.

logue took place on their way to Yi Yin's place, not after Tang's many visits. Yi Yin was not sick, but was explicitly regarded as "lowborn" (*jian* 賤, a term that is absent in *Tangqiu*). Despite these differences, there is one thing that *Mozi* and *Tangqiu* share in common: both the son of the Peng family and Fang Wei said that even if Tang summoned Yi Yin, it would still be Yi Yin's great honor. The two versions of this episode were probably modified from some common material. Compared to the *Mozi* account, *Tangqiu* does not use the story to demonstrate the importance of "exalting the worthy." It combines anecdotes and dialogues into a single narrative without having a clear agenda. While it does teach a few loosely related moral lessons in the second section, the story in the first section is not part of any philosophical argument.

More variations of this second theme can be found in late Warring States texts. In the "Nan yi" 難一 "Refutations: Part One" of the *Han Feizi* 韓非子, there is a similar story about Duke Huan 桓 of Qi (r. 685–643 BCE) visiting an untried scholar named Ji:

齊桓公時，有處士曰小臣稷。桓公三往而弗得見。桓公曰：
"吾聞布衣之士，不輕爵祿，無以易萬乘之主；萬乘之主，
不好仁義，亦無以下布衣之士。" 於是五往乃得見之。

During the reign of Duke Huan of Qi, there was an untried scholar called Lesser Servant Ji. Duke Huan visited him three times but did not get to see him. Duke Huan said: "I have heard that if a coarsely clothed scholar does not slight salary and rank, there is no way he can treat the ruler of a state with ten thousand chariots lightly, and if the ruler of a state with ten thousand chariots does not love benevolence and propriety, there is no way he can submit to a coarsely clothed scholar." Then he visited five times and finally got to see Ji.[5]

---

5   Wang Xianshen 王先慎, *Han Feizi jijie* 韓非子集解 (Beijing: Zhonghua shuju, 1998), 355–356.

A slightly different version of the story appears in the "Xia xian" 下賢 "Submitting to the Worthy" chapter of *Lüshi chunqiu*:

> 齊桓公見小臣稷，一日三至弗得見。從者曰："萬乘之主，見布衣之士，一日三至而弗得見，亦可以止矣。"桓公曰："不然。士驁禄爵者，固輕其主；其主驁霸王者，亦輕其士。縱夫子驁禄爵，吾庸敢驁霸王乎？"遂見之，不可止。
>
> Duke Huan of Qi wanted to see Lesser Servant Ji. He went three times a day but still did not get to see him. An attendant said to him: "You are the ruler of a state with ten thousand chariots. When you want to see a coarsely clothed scholar, but have failed three times in one day, you might as well stop." Duke Huan said: "Not so. A scholar who is contemptuous of salary and rank would certainly slight his ruler, and a ruler contemptuous of becoming a hegemon or king would also slight his scholar. Even though the master is contemptuous of salary and rank, how would I dare be contemptuous of becoming a hegemon or king?" Then he went to see Lesser Servant Ji and could not be stopped.[6]

Studies of the lore of Yi Yin never mention these stories because they replace Tang and Yi Yin with Duke Huan and Ji. However, they must have been inspired by the Yi Yin stories. Like Tang, Duke Huan insisted on visiting Ji, who was also a lesser servant, multiple times despite his lowly status. In "Xia xian," there was also a third person who tried to stop Duke Huan on the grounds of social hierarchy.

Additional evidence for their relationship can be found in Mengzi and Sima Qian's reports. In *Mengzi* 5A7, Wan Zhang asked Mengzi whether Yi Yin did "seek out Tang with his cooking skills" according to a popular story.

---

6   Xu Weiyu, *Lüshi chunqiu jishi*, 371. The story between Duke Huan and Ji is also quoted, with no significant variants, in Chapter 6 of the *Hanshi waizhuan* 韓詩外傳 and the "Za shi" 雜事 chapter of the *Xin xu* 新序.

Mengzi denied it and retold the story from his angle, claiming that Yi Yin could only seek out Tang with the "Way of Yao and Shun:"

> 伊尹耕於有莘之野，而樂堯舜之道焉。非其義也，非其道也，禄之以天下，弗顧也；繫馬千駟，弗視也。非其義也，非其道也，一介不以與人，一介不以取諸人。湯使人以幣聘之，囂囂然曰："我何以湯之聘幣為哉？我豈若處畎畝之中，由是以樂堯舜之道哉？"湯三使往聘之，既而幡然改曰："與我處畎畝之中，由是以樂堯舜之道，吾豈若使是君為堯舜之君哉？吾豈若使是民為堯舜之民哉？吾豈若於吾身親見之哉？……"

Yi Yin farmed in the countryside of Shen and delighted in the Way of Yao and Shun. If it was not righteous, if it was not the Way, even if you gave him the whole world as his salary, he would not consider it. Even if you gave him a thousand teams of horses, he would not glance at it. If it was not righteous, if it was not the Way, he would not give or accept from others so much as a twig. Tang sent people with gifts to invite him. Calmly, he replied: "What are the invitation gifts of Tang to me? Would I not rather work in the fields, finding joy in the way of Yao and Shun." After Tang had sent people to invite him three times, his attitude changed and he said: "Rather than dwell amidst these plowed fields and from here delight in the Way of Yao and Shun, would I not rather make this ruler into a ruler like Yao and Shun? Would I not rather make these people into people like those of Yao and Shun? Would I not rather see it myself ? … "[7]

Note that in Mengzi's account, Tang sent people to invite Yi Yin three times. The number of visits is not specified in *Tangqiu* and *Mozi*, but only in the

---

7   Jiao Xun, *Mengzi zhengyi*, 652–656. Translation modified from Van Norden trans. *Mengzi: With Selections from Traditional Commentaries*, 126–127.

two stories about Duke Huan and Ji, although in the latter case it was Duke Huan himself who went to see Ji. This seems to mean that Mengzi saw a version of the story eventually included in the *Han Feizi* with Tang and Yi Yin as the protagonists. An even more compelling piece of evidence comes from Sima Qian's report of how Yi Yin met Tang:

> 伊尹名阿衡。阿衡欲奸湯而無由，乃為有莘氏媵臣，負鼎俎，以滋味説湯，致于王道。或曰：伊尹處士。湯使人聘迎之，五反，然後肯往從湯，言素王及九主之事。湯舉任以國政。伊尹去湯適夏。既醜有夏，復歸于亳。
>
> Yi Yin's name was E-heng. E-heng wanted to seek out Tang but had no way to do so. Therefore, he made himself a dowry escort from the Shen clan, carrying a tripod and a cutting-board stand; by means of gastronomy he persuaded Tang to realize the kingly way. Some sources said that Yi Yin was an untried scholar. Tang sent someone to welcome him with presents. After five trips, he agreed to go serve Tang. He talked to Tang concerning matters of "the simple king" and "the nine rulers." Tang raised him up and let him shoulder government affairs. Yi Yin left Tang and went to Xia. Having despised Xia, he returned to Bo.[8]

In the first account given by Sima Qian, Yi Yin used his cooking skills as an excuse to approach Tang. This seems to be the version criticized by Mengzi, who argues that Yi Yin could not have been motivated by profit-seeking ends. The second one, after "Some sources said," is a variant of the *Han Feizi* story about Duke Huan and Ji. The number of Tang's visits is five in both texts. In the *Han Feizi* story, Ji is an untried scholar and lesser servant, whereas in Sima Qian's version Yi Yin becomes an untried scholar. In other words, Ji received the "lesser servant" identity from Yi Yin when the original story was recreated,

---

8   Sima Qian, *Shi ji*, 122–123.

and Yi Yin in turn received the "untried scholar" identity from Ji when the new story was confused with the earlier one. The table below summarizes the major differences between the six variants of the story:

	Character	Plot
*Tangqiu	Yi Yin, lesser servant	Tang visited Yi Yin many times and was questioned by Fang Wei.
Mozi	Yi Yin	Tang went to see Yi Yin and was questioned by the son of the Peng family before the first meeting.
Mengzi	Yi Yin	Tang sent people to invite Yi Yin, who changed his idea after three visits.
Han Feizi	Ji, untried scholar, lesser servant	Duke Huan visited Ji three times in one day but did not get to see him. He persisted and finally saw Ji after five visits.
Lüshi chunqiu	Ji, lesser servant	Duke Huan visited Ji three times and was questioned by an attendant. He persisted and finally saw Ji.
Shi ji	Yi Yin, untried scholar	Tang sent people to invite Yi Yin, who changed his idea after five visits.

After recounting the stories of Tang and Yi Yin, the narrative suddenly transitions into a dialogue between the two, written in a repetitive style reminiscent of *Chimen. Each question commences with "Tang again asked the Lesser Servant," and every response starts with "The Lesser Servant answered." Although the second section of *Tangqiu does not exhibit *Chimen's fixation on textual organization and numerology, it does arrange the questions and answers in a generally logical manner, with earlier answers often forming the basis for subsequent questions. It is likely that the narrative prologue of the first section was grafted onto the dialogue to provide a quasi-historical context. In theory, a Warring States author could have employed a similar approach with *Chimen, integrating existing stories about Tang and Yi Yin with a dialogue to contextualize its philosophical content historically.

*Tang chu yu Tangqiu 湯處於湯丘
*Tang Resided at Tang Hill

湯屋 於 湯坓 取 妻 於 又₌邦₌ 嬬 目 少₌ 臣₌ 善 爲 飤 亯 之 和
又 邦 之 女 飤 之 醬 飭

湯處於湯丘，取妻於有莘，有莘媵以小臣。小臣善爲食，烹之和。有莘之女食之，絕芳 [一]

Tang resided at Tang Hill,[9] and took a wife from the Shen clan. The Shen clan sent the Lesser Servant as her dowry escort. The Lesser Servant was good at making food and cooked it in harmony. The daughter of the Shen clan ate the food and found it extremely aromatic, [1]

---

9   The editors relate the Tang Hill to the Tang Tu 唐土 "Tang Territory" in oracle bone inscriptions.

旨 目 䏄 身 體 臊 㓆 九 宎 發 明 目 道 心 㗊 憛 快 目 恒 ___
湯 亦 飤 之 曰 允 此 可

旨以粹。身體順平，九竅發明，以導心嗌，奮快以恒。湯亦食之，曰："允！此可 [二]

savory, and pure.[10] Her body and limbs were healthy and tranquil, and her nine orifices emanated brightness, such that her heart and throat were cleared, leading to a constant state of energetic joy. Tang also ate it, and said: "Indeed! Can this [2]

---

10 I follow the editors in reading *jue* 絕 as an adverb "extremely" and *duo* 䏄 (*[t]ˤut) as a phonetic loan for *cui* 粹 (*[tsʰ]ˤu[t]-s) "pure." The second part of the sentence should be a description of the food rather than the daughter's body, because both 飭 and 䏄 have the "food" 𩙿 signific.

白 夘 中 宋 山 么 劅 曰 壴 弓 辪 山 么 杏 宮 驛 雎 半 成 山

么 又 猴 三 月 半 山 愓 反

目 和 民 虎 少 臣 僉 曰 可 乃 與 少 臣 忈 愗 郖 邦 未 成 少
臣 又 疾 三 月 不 出 湯 反

以和民乎？" 小臣答曰："可。" 乃與小臣惎謀夏邦。未成，小臣有疾，三月不出。
湯反 [三]

be used to harmonize the people?" The Lesser Servant answered: "It can."
Then together with the Lesser Servant, (Tang) plotted[11] against the state of
Xia. Before they were finished (plotting), the Lesser Servant fell ill, and did
not come out for three months. Tang went back [3]

---

11 The editor reads *ji* 忈 as *ji* 惎 "to plot against." The compound *jimou* 忈愗 (or 惎謀)
    consists of two synonyms written with the "heart" signific.

復見少臣　必夜方惟靁之乃織 ＿ 君天王是又崒
僕今少臣又疾女思吋少

復見小臣，歸必夜。方惟聞之乃箴：“君天王，是有臺僕。今小臣有疾。如思召，少 [四]

and forth to visit the Lesser Servant, never returning before nightfall. When Fang Wei heard this, he warned: "You, my lord, are the heavenly king, and such a thing should be done by attendants. Now the Lesser Servant is ill. If you want to summon him, (wait for) a brief [4]

（古文字）

閖 於 疾 朝 而 傸 之 不 猶 受 君 賜 吟 君 逞 不 目 時 逼 必
夜 繡 奉 道 迲 之 祙 民 人

間於疾，朝而訊之。不猶受君賜？今君往不以時，歸必夜。適逢道路之祟，民人 [五]

respite in his illness, and then grant him an audience to ask questions. Wouldn't he still receive a great favor from my lord? Now my lord goes out at improper times and never returns before nightfall. If you happen to be haunted along the way, what would the people [5]

霝 之 亓 胃 虐 君 可 _ 湯 曰 善 才 子 之 鼎 先= 又 言 能 亓
事 而 旻 亓 飤 是 名 曰 昌

聞之，其謂吾君何？”湯曰：“善哉！子之云。先人有言：‘能其事而得其食，是名
曰昌。[六]

say of my lord if they heard of it?" Tang said: "Excellent indeed, what you
have said! The former men had a saying: 'If those who are able to fulfill
their duties get their food, this is called prosperity. [6]

未 能 亓 事 而 昺 其 飤 是 名 曰 芒 _ 必 思 事 與 飤 相 壆
_ 今 少 臣 能 廛 章 百 義 目 和

未能其事而得其食，是名曰喪。必使事與食相當。'今小臣能展彰百義，以和 [七]

If those who are not able to fulfill their duties still get their food, this is called destruction. The work and the food must be made to fit each other.' Now the Lesser Servant is able to demonstrate and make clear the hundred proprieties, and thereby to bring harmony and [7]

利 萬 民 㠯 攸 四 時 之 正 㠯 埶 九 事 之 人 㠯 長 奉 社 稷
虐 此 是 爲 見 之 女 我 弗 見

利萬民, 以修四時之正, 以[12]設九事之人, 以長奉社稷。吾此是爲見之。如我弗見,[八]

benefit to the myriad people, to fix the correctness of the four seasons, to establish men of the nine duties, and to support the altars of soil and grain forever. This is why I visit him. If I were not to visit him, [8]

12　The character 以 is inserted in the space between 正 and 設 and is smaller in size.

夫 人 母 目 我 爲 囟 於 丌 事 虎 我 囟 於 丌 事 而 不 智 芒
虐 可 君 是 爲 ▁ 方 惟 曰 善 才

夫人毋以我爲怠於其事乎？我 [13] 怠於其事而不知喪，吾何君是爲？ ”方惟曰：“善
哉！ [九]

wouldn't the people hold me to be remiss in my duties to them? If I were
remiss in my duties to them and did not know (that this might lead to)
destruction, what kind of lord would I be?" Fang Wei said: "Excellent
indeed, [9]

---

13 The character 我 is inserted in the space between 乎 and 怠.

君 天 王 之 言 也 ＿ 唯 臣 死 而 或 生 此 言 ＿ 弗 或 可 昱
而 犤 也 ＿ 湯 曰 善 才 子 之 鼎 也

君天王之言也。雖臣死而又生，此言弗又得而聞已。" 湯曰："善哉! 子之云也。[十]

the words of my lord, the heavenly king! Even if I were to die and live again,
I would never get to hear these words again." Tang said: "Excellent indeed,
what you have said! [10]

唯 余 孤 之 與 卡= 交 剴 敢 目 衾 嬰 女 幸 余 闕 於 天 畏 朕
隹 逆 訓 是 意 ＿ 　 湯 或 矗

雖余孤之與上下交，豈敢以貪舉？如幸余間於天威，朕惟逆順是圖。"湯又問 [十一]

Even though I, the solitary one, communicate with those above and below, how would I dare to wage (war) out of greed? If perchance I win respite from the might of Heaven, I will only obey or defy these plans." Tang again asked [11]

[Oracle bone / bronze script characters]

於 少 臣 又 顕 之 悳 可 若 才 少 臣 會 又 顕 之 悳 史 貨 目
惑 蓍 䛐 改 劃 民 人 䛅 貣 型

於小臣:"有夏之德何若哉？" 小臣答:"有夏之德，吏過以惑，春秋改則，民人䛅忒，
刑 [十二]

the Lesser Servant: "What is the virtue[14] of Xia like?" The Lesser Servant
answered: "As for the virtue of Xia, the officials[15] make mistakes in confusion;
springs and autumns change their regular pattern; the people make devious
plans together;[16] punishments [12]

---

14 For the sake of consistency, I retain the "virtue" translation of *de*, although it would
    seem strange in the Lesser Servant's following description of the moral corruption of
    Xia. Nicholas Vogt translates it as "potency." See Vogt, "Consumption, Knowledge, and
    the Limits of the Body in the Xiaochen Texts," 256.
15 The editors read *shi* 史 as *shi* 使 "to cause," rendering the sentence as "The virtue of Xia
    causes (the people) to be mistaken and confused." I read *shi* 史 as *li* 吏 "official."
16 The editors read 䛅 as *qu* 趣 or 趨 "head for, run towards." However, as Wang Ning 王
    寧 points out, the *Shuowen jiezi* definition of *zou* 䛅 as "to plan together" (*ju mou* 聚謀)
    already makes good sense here. There is no need to take it as a phonetic loan. See Wang
    Ning, "Du Qinghua wu *Tang chu yu Tangqiu* sanzha" 讀清華五《湯處於湯丘》散札,
    at http://fdgwz.org.cn/Web/Show/2501, posted 21 April 2015.

止 金 傘 中 丿 ⻊ 總 兔 亢 、 罂 正 羍 杲 元 豪 、 瑙 或 素

自 心 血 空 欨 杲 巾 㝻 少 血 曽 勹 古

亡 卣 恋 民 人 皆 経 禺 𠂤 ＿ 虽 王 不 旻 亓 惪 ＿ 湯 或 矗

於 少 臣 虐 或 虽 女 勹 少 臣 會 勹 古

無 攸 赦。民 人 皆 務 偶 離，夏 王 不 得 其 圖。"湯 又 問 於 小 臣："吾 戡 夏 如 台？"小 臣 答："后 固 [十三]

are never pardoned. The people all strive to leave in groups,[17] and the king of Xia will not achieve his plans." Tang again asked the Lesser Servant: "What if I were to attack Xia?" The Lesser Servant answered: "My lord should firmly [13]

---

17 The editors read 経 as *mao* 瞀 "dim-sighted, confused" and 禺 as *ou* 偶 "couple, companion," rendering the sentence as "The people are all confused and leave in company." Wang Ning reads 経 instead as *wu* 務 "to strive." See Wang Ning, "Du Qinghua *wu Tang chu yu Tangqiu* sanzha." My translation combines their readings.

共 天 畏 敬 祀 叚 慈 我 民 若 自 史 朕 身 已 傑 之 疾 句 牆
君 又 虽 才 ＿ 湯 或 䨱 於 少 臣 古

恭天威，敬祀，淑慈我民。若自使朕身已桀之疾，后將君有夏哉！" 湯又問於少臣：
"古 [十四]

worship the might of Heaven, respect the sacrificial rites, and be good and kind to our people. If you send me myself to stop the illness of Jie,[18] my lord will rule over Xia!" Tang again asked the Lesser Servant: "As for the former [14]

---

18 The punctuation and interpretation of this sentence is based on Chen Jian's 陳劍 analysis. See Chen Jian, "Qinghua jian ziyi lingzha liangze" 清華簡字義零札兩則, in Fudan daxue chutu wenxian yu guwenzi yanjiu zhongxin 復旦大學出土文獻與古文字研究中心 eds. *Zhanguo wenzi yanjiu de huigu yu zhanwang* 戰國文字研究的回顧與展望 (Shanghai: Zhong Xi shuju, 2017), 200–203. The Lesser Servant volunteered to be a spy for Tang. To "stop the illness of Jie" echoes the story in the *Chi jiu* (see Chapter 1).

先₌聖人可目自惡 ＿ 少臣會古先₌聖人所目自惡 ＿
不 史 甹 不 屖 矣 ＿ 飤 時 不 旨 饈 五 味

之先聖人，何以自愛？" 小臣答："古之先聖人所以自愛：不事昏，不處疑。食時不
嗜珍。五味 [十五]

sages in ancient times, how did they care for themselves?" The Lesser Servant
answered: "The former sages in ancient times cared for themselves by not
serving the muddled and not dwelling on doubts. When they ate, they were
not addicted to delicacies. They arranged all five flavors [15]

165

皆 哉 不 又 所 鬒 不 備 𣏾 文 器 不 敝 鏤 不 瘥 殺 與 民 分
利 此 目 自 惡 也 ＿ 湯 或 𤔽 於 少 臣 爲 君 奚

皆載，不有所滯。不服華文，器不雕鏤。不虐殺，與民分利。此以自愛 [19] 也。” 湯又
問於小臣：“爲君奚 [十六]

without an obsession with[20] any one of them. They did not dress up in
florid patterns, and their vessels were not carved and inlaid. They did not kill
mercilessly, but shared benefits with the people. These are how they cared
for themselves." Tang again asked the Lesser Servant: "What is it like to be a
lord? [16]

---

19 The character 愛 is inserted in the space between 自 and 也.

20 Many scholars have noted that the editors' original transcription of 鬒 is wrong. The character is actually an allograph of 噬 in Chu script and appears on slip 17 of the *Tang zai Chimen*. I follow Huang Jie 黃傑 (a.k.a. Musilang 暮四郎) in reading it as *zhi* 滯 "blocked, congealed, stagnant." See Huang Jie (Musilang), "Qinghua wu *Tang chu yu Tangqiu* chudu" 清華五《湯處於湯丘》初讀 #17, at http://www.bsm.org.cn/forum/forum.php?mod=viewthread&tid=3247, posted 11 April 2015.

若 爲 臣 系 若 少 臣 倉 爲 君 㤅 民 爲 臣 共 命 湯 或 䎽 於 少 臣 㤅 民 女 紿 少 臣 倉 曰 遠 又

若？爲臣奚若？”小臣答：“爲君愛民，爲臣恭命。”湯又問於小臣：“愛民如台？”小臣答曰：“遠有 [十七]

What is it like to be a servant?” The Lesser Servant answered: “To be a lord is to care for the people. To be a servant is to worship the mandate.” Tang again asked the Lesser Servant: “What is it like to care for the people?” The Lesser Servant answered: “Those who are distant [17]

所 亟 裟 又 所 思 餤 又 所 飤 罙 刏 是 淒 高 山 是 愈 遠 民
皆 亟 是 非 㤺 民 虎 ＿ 湯 或 䢅 於 少

所極，勞有所思，飢有所食。深淵是濟，高山是逾，遠民皆極。是非愛民乎？" 湯
又問於小 [十八]

will be reached; those who toil will be thought of; those who are hungry will
have food. Crossing deep abysses and passing over high mountains, distant
people will all arrive. Isn't this caring for the people?" Tang again asked the
Lesser [18]

臣 共 命 女 **少 臣 曾 君 既 濬 明 既 受 君 命 退 不 寡 死
生 是 非 共 命 虎 _

臣:"恭命如台? "小臣答:"君既²¹ 濬明, 既受君命退, 不顧死生, 是非恭命乎! " [十九]

servant: "What is it like to worship the mandate?" The Lesser Servant answered: "Now that the lord is wise and bright, having received the lord's mandate and withdrawn,[22] (the servant) takes no heed of life or death. Isn't this to worship the mandate?" [19]

---

21 The character 既 is inserted in the space between 君 and 濬.

22 The editors punctuate after *ming* 命 "mandate" and speculate that a character *jin* 進 "to advance" is missing before *tui* 退 "to withdraw." This is possible, but not necessary if we can make sense of the sentence without the insertion. If we punctuate after 退, then the phrase 既受君命退 can simply mean "having received the lord's mandate and withdrawn."

* 湯處於湯丘

湯處於湯丘，取妻於有莘，有莘媵以小臣。小臣善爲食，烹之和。有莘之女食之，絕芳[一]旨以粹。身體順平，九竅發明，以導心嗌，奮快以恒。

湯亦食之，曰：“允！此可[二]以和民乎？”

小臣答曰：“可。”

乃與小臣惎謀夏邦。未成，小臣有疾，三月不出。湯反[三]復見小臣，歸必夜。

方惟聞之乃箴：“君天王，是有臺僕。今小臣有疾。如思召，少[四]聞於疾，朝而訊之。不猶受君賜？今君往不以時，歸必夜。適逢道路之祟，民人[五]聞之，其謂吾君何？”

湯曰：“善哉！子之云。先人有言：‘能其事而得其食，是名曰昌（*mə-tʰaŋ-s）。[六]未能其事而得其食，是名曰喪（*s-mˤaŋ-s）。必使事與食相當（*tˤaŋ）。’今小臣能展彰百義，以和[七]利萬民，以修四時之正，以設九事之人，以長奉社稷。吾此是爲見之。如我弗見，[八]夫人毋以我爲怠於其事乎？我怠於其事而不知喪，吾何君是爲？”

方惟曰：“善哉！[九]君天王之言也。雖臣死而又生，此言弗又可得而聞已。”

湯曰：“善哉！子之云也。[十]雖余孤之與上下交，豈敢以貪舉？如幸余間於天威，朕惟逆順是圖。”

湯又問[十一]於小臣：“有夏之德何若哉？”

小臣答：“有夏之德（*tˤək），吏過以惑（*[ɡ]ʷˤək），春秋改則（*[ts]ˤək），民人諏忒（*l̥ˤək），刑[十二]無攸赦。民人皆務偶離，夏王不得其圖。”

湯又問於小臣：“吾戡夏如台？”

小臣答：“后固[十三]恭天威，敬祀，淑慈我民。若自使朕身已桀之疾，后將君有夏哉！”

170

湯又問於少臣：“古[十四]之先聖人，何以自愛？”

小臣答：“古之先聖人所以自愛：不事昏，不處疑。食時不嗜珍。五味[十五]皆載，不有所滯。不服華文，器不雕鏤。不虐殺，與民分利。此以自愛也。”

湯又問於小臣：“爲君奚[十六]若？爲臣奚若？”

小臣答：“爲君愛民，爲臣恭命。”

湯又問於小臣：“愛民如台？”

小臣答曰：“遠有[十七]所極（*[g](r)ək），勞有所思（*[s]ə），饑有所食（*mə-lək）。深淵是濟，高山是逾，遠民皆極（*[g](r)ək）。是非愛民乎？”

湯又問於小[十八]臣：“恭命如台？”

小臣答：“君既濬明，既受君命退，不顧死生，是非恭命乎！”[十九]

Tang Resided at Tang Hill

Tang resided at Tang Hill, and took a wife from the Shen clan. The Shen clan sent the Lesser Servant as her dowry escort. The Lesser Servant was good at making food and cooked it in harmony. The daughter of the Shen clan ate the food and found it extremely aromatic, [1] savory, and pure. Her body and limbs were healthy and tranquil, and her nine orifices emanated brightness, such that her heart and throat were cleared, leading to a constant state of energetic joy.

Tang also ate it, and said: "Indeed! Can this [2] be used to harmonize the people?"

The Lesser Servant answered: "It can."

Then together with the Lesser Servant, (Tang) plotted against the state of Xia. Before they were finished (plotting), the Lesser Servant fell ill, and did not come out for three months. Tang went back [3] and forth to visit the Lesser Servant, never returning before nightfall.

When Fang Wei heard this, he warned: "You, my lord, are the heavenly king, and such a thing should be done by attendants. Now the Lesser Servant is ill. If you want to summon him, (wait for) a brief [4] respite in his illness, and then grant him an audience to ask questions. Wouldn't he still receive a great favor from my lord? Now my lord goes out at improper times and never returns before nightfall. If you happen to be haunted along the way, what would the people [5] say of my lord if they heard of it?"

Tang said: "Excellent indeed, what you have said! The former men had a saying: 'If those who are able to fulfill their duties get their food, this is called prosperity. [6] If those who are not able to fulfill their duties still get their food, this is called destruction. The work and the food must be made to fit each other.' Now the Lesser Servant is able to demonstrate and make clear the hundred proprieties, and thereby to bring harmony and [7] benefit

172

to the myriad people, to fix the correctness of the four seasons, to establish men of the nine duties, and to support the altars of soil and grain forever. This is why I visit him. If I were not to visit him, [8] wouldn't the people hold me to be remiss in my duties to them? If I were remiss in my duties to them and did not know (that this might lead to) destruction, what kind of lord would I be?"

Fang Wei said: "Excellent indeed, [9] the words of my lord, the heavenly king! Even if I were to die and live again, I would never get to hear these words again."

Tang said: "Excellent indeed, what you have said! [10] Even though I, the solitary one, communicate with those above and below, how would I dare to wage (war) out of greed? If perchance I win respite from the might of Heaven, I will only obey or defy these plans."

Tang again asked [11] the Lesser Servant: "What is the virtue of Xia like?"

The Lesser Servant answered: "As for the virtue of Xia, the officials make mistakes in confusion; springs and autumns change their regular pattern; the people make devious plans together; punishments [12] are never pardoned. The people all strive to leave in groups, and the king of Xia will not achieve his plans."

Tang again asked the Lesser Servant: "What if I were to attack Xia?"

The Lesser Servant answered: "My lord should firmly [13] worship the might of Heaven, respect the sacrificial rites, and be good and kind to our people. If you send me myself to stop the illness of Jie, my lord will rule over Xia!"

Tang again asked the Lesser Servant: "As for the former [14] sages in ancient times, how did they care for themselves?"

The Lesser Servant answered: "The former sages in ancient times cared for themselves by not serving the muddled and not dwelling on doubts. When they ate, they were not addicted to delicacies. They arranged all five flavors [15] without an obsession with any one of them. They did not dress up in florid patterns, and their vessels were not carved and inlaid. They did not kill mercilessly, but shared benefits with the people. These are how they cared for themselves."

Tang again asked the Lesser Servant: "What is it like to be a lord? [16] What is it like to be a servant?"

The Lesser Servant answered: "To be a lord is to care for the people. To be a servant is to worship the mandate."

Tang again asked the Lesser Servant: "What is it like to care for the people?"

The Lesser Servant answered: "Those who are distant [17] will be reached; those who toil will be thought of; those who are hungry will have food. Crossing deep abysses and passing over high mountains, distant people will all arrive. Isn't this caring for the people?"

Tang again asked the Lesser [18] Servant: "What is it like to worship the mandate?"

The Lesser Servant answered: "Now that the lord is wise and bright, having received the lord's mandate and withdrawn, (the servant) takes no heed of life or death. Isn't this to worship the mandate?" [19]

Chapter Six

Yin Gaozong wen yu San Shou 殷高宗問於三壽

The High Ancestor of Yin Asked the Three Long-Lived Ones

The Tsinghua manuscript *Yin Gaozong* was published in Volume 5 of *Qinghua daxue cang Zhanguo zhujian*. The manuscript was written on 28 slips, most of which are well preserved. Slip 3 and the top half of slip 25 are missing with a significant loss of text. The tops of slips 8 and 9 and the bottom of slip 9 are also broken, but with almost no loss of writing except for the top character on slip 8. The slips are 45cm in length, and were originally bound with three binding straps. The number of characters on each slip ranges from 28 to 34. The slips are numbered on the backs, but two of them are misplaced: according to the content of the manuscript, the slip with a number 10 on its back should be slip 15, while the slip numbered 15 should be slip 10. The title of the manuscript, *The High Ancestor of Yin Asked the Three Long-Lived Ones*, is written on the back of slip 28. There are numerous in-text punctuation marks and a text-ending mark at the end. The manuscript shows signs of proofreading, as one character is inserted in the space between regular characters on slip 12.

Codicological evidence on the slips shows that the manuscript was originally folded rather than rolled up. If the manuscript had been rolled up, we

175

would expect to see reverse impressions (*fanyin wen* 反印文) of characters on the verso of some slips. *Yin gaozong*, however, has reverse impressions only on the recto. According to Jia Lianxiang, there are a total of 39 impressions on slips 10 to 21, which indicates that the manuscript was folded on slips 15 and 16. Interestingly, there are no impressions on slips 1 to 9 and slips 22 to 28; a possible explanation for this phenomenon suggested by Jia is that these slips had already been broken off when the impressions were formed under pressure.[1] The image on p.175 above gives an example of the impression of the fifth characters on slips 15 and 16 on each other. These traces are valuable information for understanding the original physical form of the manuscript, but they also pose challenges to transcription.

Yin Gaozong can be divided into three sections. There is no obvious link between the sections, except that the main interlocutors in every case are the High Ancestor of Yin (that is, King Wu Ding 武丁 of Shang) and Ancestor Peng (Peng Zu 彭祖), a legendary figure in early China known for his longevity. We do not know whether these sections belonged together or were combined from originally independent sources. In the first section (slips 1–10), the High Ancestor asks the three Long-Lived Ones one after another the same set of questions. The first two Long-Lived Ones are anonymous, while the last one is Ancestor Peng. Each of them answers with a list of simple, unexplained terms (the Lesser Long-Lived One's answer is lost due to a missing slip). Inspired by these answers, the High Ancestor then gives his own comments in similar terms, plus a short speech stating his determination to follow the teachings. The table below shows the terms in their questions and answers:

---

1 See Jia Lianxiang 賈連翔, "Fanyin moji yu zhushu bianlian de zai renshi" 反印墨迹與竹書編連的再認識, *Chutu wenxian* 出土文獻 6 (2015): 229–245. See also Xiao Yunxiao 肖芸曉, "Qinghua jian shoujuan yanjiu juli" 清華簡收捲研究舉例, *Chutu wenxian* 出土文獻 7 (2015): 172–186.

	Long lasting	**Dangerous**	**Satisfaction**	**Detestation**
Lesser Long-Lived One	–	–	–	–
Middle Long-Lived One	Wind	Heart	Savings	Loss
Ancestor Peng	Water	Ghosts	Balance	Collapse
The High Ancestor	[Mountain]	Spears and shields	Wealth	Lack of food

The question, which gets repeated three times, is about two pairs of antonyms: "the long-lasting" is the opposite of "the dangerous," and "satisfaction" is the opposite of "detestation." Each time the answer is different. In
general, the High Ancestor is interested in how to make his state long-lasting
rather than dangerous, and how to make his people satisfied rather than
resentful. And the long-lived ones, honored for their age and experience,
provided a list of things to which he needed to pay attention.

The second section (slips 10–24) opens with a description of "eerie
occurrences and omens" (*yao xiang* 妖祥) all over the state of Yin and the
whole world. Frightened by them, the High Ancestor turns to ask Ancestor
Peng alone about the meaning of nine terms in the "the instructions left by
the past kings": "propitiousness" (*xiang* 祥, which is graphically differentiated from *xiang* as "omens" in the manuscript), "propriety" (*yi* 義), "virtue"
(*de* 德), "tone" (*yin* 音), "benevolence" (*ren* 仁), "sagacity" (*sheng* 聖), "wisdom" (*zhi* 智), "benefit" (*li* 利), and "trustworthiness" (*xin* 信). While all of
these terms are familiar keywords in early Chinese ethical thought, Ancestor
Peng's answers are not so much philosophical explanations as moral exhor-
tations. Having discussed all of them, Ancestor Peng encourages the High
Ancestor to live up to these standards and assist the spirit of Tang in replacing Xia.

The last section (slips 24–28) is another conversation between the High
Ancestor and Ancestor Peng about the people's being "ostentatious" (*yang*
揚) and "obscure" (*hui* 晦). This part is very difficult due to the loss of
about twenty characters on the broken slip 25, but the two characteristics

are clearly opposed to each other. Being ostentatious is a negative quality that will be punished by heaven, while being obscure is a positive quality that will be blessed. Ancestor Peng's discussion of the two terms is again more exhortative than philosophical. After each answer, the High Ancestor agrees with an exclamation.

A major problem in studying *Yin Gaozong* is how to contextualize it. Unlike most other manuscripts translated in this volume, *Yin Gaozong* bears no direct relationship to any other ancient text; scholars have been unable to identify textual parallels. Moreover, as Franklin Perkins suggests, *Yin Gao-zong* defies neat classification into the established categories of the Warring States "schools" — Daoism, Confucianism, and Mohism; nor does it advocate a coherent philosophical position.[2] The text is better viewed as "a collection of practical advice suitable for those in power" and as such comes close to what Matthias Richter calls a "repository of didactic materials."[3] Take the long speech of Ancestor Peng in the second section for example. It is not clear why these nine terms are treated as a group and whether there is any logic to their current order. Many of them, such as "benevolence," "propriety," "wisdom," and "trustworthiness," are Confucian cardinal virtues, but the list also has "benefit" and "tone," which are not usually grouped with the other virtues. Moreover, Ancestor Peng makes no effort to distinguish the terms from each other conceptually. His explanation of "sagacity" — "Worship the gods with respect and harmonize the people using rectitude. Bring order to the state and lay down weapons, so that those from the four directions are all tranquil. The good and the wise together come forth, so that slanders and rumors are blocked" (slip 19) — this is just a general list of good things that a ruler should do, which applies equally well to "propriety," "virtue," or "wisdom." The explanation of "benevolence," which includes "showing filial piety and parental love," "worrying about those far away and

---

2   Franklin Perkins, "*Yin Gaozong Wen Yu San Shou* 殷高宗問於三壽: Content and Context," in *Qinghua jian yanjiu* 3 (Shanghai: Zhong Xi shuju, 2019), 279–297.

3   Perkins, "*Yin Gaozong Wen Yu San Shou*: Content and Context," 294–295, n.1; Matthias Richter, *The Embodied Text: Establishing Textual Identity in Early Chinese Manuscripts* (Leiden: Brill, 2013), 171–187.

planning for close relatives," as well as "pleasing the gods and being soft with humans" (slip 18), does seem to accord with the standard understanding of the term, but it also has "dress up neatly and love trustworthiness," with "trustworthiness" being one of the nine terms.

In sharp contrast to the conceptual fuzziness of the text is its rigorous and pervasive rhyme scheme. In *Chimen* and *Tangqiu*, only some of the lines rhyme, whereas in *Yin Gaozong* virtually all speeches are written in rhyme. Since the language of *Yin Gaozong* is very difficult, paleographers often use rhymed words as clues to punctuation. The rhyming pattern of a passage almost always matches its semantic structure. Consider Ancestor Peng's answer in the first section:

I've heard that as for lasting long, nothing lasts longer than water (*s.tur?);
I've heard that as for danger, nothing is more dangerous than ghosts (*k-ʔuj?).
That which satisfies is balance (*breŋ);
That which is detestable is collapse (*[k]ʷʰeŋ).

The passage consists entirely of rhyming couplets and pairs of antonyms (as do all the answers in the first section). This means that meaning is not the sole criterion for choosing the keywords. Rather, the author needed to strike a balance between sound and meaning — that is, to find words that rhyme without too much semantic stretch. Each pair of words had to satisfy three requirements at the same time: (1) they rhyme; (2) they are antonyms or near antonyms; (3) they can be sensibly regarded as "long-lasting" and "dangerous," or "satisfying" and "detestable." Given that rhyme plays an important role in diction, we need to speak cautiously about the "philosophy" of these keywords, for they might not have been chosen for philosophical reasons alone.[4]

---

4   Cao Feng, for example, has written an article on the "view of gods and ghosts" (*guishen guan* 鬼神觀) in *Yin gaozong*, in which he considers the problem only from a philosophical point of view. See Cao Feng, "Qinghua jian *San shou Tang zai Chimen* zhong de

The second section has a different rhyme scheme, which nonetheless also corresponds to the semantic structure. The explanation of a keyword sticks to the same rhyme group determined by the word being explained. In the explanation of *xiang* 祥 "propitiousness" (*s.ɢaŋ), for example, every sentence ends in *-aŋ:

> Be receptive to Heaven's constancy (*[d]aŋ)
> And revere the gods' brilliance (*mraŋ).
> Exalt the *zhao* and obey the *mu* tablets,
> And respect the people's conduct (*[g]ˤraŋ-s).
> Make abundant offerings and present achievements,
> Quickly turning back eerie occurrences and omens (*s.ɢaŋ).
> Such is named propitiousness (*s.ɢaŋ).

The preoccupation with rhymes may partially account for the conceptual sloppiness of *Yin gaozong*. To maintain the rhyme pattern, the author must have found it necessary to sacrifice semantic accuracy or syntactic parallelism in some cases. An interesting example of this kind is the explanation of the last keyword "trustworthiness" (*s-ni[ŋ]-s). As mentioned above, the rhyme group of an explanation is determined by the sound of the keyword, and yet here the whole passage rhymes with the first keyword "propitiousness" (*s.ɢaŋ):

> In encouraging and approaching the bright and perceptive (*mraŋ),
> Be gentle and tactful in voice and countenance,
> But be intelligent and valiant without deception (*maŋʔ).
> Emulate the pure and plan for the long term;
> Shepherd the people and defend the king (*ɢʷaŋ).
> All under heaven examine and commend (you),

---

guishen guan" 清華簡《三壽》《湯在啻門》中的鬼神觀, *Sichuan daxue xuebao (zhexue shehui kexue ban)* 四川大學學報(哲學社會科學版) 2016.5, 33–40.

Making announcements in the four directions (*C-paŋ).
Such is named intelligent and trustworthy conduct (*[g]ˤraŋ-s).

By choosing a different rhyme group, the author had no choice but to change the last sentence from "Such is named trustworthiness" to "Such is named intelligent and trustworthy conduct," breaking the formulaic pattern. But why switch to a different rhyme group? He might have found it difficult to construct a meaningful passage that totally rhymed with "trustworthiness." It is also likely that he was trying to make Ancestor Peng begin and finish his speech in the euphonic *-aŋ.

All this is not to suggest that we cannot speak about the intellectual content of *Yin gaozong*. Although the text has no coherent argument, it is possible to identify recurrent themes. One example noted by Cao Feng is the frequent coupling of *min* 民 "people" (or occasionally *ren* 人 "humans") with *shen* 神 "gods" in the second and third sections:[5]

> … revere the gods' brilliance … and respect the people's conduct. (slip 14)
> … covered with gods' blessings and joined with the strength of the people. (slip 16)
> Please the gods and be soft with humans. (slip 18)
> Worship the gods with respect and harmonize the people using rectitude. (slip 19)
> neither the gods nor the people can blame (you) (slip 20)
> The gods and people together condemn (them) (slip 26)
> Worship the gods and reward the people (for their toil) (slip 28)

Since the speeches are all addressed to the king, the text seems to view the king as a mediator between the divine and human world, whose job it is to

---

5   Cao Feng, "Qinghua jian *San shou Tang zai Chimen* zhong de guishen guan," 35; Perkins, "*Yin Gaozong Wen Yu San Shou*: Content and Context," 296.

make both happy. All the instructions are embedded in this implicit framework of gods, the king, and the people. This being the case, *Yin Gaozong* makes no effort to turn this framework into a conceptually organized cosmology, like the one found in **Chimen*. It cares more about rhyme and formal parallels than conceptual structure.

Yin Gaozong wen yu San Shou 殷高宗問於三壽
The High Ancestor of Yin Asked the Three Long-Lived Ones

高 宗 觀 於 匋 水 之 上 ＿ 參 壽 與 從 ＿ 高 宗 乃 矗 於 少
壽 曰 尔 是 先 生 尔 是

高宗觀於洹水之上，三壽與從。高宗乃問於少壽曰："爾是先生，爾是 [一]

The High Ancestor was sightseeing on the Huan River, and the Three Long-Lived Ones went along with him. The High Ancestor then asked the Lesser Long-Lived One, saying: "You were born before me, and thus you [1]

183

智 二 又 邺 之 請 _ 敢 馪 人 可 胃 長 _ 可 胃 墮 _ 可 胃
肩 _ 可 胃 亞 _ 少 壽 會 曰 虗

知二有國之情。敢問人何謂長? 何謂險? 何謂厭? 何謂惡? ” 少壽答曰: “吾 [二]

know the situation of the two states.[6] May I ask what people mean by lasting long? What they mean by danger? What they mean by satisfaction? What they mean by detestation?" The Lesser Long-Lived One answered, saying: "I've [2]

6　The two states must be Xia and Shang/Yin.

[聞夫長莫長於□，吾聞夫險莫險於□。厭彼□，惡彼□。" 高宗乃或問於] [三]

[heard that as for lasting long, nothing lasts longer than … ; I've heard that as for danger, nothing is more dangerous than … That which satisfies is … ; that which is detestable is … " The High Ancestor then asked][7] [3]

---

7   Slip 3 is missing, but most of its content can be guessed from the High Ancestor's parallel questions.

审 壽 曰 敢 䎷 人 可 胃 長 ＿ 可 胃 墮 ＿ 可 胃 肩 ＿ 可 胃
亞 ＿ 审 壽 僉 曰 虐 䎷 夫 長 莫

中壽曰："敢問人何謂長？何謂險？何謂厭？何謂惡？" 中壽答曰："吾聞夫長莫 [四]

the Middle Long-Lived One, saying: "May I ask what people mean by lasting
long? What they mean by danger? What they mean by satisfaction? What
they mean by detestation?" The Middle Long-Lived One answered, saying:
"I've heard that as for lasting long, nothing [4]

長於風＿虐羸夫墮莫墮於心＿肩非艰＿
亞非芒＿高宗乃或羸於彭且曰高

長於風，吾聞夫險莫險於心。厭彼藏，惡彼喪。" 高宗乃或問於彭祖曰："高 [五]

lasts longer than the wind; I've heard that as for danger, nothing is more dangerous than the heart. That which satisfies is[8] savings; that which is detestable is loss." The High Ancestor then asked Ancestor Peng, saying: "Culturally Accomplished High [5]

---

8   Following Huang Jie 黃傑 (a.k.a. Musilang 暮四郎), I take *fei* 非 (*pəj) "not" as a loan for *bi* 彼 (*pajʔ) "that." See Huang Jie (Musilang), "Qinghua wu *Yin gaozong wen yu san shou* chudu" 清華五《殷高宗問於三壽》初讀 #5, at http://www.bsm.org.cn/forum/forum.php?mod=viewthread&tid=3249, posted 10 April 2015. It is also possible to read *fei* (1) simply as "not" or (2) as a loan for *bi* 必 "must, necessarily." For discussions and comparisons of alternative readings, see Liu Chuanbin 劉傳賓, "Qinghua wu *Yin Gao Zong wen yu san shou* jian 1–8 jiexi" 清華五《殷高宗問於三壽》簡1–8解析, *Guwenzi yanjiu* 31 (2016): 391–396; Franklin Perkins, "*Yin Gaozong Wen Yu San Shou*: Content and Context," 283–286. Baxter argues against the *bi* 必 reading because 非 (*pəj) and 必 (*pit) have different main vowels and codas. See William H. Baxter, "Guanyu Qinghua jian (wu) san pian de yixie biji" 關於清華簡（伍）三篇的一些筆記, in *Qinghua jian yanjiu* 3 (Shanghai: Zhong Xi shuju, 2019), 33.

文成且敢羴人可胃長可胃隍可胃肩可胃亞彭且
會曰虐羴夫長莫

文成祖，敢問人何謂長？何謂險？何謂厭？何謂惡？" 彭祖答曰："吾聞夫長莫 [六]

Ancestor, May I ask what people mean by lasting long? What they mean by danger? What they mean by satisfaction? What they mean by detestation?" Ancestor Peng answered, saying: "I've heard that as for lasting long, nothing [6]

長 於 水 _ 虗 䎽 夫 隥 莫 隥 於 褱 _ 肩 非 坪 _ 亞 非 𦗏
高 宗 乃 言 曰 虗 䎽 夫 長 莫 長 於

長於水，吾聞夫險莫險於鬼。厭彼平，惡彼傾。” 高宗乃言曰：“吾聞夫長莫長於 [七]

lasts longer than water; I've heard that as for danger, nothing is more dangerous than ghosts. That which satisfies is balance; that which is detestable is collapse."[9] The High Ancestor then spoke, saying: "I've heard that as for lasting long, nothing lasts longer than [7]

9 The editors read 𦗏 , whose phonophore is 聖, as *qing* 傾 "collapse." Baxter, on the other hand, argues that *sheng* 聖 (*l̥eŋ-s) cannot be a loan for *qing* 傾 (*[k]ʷʰeŋ) because the initials are very different. See Baxter, "Guanyu Qinghua jian (wu) san pian de yixie biji," 33. He does not, however, consider the graphic form and meaning at all. The signific of this character  is the bottom left component  , which, as mentioned in p.64, n.28, is an inverted 山 meaning "overturn, collapse." As such, it corresponds very well with the *qing* 傾 reading. Moreover, this reading works perfectly in context as an antonym of *ping* 平 "balance." A similar contrast can be found in the "Dao shu" 道術 "Techniques of the Way" chapter of Jia Yi's 賈誼 *Xin shu* 新書 *New Writings*: "To occupy an appropriate position without collapse is called balance; the opposite of balance is danger" (據當不傾謂之平, 反平為險). See Yan Zhenyi 閻振益 and Zhong Xia 鍾夏, *Xinshu jiaozhu* 新書校注 (Beijing: Zhonghua shuju, 2000), 303. Moreover, as Zhang Fuhai 張富海 points out, the character *xin* 馨 (*qʰˤeŋ) is sometimes written with a 聖 phonophore. On the Western Zhou Si 獄 *gui*, 馨 appears in the phrase *xin xiang* 馨香 "fragrance" and is written with a 聖 and a 鬯, where 鬯 is obviously the signific. Baxter and Sagart's reconstruction of 聖 (*l̥eŋ-s) does not take into account this example. See Zhang Fuhai, "Li yong xiesheng gouni shanggu yin yinggai zhuyi de jige wenti," 138. For the Si 獄 *gui*, see Wu Zhenfeng 吴鎮烽, "Si qi mingwen kaoshi" 獄器銘文考釋, *Kaogu yu wenwu* 考古與文物 2006.6: 58–65.

□ ＿ 虐 舋 夫 墜 非 矛 返 干 ＿ 肩 非 稟 ＿ 亞 非 亡 飤 ＿
句 我 與 尔 相 念 相 愍 ＿ 殜＝ 至 於 後 飤 我 思

[山]，吾聞夫險彼矛及干。厭彼富，惡彼無食。苟我與爾相念相謀，世世至於後嗣。
我思 [八]

[mountains];[10] I've heard that as for danger, it is spears and shields. That
which satisfies is wealth; that which is detestable is lack of food. If you and
I consider and plan with each other, (our legacy will last) generation after
generation to posterity.[11] When I think of [8]

10　The top character on this slip is missing. Wang Ning 王寧 suggests that the missing
　　character is *shan* 山 (*s-ŋrar) "mountain." Semantically it corresponds with the "wind"
　　and "water" in the parallel answers. Phonetically it rhymes with *gan* 干 (*kˤa[r]) "shield."
　　See Wang Ning, "Du *Yin gaozong wen yu san shou* sanzha" 讀《殷高宗問於三壽》散札,
　　at http://www.fdgwz.org.cn/Web/Show/2525, posted 17 May 2015.
11　The editors read 食 as *si* 嗣, the compound *housi* meaning "posterity."

天風 既富 或击虐 孛 自印 畏 以 敬 夫 孳 怠 ＿ 孳= 而 不
譯 箸 占 ＿ 則 若 尖= 之 瘧 痖 而

天風，既回又止，吾勉自抑畏，以敬夫滋怠。君子而不讀書占，則若小人之聾狂而 [九]

the heavenly wind, now whirling and now stopping, I strive on my own to suppress the fear[12] and to be on guard against increasing laziness.[13] If a gentleman does not read written prognostications, then, like a petty person who is deaf and crazy, [9]

---

12 I follow the editors and punctuate after *wei* 畏 "fear," because, as they point out, there is a similar phrase "able to suppress one's own fear" (克自抑畏) in the "Wu yi" 無逸 chapter of *Shang shu*.

13 The last two characters of this sentence are difficult. The first 孳 is often seen in early manuscripts and usually means *zi* 茲 "this," *zi* 滋 "increase," or *zai* 哉 (a sentence-final particle). It cannot be *zai*, because there is a punctuation mark after the next character, and it is unlikely that this one is a sentence-final particle. The second character in fact cannot be identified clearly. I agree with Ma Nan that it looks very much like a 怠. See Qinghua daxue chutu wenxian dushuhui 清華大學出土文獻讀書會, "Qinghua jian diwu ce zhengli baogao buzheng" 清華簡第五冊整理報告補正, at https://www.ctwx. tsinghua.edu.cn/info/1081/2214.htm, posted 8 April 2015. Possible readings of it are *dai* 怠 "lazy," *dai* 殆 "danger, nearly," and *shi* 始 "beginning." Yegor Grebnev suggests (in an online discussion) taking the phrase as *zidai* 滋怠 "increasing laziness."

不吝_ 醫邦之蚤蓳并记 八絹 則緇四厰酒行四昚
之㠯 則复九牧_ 九矣酒㞢 娃=

不友。"殷邦之妖祥并起。八紀則紊，四巖將行。四海之夷則作，九牧九畡將喪。
枉矢 [+]

he will have no friends."[14] Eerie occurrences and omens together arose in
the state of Yin. The Eight Cords were then disturbed, and the Four Cliffs
were about to move. Barbarians of the Four Seas then rose up, and the
Nine Pastoral Grounds and the Nine Domains[15] were about to be lost. The

---

14 Since the manuscript has no quotation mark, an important question is where the High
Ancestor's speech stops. I believe the paragraph describing "eerie occurrences and
omens" begins another section of the nine ethical terms. The High Ancestor's speech
from slips 7–9 has the same rhyme scheme. Starting from slip 10, the rhyme scheme
changes and remains consistent until when the High Ancestor speaks again on slip 11.
The only exception is the first sentence "Eerie occurrences and omens together arose in
the state of Yin." It rhymes with the last paragraph and continues the topic of divination.

15 The editors read 矣 as *you* 有 "realm." A contrast between the Nine Realms and the
Nine Pastoral Grounds can be found in the "Jie bi" 解蔽 "Removing Obsession" chapter of *Xunzi* 荀子, where King Tang of Shang is said to have "replaced the king of Xia (i.e.
Jie 桀) and received the Nine Realms" (代夏王而受九有也), and King Wen of Zhou
is said to have "replaced the king of Yin (i.e. Zhòu 紂) and received the Nine Pastoral
Grounds" (代殷王而受九牧也). Both terms were glossed as "Nine Regions" (*jiuzhou*
九州) by Yang Liang 楊倞 (fl. c. 800). Wang Xianqian 王先謙, *Xunzi jijie* 荀子集解
(Beijing: Zhonghua shuju, 1988), 389. Baxter disagress with this reading and points out
that 矣 (*qəʔ) and 有 (*[ɢ]ʷəʔ) have quite different initials. He supports Wang Ning's
reading *gai* 畡/垓 (*[k]ˤə) "domain." The term *jiugai* 九畡 (or 九垓) "Nine Domains"
is also attested in early texts. See Wang Ning, "Du *Yin gaozong wen yu san shou* sanzha;"
Baxter, "Guanyu Qinghua jian (wu) san pian de yixie biji," 36.

Crooked Arrow[16] [10] [17]

先 反 大 茗 甬 見 兵 龜 筮 孚 貣 五 寶 兌 色 而 星 月 躙 行
高 宗 恭 愳 乃 專 語 彭 且

先反，大路用見兵。龜筮孚忒，五寶變色，而星月亂行。高宗恐懼，乃敷語彭祖 [十一]

returned first, and armies thus appeared on thoroughfares. Shell and stalk divinations were not credible; the Five Treasures[18] changed color; the stars and the moon moved in disorder. The High Ancestor was terrified and then spoke at length to Ancestor Peng, [11]

16 I follow Wang Ning in reading this character as the combination of *wangshi* 枉矢 "Crooked Arrow," which refers to a shooting star moving along a winding path. See Wang Ning, "Du *Yin gaozong wen yu san shou* sanzha." This can be one of the "eerie omens" mentioned before. For a detailed discussion of historical records of the Crooked Arrow, see Zhuang Tianshan 莊天山, "Lun Tiangou, Wangshi de shizhi ji qita" 論天狗、枉矢的實質及其他, in Zhongguo tianwenxue shi zhengli yanjiu xiaozu 中國天文學史整理研究小組 eds. *Kejishi wenji* 科技史文集 10 (Shanghai: Shanghai kexue jishu chubanshe, 1983), 151–169.

17 The number on the back of this slip is 15, while the number on the current slip 15 is 10. According to the textual content, however, they are obviously misplaced.

18 It is not clear what the "Five Treasures" refers to. It seems to be an astronomical phenomenon.

曰 於 虔 彭 且 古 民 人 迷 䚫 兔 矛 康 歎 而 不 智 邦 之 牆 㞷 敢 䎩 先 王 之 遺 忍

曰:"嗚呼, 彭祖! 古民人迷亂, 逸務康懋, 而不 [19] 知邦之將喪。敢問先王之遺訓,[十二]

saying: "Aha, Ancestor Peng! The people of old were perplexed and disordered, idle at work and complacent in their efforts.[20] They did not know that the state was about to be lost. May I ask about the instructions left by the past kings? [12]

---

19 The character 不 is inserted in the space between 而 and 知.

20 The four characters 兔矛康歎 provoke considerable controversy, and numerous readings have been proposed. The editors transcribe the first character as *xiang* 象 rather than *tu* 兔 (the two characters look very similar in Chu script and are often confused). I agree with Huang Jie that it should be 兔. See Huang Jie (Musilang), "Qinghua wu *Yin gaozong wen yu san shou* chudu" #6, posted 10 April 2015. By transcribing it as 兔 and reading it as *yi* 逸 "idle," we get a nice parallel between this and the third word *kang* 康 "complacent." The second and fourth characters also seem to parallel each other, for both have *mao* 矛 as the phonetic. They can be read either as *wu* 務 "work" or *mao* 懋 "effort," both also having 矛 as the phonetic. Therefore, I take the four characters as two synonymous phrases, "idle at work" and "complacent in efforts."

可 胃 恙 可 胃 義 ＿ 可 胃 悳 ＿ 可 胃 音 ＿ 可 胃 訡 ＿ 可
胃 惡 ＿ 可 胃 智 可 胃 利 可 胃

何謂祥? 何謂義? 何謂德? 何謂音? 何謂仁? 何謂聖? 何謂知? 何謂利? 何謂 [十三]

What is meant by propitiousness? What is meant by propriety? What is meant by virtue? What is meant by tone? What is meant by benevolence? What is meant by sagacity? What is meant by wisdom? What is meant by benefit? What is meant by [13]

訏 彭 且 會 曰 霯 天 之 棠 鼎 神 之 明 走 卲 心 穆 而 敬 民
之 行 余 言 獻 社 遚 還 蚕

信? " 彭祖答曰: "聞天之常, 祇神之明。尚昭順穆, 而敬民之行。餘享獻功, 遚還
妖 [十四]

trustworthiness?" Ancestor Peng answered, saying: "Be receptive to Heaven's constancy and revere the gods' brilliance. Exalt the *zhao* and obey the *mu* tablets, and respect the people's conduct. Make abundant offerings and present achievements, quickly turning back eerie occurrences [14]

[bronze/seal script line 1]

[bronze/seal script line 2]

蓋 寺 名 曰 恙 邇 則 文 之 愚 萬 象 天 寺 棓 厇 毋 諟 戈 豐

騪 怳 專 民 之 恷 民 騪 毋 皮

祥。是名曰祥。邇則文之偽。曆象天時，往度毋徙。申禮勸技，輔民之化。民勸毋疲，[十五]

and omens. Such is named propitiousness.[21] Closely model yourself on the artifices[22] of culture. Make calendars to depict Heaven's time and do not change past standards. Extend the rites and encourage the crafts to facilitate the transformation of the people, and the people will exert themselves tirelessly. [15]

---

21 The two characters transcribed as 祥 on slip 15 are distinguished by their signific: one has 虫 "insect" and the other has 心 "heart." Although paleographers generally believe that significs do not play any semantic role in Warring States manuscripts, in this case they are certainly meaningful. The distinction between these two significs is maintained throughout the manuscript. The character 蓋 (slips 10 and 15) always means "eerie omen," whereas the character 恙 (slips 13, 15, and 27) always has positive (though not exactly the same) meanings. The *Yin gaozong* seems more attentive to orthography than other manuscripts around the same time. See p.205, n.32 below for another example of this kind.

22 The editors read *wei* 愚 "artifice" as *hua* 化 "transformation," but there is a *hua* 恷 on the same slip that is almost certainly "transformation."

197

寺 名 曰 義 ＿ 樸 宋 水 臾 不 力 寺 型 罰 詠 ＿ 晨 若 敘 態
冒 神 之 福 同 民 之 力 寺

是名曰義。揆中水衡不力。時刑罰赦，振若除慝。冒神之福，同民之力。是 [十六]

Such is named propriety. Measure the middle using the level and balance
without force. Exempt (the people from) punishments in a timely manner,[23]
stimulating the agreeable and eliminating the wicked. (Then you will be)
covered with the gods' blessings and joined with the strength of the people.
Such is [16]

---

23 As for the string of ten characters 揆宋水臾不力寺型罰詠 between the two punctuation
marks, the editors punctuate after 不力 and speculate that two characters are missing
before 不力, so that the definition of "virtue" consists of tetrasyllabic lines only: 揆中
準衡, □□不力, 時刑罰赦. The punctuation, motivated by the rhyme scheme of this
part (力, 慝, and 福), seems reasonable, but there is no strong reason to believe that the
text must conform to a tetrasyllabic pattern. The definitions of "propriety" and "benefit,"
for example, are not consistently tetrasyllabic. Therefore, I follow Bubai 補白 in taking
揆中水衡不力 as a single sentence. See Bubai, "Qinghua jian *Yin gaozong wen yu san
shou* yishuo size" 清華簡《殷高宗問於三壽》臆說四則, at http://fdgwz.org.cn/Web/
Show/2497, posted 16 April 2015. The phrase *kui zhong* 揆中, literally "to measure the
middle" also appears on slip 28. It seems to be a metaphor for making balanced judg-
ments in adjudication.

名 曰 惪 惠 民 由 壬 均 寶 傑 怪 闢 義 和 藥 非 裹 于 惵 四
方 飄 孝 監 莞 莫 淦

名曰德。惠民由任，徇詢揭淫。宣義和樂，非懷于耽。四方勸教，濫媚莫感。[十七]

named virtue. Be generous to the people and employ those who are responsible; expose the disgraceful and disclose the licentious.[24] Proclaim decorum and harmonize music; repudiate (the practice of) cherishing indulgence. Encourage and educate those from the four directions, so that no one will be moved by extravagant and alluring (music). [17]

---

24 The meaning of 均寶傑怪 is highly controversial. I follow Wang Ning in taking this line as two synonymous verb-object phrases. He reads the first character 均 as *xun* 徇 "to expose, to display publicly" so that it parallels the third character 傑, which is read as *jie* 揭 "to unveil, to disclose." As for the second character, he points out that it also appears on slip 26 (the fourth character) and should be read as *gou* 詢 (also written as 詬) "disgrace" in both places. This meaning echoes the fourth character *yin* 淫 "licentious". See Wang Ning, "Du *Yin gaozong wen yu san shou* sanzha."

寺 名 曰 音 ＿ 衣 備 耑 而 好 訐 丂 杰 而 衮 罙 屾 遠 而 忶
新 ＿ 憙 神 而 順 人 寺 名 曰 訫 ＿ 龏

是名曰音。衣服端而好信。孝慈而哀鰥。恤遠而謀親。喜神而柔人。是名曰仁。恭 [十八]

Such is named tone. Dress up neatly and love trustworthiness. Show filial
piety and parental love; feel pity for widowed people. Worry about those far
away and plan for close relatives. Please the gods and be soft with humans.
Such is named benevolence. Worship [18]

神 以 敬 和 民 甬 政 ＿ 畱 邦 晏 兵 四 方 達 盉 元 折 并 進
譆 繇 則 救 ＿ 寺 名 曰 惡 ＿ 昔 勤

神以敬，和民用正。留邦偃兵，四方達寧。元哲并進，讒謠則屏。是名曰聖。昔勤 [十九]

the gods with respect and harmonize the people using rectitude. Bring order to the state[25] and lay down weapons, so that those from the four directions are all tranquil. The good and the wise together come forth, so that slanders and rumors are blocked. Such is named sagacity. Don't be content with past effort, [19]

---

25   The editors point out that *liu* 留 is glossed as *zhi* 治 "to govern, to bring order to, to work on" in Wei Zhao's 韋昭 (204–273) commentary to *Guo yu*.

不 居 虜 臡 不 易 共 椹 思 坙 内 諫 受 訾 神 民 莫 責 寺 名
曰 智 内 臸 而 外 比 上 下 毋 倉

不居，狎祇不易。恐枉思修，納諫受訾，神民莫責，是名曰智。內甚而外比。上下
毋爽，[二十]

and habitually show reverence without change. Fear crookedness and wish
to correct it; accept remonstrance and take criticism, so that neither the gods
nor the people can blame (you). Such is named wisdom. Those on the inside
make plans and those from outside follow along.[26] Those above and below
should not be mistaken; [20]

---

26 Tang Pui-ling 鄧佩玲 takes *nei* 内 "inside" and *wai* 外 "outside" as referring to domestic
and foreign affairs. See Tang Pui-ling, "Qinghua jian (wu) *Yin gaozong wen yu san shou
youguan* 'zhi' 'li' 'xin' *sanduan jianwen kaoshi*" 清華簡(伍)《殷高宗問於三壽》有關
"智""利""信"三段簡文考釋, *Chutu wenxian* 11 (2017): 198.

发=愚比弜救丩出經緯忑齊土悁毋复而天目毋屒
寺名曰利 _ 勴臺恩明音色 _

左右謀比。強屏糾黜，經緯順齊。妒怨毋作，而天目毋睨。是名曰利。勸就聰明。
音色 [二十一]

those on the left and right seek to follow along.[27] The violent are blocked and the twisted banished,[28] so that social fabric[29] will be smooth and even. Envy and resentment should not arise, and the heavenly eye should not look sideways.[30] Such is named benefit. In encouraging and approaching the bright and perceptive, be gentle and tactful [21]

---

27 "Those on the left and right" is a metaphor for the close attendants of a ruler. The literal translation is meant to preserve the three contrasts between inside and outside, above and below, and left and right.

28 I take 弜救丩出 as two synonymous phrases. Following Huang Jie (Musilang), I read 救 (which also appears on slip 19) as *ping* 屏 "to block" and 出 as *chu* 黜 "to banish." See Huang Jie (Musilang), "Qinghua wu *Yin gaozong wen yu san shou* chudu" #32, posted 13 April 2015. If that is the case, then 弜 (a variant form of *qiang* 強 "violent") and 丩 must be both negative. The editors read 丩 as *jiu* 糾 in the sense of "to examine." Adopting this reading, I gloss *jiu* as "twisted," an uncommon meaning attested in the "Yi bing" 議 兵 "Discussing Military Affairs" chapter of *Xunzi*: "Those who are of the boastful, twist-ed, constrained, and devious type will transform for him and become concordant" (矜糾 收繚之屬為之化而調). Obviously, in this sentence, being *jiu* is the opposite of being "concordant." Wang Xianqian, *Xunzi jijie*, 288.

29 Literally "warp and weft," a metaphor for social order or the act of maintaining order.

30 Tang Pui-ling reads 屒 as *yi* 睨 "to look sideways." See Tang Pui-ling, "Qinghua jian (wu) *Yin gaozong wen yu san shou* youguan 'zhi' 'li' 'xin' sanduan jianwen kaoshi," 200–201.

柔丂而觀武不罔天屯佢猷 ＿ 牧民而駢王天下覒
丏以晕四方寺名曰觀訐之

柔巧，而叡武不罔。效純桓猷，牧民而禦王。天下甄稱，以誥四方。是名曰叡信之 [二十二]

in voice and countenance, but be intelligent and valiant without deception. Emulate the pure and plan for the long term;[31] shepherd the people and defend the king. All under heaven examine and commend (you), making announcements in the four directions. Such is named intelligent and trustworthy [22]

31　The editors read 佢猷 as *xuan you* 宣猷 "to announce plans," but on slip 17, a different character 閒 is read as *xuan* 宣 already. It is not totally impossible that two different characters are used for the same word in a manuscript, but "announce plans" does not work that well in this context either. I suspect that 佢猷 is just the 趄慕 (read as *huan mo* 桓謨 "great plans") or *yuan you* 遠猷 "to plan for the long term" in the Qiang 墻 *pan* (10175) bronze inscription. The phrase *yuan you* 遠猷 also appears in the Hu 默 *gui* (4317) inscription. The bronze inscriptions are cited by their numbers in the *Yin Zhou jinwen jicheng (zengbu xiuding ben)*. See p.31, n.7 in the introduction to this volume for full bibliographic information. There is textual support for reading 佢 as *yuan* 遠 "distant" in the Mawangdui *Zhouyi* 周易: in the "Zhun" 屯 hexagram, for the manuscript's 半遠, the received text reads 磐桓. See Chen Jian 陳劍 ed. "Zhouyi jingzhuan" 周易經傳, in Hunan sheng bowuguan 湖南省博物館 and Fudan daxue chutu wenxian yu guwenzi yanjiu zhongxin 復旦大學出土文獻與古文字研究中心 eds. *Changsha Mawangdui Hanmu jianbo jicheng* 長沙馬王堆漢墓簡帛集成 vol. 3 (Beijing: Zhonghua shuju, 2014), 21. See also Edward L. Shaughnessy, *I Ching (The Classic of Changes)* (New York: Ballantine Books, 1996), 82–83.

行　 彭且曰於虔我均晨共孳九厎覾頋之逴商方
曼于茗甬肎卲句成湯弌傑

行。" 彭祖曰: "嗚呼! 我均震恐茲九度，甄夏之歸商。方勉于路，用乂召后成湯，
代桀 [二十三]

conduct." Ancestor Peng said: "Aha! I'm equally shocked and terrified by these nine standards[32] when examining Xia's surrender to Shang. (The Shang people were) about to strive on the road to assist Lord Cheng Tang, replacing Jie [23]

---

32 The meaning of 我均晨共孳九厎 is controversial. The editors' original reading, *e yin chen jiang zai jiu zhai* 俄寅晨降在九宅 "suddenly at dawn coming down to the Nine Dwellings," is totally wrong. Wang Ning argues that 我 should simply be read as *wo* 我 "we" rather than *e* 俄 "suddenly," and the Tsinghua Reading Group later corrected their own reading, now taking 九厎 as *jiu du* 九度 "nine standards" and 孳 as *zi* 茲 "this/these." The "nine standards" seem to refer to the nine ethical terms just defined. All of these are clear enough, but the meaning of 均晨 (which also appear on slip 17 and 16 respectively) is very problematic. Since everyone reads 共 as *gong* 恭 "to respect," they mostly take 均晨 as an adverbial phrase modifying the verb. Huang Jie (Musilang) reads it as *chun shen* 惇慎 "earnestly and cautiously," pointing out that the phrase appears in the "Jun zi" 君子 chapter of the *Xunzi*. Shi Xiaoli 石小力 reads it as *yin zhi* 寅祗, both characters meaning "respectful." See Huang Jie (Musilang) "Qinghua wu *Yin gaozong wen yu san shou chudu*" #77, posted 4 May 2015; Shi Xiaoli, "Qinghua wu *Yin gaozong wen yu san shou* chudu" #14, at http://www.bsm.org.cn/forum/forum.php?mod=viewthread&tid=3249, posted 11 April 2015. The problem of these readings is that they do not work phonologically: 均晨 (*C.qʷi[n], *[d]ər) sounds very different from 惇慎 (*tˤur, *[d]i[n]-s) and 寅祗 (*[ɢ](r)ər, *tˤij?) in Old Chinese. The "respectful" reading is also semantically redundant (why put three words meaning "respect" in a row?). I believe the reason why this phrase is so difficult is that all scholars assume that the following character 共 should be read as *gong* 恭 "to respect" rather than *kong* 恐 "to fear." As mentioned in note 207, *Yin gaozong* is careful about orthography. It *always* uses the character 龏 for *gong* 恭 "to respect" (slips 18, 26, and 27) and the character 共, or whatever character that has 共 as the phonophore, for *kong* 恐 "to fear" (slips 11 and 20). The five occurrences are enough evidence of a consistent distinction. If we read the 共 here also as *kong* 恐, then 晨共 can be read simply as *zhen kong* 震恐 (or 振恐) "shocked and terrified," a very common phrase in early texts. This meaning echoes the High Ancestor's fear on slip 11, which begins Ancestor Peng's discussion of the nine standards. It also works well in the context of examining Xia's surrender to Shang. For an extended discussion on this reading, see Zhou Boqun 周博群, "Qinghua wu *Yin gaozong wen yu san shou bushi*" 清華五《殷高宗問於三壽》補釋, *Chutu wenxian* 出土文獻 (forthcoming).

尃 又 下　方 高 宗 或 羴 於 彭 且 曰　高 文 成 且 敢 羴 疋 民
古 曰 易﹦ 則 舌 逯 亡 棠 ＿ 古 曰 昏﹦ 則

敷有下方。"高宗或問於彭祖曰："高文成祖，敢問斯民胡曰揚？揚則攝佚無常。胡
曰晦？晦則 [二十四]

and broadly having (the territories) below." The High Ancestor asked Ancestor Peng, saying: "Culturally Accomplished High Ancestor, may I ask as for
the people, how they are called ostentatious? When (they are) ostentatious,
(they are sometimes) restrained and (sometimes) dissolute[33] without constancy. How they are called obscure? When (they are) obscure, [24]

---

33 Wang Ning reads 舌逯 as *she yi* 攝佚 "restrained and dissolute." See Wang Ning, "*Du
Yin gaozong wen yu san shou* sanzha."

☑ 𝕒𝕓𝕔𝕕𝕖𝕗𝕘𝕙𝕚𝕛𝕜

☑ 戲 悷 自 嘉 而 不 縷 淾 高 玟 寠

[⋯彭祖曰：“民之有揚⋯] 戲淫自嘉而不數。感高文富 [二十五]

[… Ancestor Peng said: "As for the people's being ostentatious …][34] wallow in licentiousness, congratulating but never censuring themselves. (They are) moved by high class and decorated with wealth, [25]

---

34 The first twenty or so characters are missing on this slip. The punctuation, reading, and translation of the remaining text on slip 25 are all tentative. I shall not venture any hypothetical reconstruction of the missing part, although it certainly includes the transition from the High Ancestor's question to Ancestor Peng's answer.

而 昏 忘 實 返 利 ＿ 嚚 神 慕 犇 而 不 夤 于 逡 ＿ 神 民 并
盞 而 九 惆 所 聚 天 罰 是 加 甬 兌 以 見

而昏忘詢。急利嚚神莫恭而不顧于後。神民并尤，而仇怨所聚。天罰是加，用兌以
見 [二十六]

muddled and forgetful of disgrace. Eager for profits, (they) clamor before
the gods without worshipping them and have no regard for descendants.[35]
The gods and people together condemn (them), on whom hatred and
resentment accumulate. Heavenly punishments will be inflicted, and because
of the disasters (they) are [26]

---

35 I follow the editors' punctuation of the two sentences: 感高文富而昏忘詢。急利嚚神
莫恭而不顧于後。 This punctuation plan is motivated by the rhymed words 詢 (*qʰˤ(r)
o-s) and 後 (*[ɢ]ˤ(r)oʔ). However. I think it is also possible to punctuate the text as 感高
文富而昏，忘詢急利。嚚神莫恭，而不顧于後, which can be translated as "Affected
by high class and decorated with wealth, (they are) muddled. (They) forget about disgrace
and rush to profits. Clamoring before the gods without worshipping them, (they) have
no regard for descendants." There is no significant difference in meaning. This second
punctuation plan does not preserve all the rhymes, but it foregrounds a potential syntactic parallelism between Ancestor Peng's two replies in this section:

嚚神莫恭，而不顧于後。神民并尤，而仇怨所聚。(slip 26)
Clamoring before the gods without worshipping them, (they) have no regard for
descendants. The gods and people together condemn (them), on whom hatred and
resentment accumulate.
恭神勞民，揆中而象常。束柬和謨，補缺而救枉。(slip 28)
Worship the gods and reward the people (for their toils); measure the middle and
emulate the constant. Gather together remonstrances and plan harmoniously;
supplement what is lacking and save the crooked.

訽 _ 曰 於 虖 若 寺 _ 民 之 有 畱= 而 本 由 生 光 則 佳 小
心 翼= 募 復 亐 𩒨 𩫖 孝 𢙁 舍 敬 恙 𦋅

訽。" 曰: "嗚呼! 若是。" "民之有晦，晦而本由生光。則唯小心翼翼，顧復勉祗。
聞教訓，餘敬養。恭 [二十七]

disgraced." (The High Ancestor) said: "Aha! (It is indeed) like this." "As
for the people's being obscure, their obscurity is the root from which light
grows.[36] Therefore, be cautious and reverent, look after[37] (the people) and
strive to be reverent; be receptive to teachings and instructions, and abundantly respect and care for (the people). Worship [27]

---

36 This sentence about obscurity is itself obscure, and my translation is again tentative. It
could also mean "Although the people are obscure, at their root brightness grows."

37 As Wang Ning and Huang Jie (Musilang) point out, the compound *gufu* 顧復 "to look
after and cover" appears in the "Liao e" 蓼莪 poem of *Shi jing*, in a stanza about parental care: (They) caress and feed me, nurture and rear me, look after and cover me (拊我
畜我, 長我育我, 顧我復我). The stanza lists a series of synonyms for "nurture" "rear"
or "care for." See Wang Ning, "Du *Yin gaozong wen yu san shou* sanzha." Huang Jie
(Musilang), "Qinghua wu *Yin gaozong wen yu san shou* chudu" #41.

神 燊 民 樸 宷 而 象 裳 棘 束 和 莫 専 歆 而 救 桂 天 募 復
之 甬 休 唯 侌 或 明 曰 於 虘 若 寺 ╱

神勞民，撲中而象常。束棘和謨，補缺而救枉。天顧復之，用休雖陰又明。"曰："嗚
呼！若是。"[二十八]

the gods and reward the people (for their toils); measure the middle and emulate the constant. Gather together remonstrances and plan harmoniously;[38]
supplement what is lacking and rescue the crooked. Heaven will look after
them, and because of the blessings even darkness will turn bright."[39] (The
High Ancestor) said: "Aha! (It is indeed) like this." [28]

---

38 I follow Bubai 補白 in reading 棘束和莫 as *shu jian he mo* 束棘和謨 "gather together
remonstrances and plan harmoniously." See Bubai, "Qinghua jian *Yin gaozong wen yu
san shou* yishuo size." The literal meaning of *shu* 束 is "to bind," but it is sometimes
glossed metaphorically as *ju* 聚 or *lian* 斂 "to put together, to collect, to gather." The
subject of this sentence should be the ruler. By heeding advise and making plans accordingly, the ruler can "supplement what is lacking and save the crooked" as the next sentence says. On slip 20, it is also advised that the king should "accept remonstrance" (*najian*
納諫).
39 The editors' punctuation of this sentence is 天顧復之用休，雖陰又明, but there seems
to be a parallel between this ending and the ending of Ancestor Peng's last answer on
slips 26–27:

> 天罰是加，用兇以見詢。
> "Heavenly punishments will be inflicted, and because of the disasters (they) are
> disgraced."
> 天顧復之，用休雖陰又明。
> "Heaven will look after them, and because of the blessings even darkness turns
> bright."

"Disaster" refers to the heavenly punishments, while "blessing" refers to the care provided by Heaven. The transformation from darkness to brightness echoes the earlier theme
of light growing out of obscurity on slip 27.

VERSO

一

一【一背】

1【1V】

二

二【二背】

2【2V】

四

四【四背】

4【4V】

五

五【五背】

5【5V】

六

六【六背】

6【6V】

七

七【七背】

7【7V】

八

八【八背】

8【8V】

九

九【九背】

9【9V】

十五

十五【十背】

15【10V】

十一

十一【十一背】

11【11V】

十二

十二【十二背】

12【12V】

十三

十三【十三背】

13【13V】

十四

十四【十四背】

14【14V】

十

十【十五背】

10【15V】

十六

十六【十六背】

16【16V】

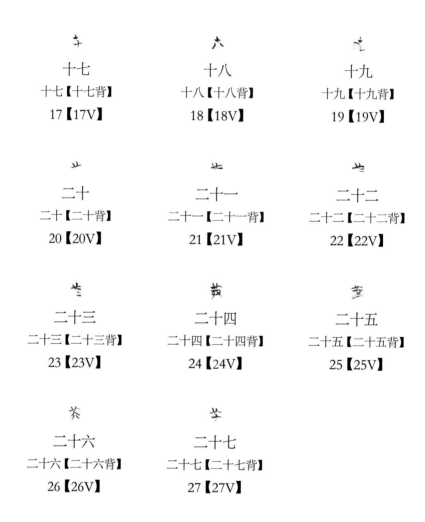

十七
十七【十七背】
17【17V】

十八
十八【十八背】
18【18V】

十九
十九【十九背】
19【19V】

二十
二十【二十背】
20【20V】

二十一
二十一【二十一背】
21【21V】

二十二
二十二【二十二背】
22【22V】

二十三
二十三【二十三背】
23【23V】

二十四
二十四【二十四背】
24【24V】

二十五
二十五【二十五背】
25【25V】

二十六
二十六【二十六背】
26【26V】

二十七
二十七【二十七背】
27【27V】

罄高宗歸於三晨　二十八
殷高宗問於三壽。二十八【二十八背】

The High Ancestor of Yin Asked the Three Long-Lived Ones. Twenty-eight
【28 V】

殷高宗問於三壽

高宗觀於洹水之上，三壽與從。

高宗乃問於少壽曰：

　　　　"爾是先生，爾是 [一] 知二有國之情。

　　　　敢問人何謂長？何謂險？何謂厭？何謂惡？"

少壽答曰：

　　　　"吾 [二] [聞夫長莫長於□，

　　　　吾聞夫險莫險於□。

　　　　　　　　厭彼□，

　　　　　　　　惡彼□。"

高宗乃或問於] [三] 中壽曰：

　　　　"敢問人何謂長？何謂險？何謂厭？何謂惡？"

中壽答曰：

　　　　"吾聞夫長莫 [四] 長於風（*prəm），

　　　　吾聞夫險莫險於心（*səm）。

　　　　　　　厭彼藏（*m-tsʰˤaŋ-s），

　　　　　　　惡彼喪（*s-mˤaŋ-s）。"

高宗乃或問於彭祖曰：

　　　　"高 [五] 文成祖，敢問人何謂長？何謂險？何謂厭？何

　　　　謂惡？"

彭祖答曰：

　　　　"吾聞夫長莫 [六] 長於水（*s.turʔ），

　　　　吾聞夫險莫險於鬼（*k-ʔujʔ)。

　　　　　　　厭彼平（*breŋ），

　　　　　　　惡彼傾（*[k]ʷʰeŋ)。"

高宗乃言曰：

　　　　"吾聞夫長莫長於 [七] [山]（*s-ŋrar），

　　　　吾聞夫險彼矛及干（*kˤa[r]）。

　　　　　　　厭彼富（*pək-s），

213

惡彼無食（*mə-lək）。

苟我與爾相念相謀，世世至於後嗣（*sə.lə-s）。

我思[八]天風，既回又止（*təʔ），

吾勉自抑畏，以敬夫滋怠（*lʕəʔ）。

君子而不讀書占，則若小人之聾狂而[九]不友（*[ɢ]ʷəʔ）。"

殷邦之妖祥并起（*khəʔ）。

八紀則紊，四巖將行（*Cə.[g]ʕraŋ）。

四海之夷則作，九牧九晐將喪（*smâŋ）。

枉矢[十]先反，大路用見兵（*praŋ）。

龜筮孚忒（*lhə̂k），

五寶變色（*srək），

而星月亂行（*Cə.[g]ʕraŋ）。

高宗恐懼，乃敷語彭祖[十一]曰：

"嗚呼，彭祖！古民人迷亂，逸務康戀，而不知邦之將喪。

敢問先王之遺訓，[十二]何謂祥？何謂義？何謂德？何謂音？何謂仁？何謂聖？何謂知？何謂利？何謂[十三]信？"

彭祖答曰：

"聞天之常（*[d]aŋ），

祇神之明（*mraŋ）。

尚昭順穆，而敬民之行（*[g]ʕraŋ-s）。

餘享獻功，遻還妖[十四]祥（*s.ɢaŋ）。

是名曰祥（*s.ɢaŋ）。

邁則文之偽（*m-ɢʷ(r)aj-s）。

曆象天時，往度毋徙（*[s]ajʔ）。

申禮勸技，輔民之化（*qʷhʕraj-s）。

民勸毋疲，[十五]是名曰義（*ŋ(r)aj-s）。

揆中水衡不力（*k.rək）。
時刑罰赦，振若除慝（*n̥ˤək）。
冒神之福（*pək），
同民之力（*k.rək）。
是[十六]名曰德（*tˤək）。

惠民由任（*n[ə]m-s），
徇詢遏淫（*N.r[ə]m）。
宣儀和樂，非懷于耽（*[t-q]ˤ[ə]m）。
四方勸教，濫媚莫感（*kˤ[ə]mʔ）。[十七]
是名曰音（*[q](r)əm）。

衣服端而好信（*s-ni[ŋ]-s）。
孝慈而哀鰥（*[k]ʷˤrə[n]）。
恤遠而謀親（*[tsʰ]i[n]）。
喜神而柔人（*ni[ŋ]）。
是名曰仁（*niŋ）。

恭[十八]神以敬（*kreŋ(ʔ)-s），
和民用正（*teŋ-s）。
留邦偃兵，四方達寧（*nˤeŋ）。
元哲并進，讒謠則屏（*[b]ˤeŋ）。
是名曰聖（*l̥eŋ-s）。

昔勤[十九]不居，狎祗不易（*lek）。
恐枉思修，納諫受訾（*s-N-tse(j)）。
神民莫責（*s-tˤrek），
是名曰智（*tre-s）。

内慧而外比（*pij-s）。

215

上下毋爽，[二十] 左右謀比（*pij-s）。
強屏糾黜，經緯順齊（*[dz]ˤəj）。
妒怨毋作，而天目毋睇（*ləj）。
是名曰利（*C.ri[t]-s）。

勸就聰明（*mraŋ），
音色[二十一] 柔巧，而叡武不罔（*maŋʔ）。
效純桓猷，牧民而禦王（*ɢʷaŋ）。
天下甄稱，以誥四方（*C-paŋ）。
是名曰叡信之[二十二] 行（*[g]ˤraŋ-s）。"

彭祖曰：

"嗚呼！
我均震恐茲九度（*[d]ˤak-s），
甄夏之歸商（*s-taŋ）。
方勉于路（*Cə.rˤak-s），
用乂召后成湯（*r̥ˤaŋ），
代桀[二十三] 敷有下方（*C-paŋ）。"

高宗或問於彭祖曰：

"高文成祖，敢問斯民
胡曰揚（*laŋ）？
揚則攝佚無常（*[d]aŋ）。
胡曰晦？
晦則 […][二十四]
[…彭祖曰：

"民之有揚…]
戲淫自嘉而不數（*s-roʔ）。
感高文富[二十五] 而昏忘詢（*qʰˤ(r)o-s）。
急利囂神莫恭而不顧于後（*[ɢ]ˤ(r)oʔ）。
神民并尤，而仇怨所聚（*m-tsʰoʔ）。
天罰是加，用兇以見[二十六] 詢（*qʰˤ(r)o-s）。"

216

曰："嗚呼！若是。"

　　"民之有晦，晦而本由生光（*kʷˤaŋ）。

　　則唯小心翼翼，顧復勉祇。聞教訓，餘敬養（*[ɢ]
　　aŋʔ）。

　　恭[二十七]神勞民，揆中而象常（*[d]aŋ）。

　　束束和謨，補缺而救枉（*qʷaŋʔ）。

　　天顧復之，用休雖陰又明（*mraŋ）。"

曰："嗚呼！若是。"[二十八]

217

The High Ancestor of Yin Asked the Three Long-Lived Ones

The High Ancestor was sightseeing on the Huan River, and the Three Long-Lived Ones went along with him.

The High Ancestor then asked the Lesser Long-Lived One, saying:

"You were born before me, and thus you [1] know the situation of the two states.

May I ask what people mean by lasting long?

What they mean by danger?

What they mean by satisfaction?

What they mean by detestation?"

The Lesser Long-Lived One answered, saying:

"I've [2] [heard that as for lasting long, nothing lasts longer than … ;

I've heard that as for danger, nothing is more dangerous than …

That which satisfies is … ;

that which is detestable is … "

The High Ancestor then asked] [3] the Middle Long-Lived One, saying:

"May I ask what people mean by lasting long?

What they mean by danger?

What they mean by satisfaction?

What they mean by detestation?"

The Middle Long-Lived One answered, saying:

"I've heard that as for lasting long, nothing [4] lasts longer than the wind;

I've heard that as for danger, nothing is more dangerous than the heart.

That which satisfies is savings;

that which is detestable is loss."

The High Ancestor then asked Ancestor Peng, saying:

"Culturally Accomplished High [5] Ancestor,

May I ask what people mean by lasting long?

What they mean by danger?

What they mean by satisfaction?

What they mean by detestation?"

Ancestor Peng answered, saying:

"I've heard that as for lasting long, nothing [6] lasts longer than water;

I've heard that as for danger, nothing is more dangerous than ghosts.

That which satisfies is balance;

that which is detestable is collapse."

The High Ancestor then spoke, saying:

"I've heard that as for lasting long, nothing lasts longer than [7] [mountains];

I've heard that as for danger, it is spears and shields.

That which satisfies is wealth;

that which is detestable is lack of food.

If you and I consider and plan with each other, (our legacy will last) generation after generation to posterity.

When I think of [8] the heavenly wind, now whirling and now stopping,

I strive on my own to suppress the fear and to be on guard against increasing laziness.

If a gentleman does not read written prognostications, then, like a petty person who is deaf and crazy, [9] he will have no friends."

Eerie occurrences and omens together arose in the state of Yin.

The Eight Cords were then disturbed, and the Four Cliffs were about to move.

Barbarians of the Four Seas then rose up, and the Nine Pastoral Grounds and the Nine Domains were about to be lost.

The Crooked Arrow [10] returned first, and armies thus appeared on thoroughfares.

Shell and stalk divinations were not credible;

the Five Treasures changed color;

the stars and the moon moved in disorder.

The High Ancestor was terrified and then spoke at length to Ancestor
Peng, [11] saying:

> "Aha, Ancestor Peng! The people of old were perplexed and dis-
> ordered, idle at work and complacent in their efforts. They did
> not know that the state was about to be lost. May I ask about the
> instructions left by the past kings? [12] What is meant by propitious-
> ness? What is meant by propriety? What is meant by virtue? What
> is meant by tone? What is meant by benevolence? What is meant
> by sagacity? What is meant by wisdom? What is meant by benefit?
> What is meant by [13] trustworthiness?"

Ancestor Peng answered, saying:

> "Be receptive to Heaven's constancy and revere the gods' brilliance.
> Exalt the *zhao* and obey the *mu* tablets, and respect the people's
> conduct. Make abundant offerings and present achievements,
> quickly turning back eerie occurrences [14] and omens. Such is named
> propitiousness.
>
> Closely model yourself on the artifices of culture. Make calendars
> to depict Heaven's time and do not change past standards. Extend
> the rites and encourage the crafts to facilitate the transformation of
> the people, and the people will exert themselves tirelessly. [15] Such is
> named propriety.
>
> Measure the middle using the level and balance without force.
> Exempt (the people from) punishments in a timely manner, stimu-
> lating the agreeable and eliminating the wicked. (Then you will be)
> covered with the gods' blessings and joined with the strength of the
> people. Such is [16] named virtue.
>
> Be generous to the people and employ those who are responsible;
> expose the disgraceful and disclose the licentious. Proclaim deco-

rum and harmonize music; repudiate (the practice of) cherishing indulgence. Encourage and educate those from the four directions, so that no one will be moved by extravagant and alluring (music). [17] Such is named tone.

Dress up neatly and love trustworthiness. Show filial piety and parental love; feel pity for widowed people. Worry about those far away and plan for close relatives. Please the gods and be soft with humans. Such is named benevolence.

Worship [18] the gods with respect and harmonize the people using rectitude. Bring order to the state and lay down weapons, so that those from the four directions are all tranquil. The good and the wise together come forth, so that slanders and rumors are blocked. Such is named sagacity.

Don't be content with past effort, [19] and habitually show reverence without change. Fear crookedness and wish to correct it; accept remonstrance and take criticism, so that neither the gods nor the people can blame (you). Such is named wisdom.

Those on the inside make plans and those from outside follow along. Those above and below should not be mistaken; [20] those on the left and right seek to follow along. The violent are blocked and the twisted banished, so that social fabric will be smooth and even. Envy and resentment should not arise, and the heavenly eye should not look sideways. Such is named benefit.

In encouraging and approaching the bright and perceptive, be gentle and tactful [21] in voice and countenance, but be intelligent and valiant without deception. Emulate the pure and plan for the long term; shepherd the people and defend the king. All under heaven examine and commend (you), making announcements in the four directions. Such is named intelligent and trustworthy [22] conduct."

Ancestor Peng said:

"Aha! I'm equally shocked and terrified by these nine standards when examining Xia's surrender to Shang. (The Shang people were) about to strive on the road to assist Lord Cheng Tang, replacing Jie [23] and broadly having [the territories] below."

The High Ancestor asked Ancestor Peng, saying:

"Culturally Accomplished High Ancestor, may I ask as for the people, how they are called ostentatious?

When (they are) ostentatious, (they are sometimes) restrained and (sometimes) dissolute without constancy.

How they are called obscure? When (they are) obscure, [24] [···

Ancestor Peng said:

"As for the people's being ostentatious ···] wallow in licentiousness, congratulating but never censuring themselves. (They are) moved by high class and decorated with wealth, [25] muddled and forgetful of disgrace. Eager for profits, (they) clamor before the gods without worshipping them and have no regard for descendants. The gods and people together condemn (them), on whom hatred and resentment accumulate. Heavenly punishments will be inflicted, and because of the disasters (they) are [26] disgraced."

(The High Ancestor) said: "Aha! (It is indeed) like this."

"As for the people's being obscure, their obscurity is the root from which light grows. Therefore, be cautious and reverent, look after (the people) and strive to be reverent; be receptive to teachings and instructions, and abundantly respect and care for (the people). Worship [27] the gods and reward the people (for their toils); measure the middle and emulate the constant. Gather together remonstrances and plan harmoniously; supplement what is lacking and rescue the crooked. Heaven will look after them, and because of the blessings even darkness will turn bright."

(The High Ancestor) said: "Aha! (It is indeed) like this." [28]

The High Ancestor of Yin Asked the Three Long-Lived Ones. Twenty-eight. [28V]

222

Appendix A

Lüshi Chunqiu

"Shen da" (Being Careful When the State Is Large)

The "Shen da" chapter of *Lüshi chunqiu* is a warning against the complacency and arrogance of a ruler who governs a large state. It begins with the claim that the more powerful a state is, the more enemies it will have, and the more cautious its ruler should be. Then it illustrates the claim with three historical examples: Tang's conquest of Xia, King Wu's conquest of Shang, and Master Xiang 襄 of Zhao's conquest of Zuoren 左人 and Zhongren 中人. In each case, the winner learned a lesson from the failure of their opponents and worried about potential dangers. Having quoted Confucius's praise of Master Xiang, the chapter concludes that holding on to what one has conquered is more difficult than prevailing in war. In the first example translated here, Yi Yin allied himself with Tang and spied on Xia for him. The story can be compared with the Tsinghua manuscript *Yin zhi*.

Text and Translation[1]

桀為無道，暴戾頑貪，天下顫恐而患之。言者不同，紛紛分分，其情難得。干辛任威，凌轢諸侯，以及兆民，賢良鬱怨。殺彼龍逢，以服群凶。衆庶泯泯，皆有遠志，莫敢直言，其生若驚。大臣同患，弗周而畔。桀愈自賢，矜過善非。主道重塞，國人大崩。

湯乃惕懼。憂天下之不寧，欲令伊尹往視曠夏。恐其不信，湯

---

1   The translation here is modified from John Knoblock and Jeffrey Riegel trans. *The Annals of Lü Buwei* (Stanford: Stanford University Press, 2000), 338–339.

223

由親自射伊尹。伊尹奔夏三年，反報于亳，曰："桀迷惑於末嬉，好彼琬、琰。不恤其衆，衆志不堪。上下相疾，民心積怨，皆曰'上天弗恤，夏命其卒'。"湯謂伊尹曰："若告我曠夏盡如詩。"湯與伊尹盟，以示必滅夏。伊尹又復往視曠夏，聽於末嬉。末嬉言曰："今昔天子夢西方有日，東方有日。兩日相與鬥，西方日勝，東方日不勝。"伊尹以告湯。

商涸旱，湯猶發師，以信伊尹之盟。故令師從東方出於國，西以進。未接刃而桀走，逐之至大沙，身體離散，為天下戮。不可正諫，雖後悔之，將可奈何？湯立為天子，夏民大說，如得慈親。朝不易位，農不去疇，商不變肆，親郼如夏。此之謂至公，此之謂至安，此之謂至信。盡行伊尹之盟，不避旱殃。祖伊尹世世享商。

Jie acted against the Way with violence and greed, and all under heaven shivered in fear and were distressed by him. Advisors disagreed among themselves in confusion, and it was difficult to determine the truth of their words. Gan Xin relied on the authority (of Jie) to oppress and maltreat the feudal lords and even millions of people, so that the worthy and good were depressed and resentful. Jie murdered Guan Longpeng in order to quell all opposition. The officials grew restive, all with the intention to go far away. No one dared say an honest word, being alarmed in their lives. The great ministers, sharing their distress, did not remain loyal and turned to open rebellion. Jie grew ever more convinced of his worthiness, boasting about his faults and praising his errors. The Way of ruling was repeatedly obstructed, and the people of the state were about to collapse.

Tang then grew vigilant and terrified. Worrying about the unrest in the world, he wanted to send Yi Yin to observe the ferocious Xia. Fearing (that Yi Yin would) not be trusted (by Xia), Tang himself shot arrows at Yi Yin. Three years after Yi Yin had fled to Xia, he returned to the Shang capital at Bo and reported: "Jie is entranced by Mo Xi and favors the women Wan and Yan. He shows no pity for his multitudes, who are no longer willing to tolerate (such treatment). Superiors and subordinates hate each other, and the people accumulate ever greater resentment in their hearts, all saying, 'Heaven on high shows no pity. May the mandate of Xia expire.'" Tang said to Yi Yin: "You are telling me that the ferocious Xia is all like this." Tang and Yi Yin swore a covenant to demonstrate their determination to annihilate Xia. Yi Yin once again went to observe the ferocious Xia, and he heeded the words of Mo Xi. Mo Xi said: "Just last evening the Son of Heaven dreamt that there was a sun in the west and a sun in the east and that these two suns fought. The sun in the west was victorious and the sun in the east did not win." Yi Yin reported this to Tang.

Shang was suffering from a drought, but Tang still sent out an army to stand by his covenant with Yi Yin. Accordingly, he ordered the army to leave the state from the east and advance from the west. Without the crossing of any blades, Jie fled. Tang pursued him to Dasha where his body and limbs were torn apart, and he was disgraced before all under heaven. Since Jie could not be chastened and would heed no remonstrance, although he later regretted his actions, what else could he do? Tang was established as the Son of Heaven, and the people of Xia were greatly pleased, as if they had found a loving relative. Those at court did not leave their positions, farmers did not abandon their fields, merchants did not alter their places of business, and the people felt the same allegiance to the state of Yi[2] that they had had to Xia. This is what is meant by "supreme impartiality," "supreme security" and "supreme trustworthiness." Tang fully carried out the terms of his covenant with Yi Yin and did not try to renounce them because of the catastrophe of the drought. The descendants of Yi Yin for generations thereafter enjoyed offerings from Shang.

---

2   An alternative name of the state of Shang.

Appendix B

Lüshi Chunqiu

"Ben wei" (Root of Flavors)

The "Ben wei" chapter of *Lüshi chunqiu* tells two stories about Yi Yin. In the first story, which can be compared with the Tsinghua manuscript *Tangqiu*, baby Yi Yin was found in the hollow trunk of a mulberry tree and taken to the Shen clan, where he grew to be a worthy man. When Tang heard about Yi Yin, he took a wife from the Shen clan so that he could employ Yi Yin. In the second story, after Yi Yin had joined Tang, he gave Tang a long lecture on how to bring out the finest flavors and where to find the best raw materials, but did not relate the skills to governance. The point of including the second story is not clear, because it is the only story in the chapter that does not illustrate its main argument put forward at the beginning, namely, that "obtaining the worthy" is the key to great fame and achievements. Even though the title "Root of Flavors" is taken from the second Yi Yin story, the majority of this chapter has nothing to do with the philosophy of cooking.

Text and Translation[3]

求之其本，經旬必得。求之其末，勞而無功。功名之立，由事之本也，得賢之化也。非賢其孰知乎事化？故曰其本在得賢。

有侁氏女子採桑，得嬰兒于空桑之中，獻之其君。其君令烰人

---

3 The translation here is modified from Knoblock and Riegel trans. *The Annals of Lü Bu-wei*, 306–311.

養之。察其所以然，曰："其母居伊水之上，孕，夢有神告之曰：'臼出水而東走，毋顧。'明日，視臼出水，告其鄰，東走十里，而顧其邑盡為水。身因化為空桑。故命之曰伊尹。"此伊尹生空桑之故也。

長而賢。湯聞伊尹，使人請之有侁氏。有侁氏不可。伊尹亦欲歸湯，湯於是請取婦為婚。有侁氏喜，以伊尹為媵送女。

故賢主之求有道之士，無不以也；有道之士求賢主，無不行也。相得然後樂。不謀而親，不約而信，相為殫智竭力，犯危行苦，志懽樂之，此功名所以大成也。固不獨。士有孤而自恃，人主有奮而好獨者，則名號必廢熄，社稷必危殆。故黃帝立四面，堯、舜得伯陽、續耳然後成。

凡賢人之德，有以知之也。伯牙鼓琴，鍾子期聽之，方鼓琴而志在太山，鍾子期曰："善哉乎鼓琴，巍巍乎若太山。"少選之間，而志在流水，鍾子期又曰："善哉乎鼓琴，湯湯乎若流水。"鍾子期死，伯牙破琴絕弦，終身不復鼓琴，以為世無足復為鼓琴者。非獨琴若此也，賢者亦然。雖有賢者，而無禮以接之，賢奚由盡忠？猶御之不善，驥不自千里也。

湯得伊尹，袚之於廟，爝以爟火，釁以犧猳。明日，設朝而見之，說湯以至味。湯曰："可得而為乎？"對曰："君之國小，不足以具之，為天子然後可具。夫三群之蟲，水居者腥，肉玃者臊，草食者羶，臭惡猶美，皆有所以。凡味之本，水最為始。五味三材，九沸九變，火為之紀。時疾時徐，滅腥去臊除羶。必以其勝，無失其理。調和之事，必以甘酸苦辛鹹，先後多少，其齊甚微，皆有自起。鼎中之變，精妙微纖，口弗能言，志不能喻。若射御之微，陰陽之化，四時之數。故久而不弊，熟而不爛，甘而不噥，酸而不酷，鹹而不減，辛而不烈，澹而不薄，肥而不膄。

肉之美者：猩猩之脣，獾獾之炙，雋觾之翠，述蕩之踵，旄象之約。流沙之西，丹山之南，有鳳之丸，沃民所食。

魚之美者：洞庭之鱄，東海之鮞。醴水之魚，名曰珠鱉，六足，有珠百碧。雚水之魚，名曰鰩，其狀若鯉而有翼，常從西海夜飛，游於東海。

菜之美者：崑崙之蘋，壽木之華。指姑之東，中容之國，有赤木玄木之葉焉。餘瞀之南，南極之崖，有菜，其名曰嘉樹，其色若碧。

陽華之芸。雲夢之芹。具區之菁。浸淵之草，名曰土英。

和之美者：陽樸之薑，招搖之桂，越駱之菌，鱣鮪之醢，大夏之鹽，宰揭之露，其色如玉，長澤之卵。

飯之美者：玄山之禾，不周之粟，陽山之穄，南海之秬。

水之美者：三危之露；崑崙之井；沮江之丘，名曰搖水；白山之水；高泉之山，其上有涌泉焉，冀州之原。

果之美者：沙棠之實；常山之北，投淵之上，有百果焉，群帝所食；箕山之東，青鳥之所，有甘櫨焉；江浦之橘；雲夢之柚。漢上石耳。

所以致之：馬之美者，青龍之匹，遺風之乘。非先為天子，不可得而具。天子不可彊為，必先知道。道者止彼在己，己成而天子成，天子成則至味具。故審近所以知遠也，成己所以成人也。聖人之道要矣，豈越越多業哉！"

Seek things in their root, and in the course of a ten-day period you are certain to obtain them. Seek things in nonessential branches, and you will toil but achieve nothing. Establishing achievements and fame is a matter of following the root of affairs and acquiring the transforming influence of the worthy. Who other than the worthy understands the transformation of affairs? Therefore, it is said, "Its root lies in obtaining the worthy."

While picking mulberry leaves, a woman of the Shen clan found a baby in the hollow trunk of a mulberry tree and presented it to her lord. Her lord ordered a cook to raise it. Having investigated how it came to be so, (the cook) said, "Its mother lived on the banks of the Yi river, became pregnant, and dreamt that a spirit announced to her, 'When your mortar produces water, move to the east and do not look back.' The next day, seeing that her mortar did produce water, she told her neighbor about it, went east ten *li* and, looking back, saw that her town was completely inundated. For that reason, she was changed into a hollow mulberry. Hence they called him 'Yi Yin.'" This is how Yi Yin came to be born in a hollow mulberry.

Yi Yin grew to be a worthy man. When Tang heard about him, he sent a messenger to request him from the Shen clan. The Shen clan would not agree. Yi Yin also wished to join Tang, so Tang asked the family to grant him a wife in marriage. The Shen clan was overjoyed and sent Yi Yin as the girl's dowry escort.

Therefore, there is nothing that a worthy ruler will not do when he seeks a scholar who possesses the Dao; and there is nothing that a scholar who possesses the Dao will not do when he seeks a worthy ruler. Only when they find one another are they happy. They are close without planning to be so and trust each other without making any agreement. For the sake of the other each uses all his knowledge and exhausts his strength, confronts danger and endures hardship, and each feels great pleasure and happiness. This is how achievements and fame are perfected. Achievements and fame absolutely cannot be perfected alone. If a scholar is isolated and relies on himself, or if a ruler is proud and enjoys being alone, his fame is certain to diminish and be snuffed out, and the altars of soil and grain will surely be gravely endangered. Therefore, the Yellow Thearch sought worthies in the four directions, and only after Yao and Shun got Bo Yang and Xu Er were they successful.

As a general rule, there are means to recognize the virtue of the worthy man. Whenever Bo Ya played the lute, Zhong Ziqi would listen to him. Once he was playing the lute, his thoughts turned to Mount Tai. Zhong Ziqi said, "How splendidly you played the lute! Lofty and majestic like Mount Tai!" A short time later, when his thoughts turned to rolling waters, Zhong Ziqi said, "How splendidly you played the lute! Rolling and swelling like a rushing river!" When Zhong Ziqi died, Bo Ya smashed the lute and cut its strings. To the end of his life, he never played the lute again because he felt that there was no one in the world worth playing for. This applies not only to the lute, but to worthiness as well. Although a man is worthy, if he is not received by a ruler with due courtesy, why should he devote his full loyalty to him? It is like the fleet-footed horse that will not go a thousand *li* by itself when the driver is not skilled.

When Tang got Yi Yin, he performed rites of purgation on him in the ancestral temple, lighting a bundle of wood to eliminate noxious influences, and smearing him with the blood of a sacrificial pig. The next day he gave an audience to Yi Yin at his court. Yi Yin spoke to Tang about the finest flavors. Tang asked, "Can they be acquired and prepared?" Yi Yin replied, "The small size of my lord's state is insufficient to supply them. Only after you have become Son of Heaven can they be supplied. Now, there are three tribes of creatures: the water dwellers, which smell fishy; the carnivores, which smell rank; and the herbivores, which have a fetid smell. Although malodorous and evil smelling, they can be refined when each is properly used. As a general rule, the root of flavors begins first with water. For the five flavors and three materials, as well as the nine simmerings and nine transformations, fire serves as the regulator. At times quick and at times slow, it eliminates fishiness, removes rankness, and eradicates fetidness. One must overcome these with it but not lose the principle. In the task of harmonizing and blending one must use the sweet, sour, bitter, acrid, and salty. The balancing of what should be added first or last and of whether to use more or less is very subtle, and each variation gives rise to its own effect. The transformation within the cauldron is quintessential, marvelous, extremely fine, and delicate. The mouth cannot describe it, and the feeling cannot be conveyed. It is like the subtle art of archery and horsemanship, the transformations of Yin and Yang, and the numbers of the four seasons. Therefore, it keeps for a long time and does not ruin, is thoroughly cooked but not mushy, sweet but not cloying, sour but not excessively so, salty but not deadening, acrid but not caustic, mild but not bland, rich with fat but not greasy."

"The finest of the meats are the lips of the ape; the feet of the *huanhuan* bird; the fleshy tail of the *junyan* bird; the paws of the *shudang* beast; the short tail of the grunting ox and the elephant. West of the Flowing Sands and south of the Cinnabar Peak are phoenix eggs eaten by the Wo people.

The finest of the fish are the perch of Lake Dongting and the miniature fish of the Eastern Sea; a fish in the Li River called Pearl Turtle, which has six feet and hundreds of jade-colored, pearl like nodules; and a fish in the Guan River called the 'flying fish,' which is shaped like a carp with wings and which flies nightly from the Western Sea to the Eastern Sea.

The finest of the edible plants are the crest of Mount Kunlun and the flower of the Longevity Tree. The leaves of the Red Tree and the Black Tree that grow east of Zhigu in the state of Zhongrong; an edible plant colored like green jade, called the 'luck tree,' that grows to the south of Yumao, on a cliff at the edge of the southern limit; the fragrant cress of Yanghua; the celery of Yunmeng; the kale of Juqu; and a grass of Jinyuan called 'flower of the soil.'

The finest of the seasoning agents are the ginger from Yangpu; the cinnamon from Zhaoyao; bamboo shoots from Yueluo; the vinegar made from *zhanwei* sturgeon; the salt from Daxia; the dewy waters from Zaijie, which have the color of white jade; and the eggs from Changze.

The finest of the grains are the millet of Dark Mountain; the foxtail millet of Mount Buzhou; the panicled millet of Bright Mountain; and the black glutinous panicled millet of the Southern Sea.

The finest of the waters are the dew waters of Sanwei Peak; the well water of Mount Kunlun; the spring named Jade Pond, located on a hillock by the Zhu river; the stream White Mountain; the bubbling spring high on the Mountain of Lofty Spring; and the source in Jizhou.

The finest of the fruits are those of the Shatang tree; the hundred fruits eaten by all the Sovereigns, which grow north to Mount Chang, atop the Tou Gorge; the sweet berries found east of Mount Ji, in the nesting place of the Azure Bird; the tangerines from the banks of the Yangzi; the pomelos of Yunmeng; and the stone ears from the banks of the Han river.

For obtaining these, there are the finest horses, the Green Dragon and the Steed that Leaves Wind Behind. A man who has not first become Son of Heaven cannot have all these things supplied him. Since he cannot become the Son of Heaven by force, he must first know the Way. The Way leaves others behind and concentrates on the inner self. When the inner self is perfected, the position of Son of Heaven is realized. When the position of Son of Haven is realized, the perfect flavors are supplied. Thus, by examining what is near, a person may know what is distant, and by perfecting the inner self, he may perfect others. The Way of the Sage is restricted to the essentials, how could he toil at numerous things!"

Appendix C

Mozi

"Gui yi" (Valuing Propriety)

As mentioned in the introduction to this volume, Mozi first treated Tang and Yi Yin as exemplars of "exalting the worthy." According to the "Gui yi" chapter, Mozi went to see King Xianhui of Chu and met the king's minister Mu He 穆賀. Mu He was greatly impressed by Mozi's teachings, but feared that his low social status would cause him to be neglected by the king. In response, Mozi told a story about Tang and Yi Yin to show that a true king, in searching for ministers, would only care about one's worthiness. The story can be compard with the Tsinghua manuscript *Tangqiu*.

Text and Translation[4]

　　子墨子南游於楚，見楚獻惠王。獻惠王以老辭，使穆賀見子墨子。子墨子說穆賀。穆賀大說，謂子墨子曰："子之言則成善矣！而君王，天下之大王也，毋乃曰'賤人之所為'，而不用乎？"

　　子墨子曰："唯其可行，譬若藥然。草之本，天子食之以順其疾。豈曰'一草之本'而不食哉？今農夫入其稅於大人，大人為酒醴粢盛以祭上帝鬼神。豈曰'賤人之所為'而不享哉？故雖賤人也，上比之農，下比之藥，曾不若一草之本乎？

　　且主君亦嘗聞湯之說乎？昔者，湯將往見伊尹，令彭氏之子御。彭氏之子半道而問曰：'君將何之？'湯曰：'將往見伊尹。'彭氏之

4　The translation here is modified from Ian Johnston trans. *The Mozi: A Complete Translation* (Hong Kong, The Chinese University Press, 2010), 661–663.

子曰：'伊尹，天下之賤人也。若君欲見之，亦令召問焉。彼受賜矣。'
湯曰：'非女所知也。今有藥此，食之則耳加聰，目加明，則吾必説
而强食之。今夫伊尹之於我國也，譬之良醫善藥也。而子不欲我見
伊尹，是子不欲吾善也。'因下彭氏之子，不使御。彼苟然，然後
可也。"

Master Mozi travelled south to Chu to see King Xianhui of Chu.[5] King Xianhui declined (to see him) on the grounds of age, sending Mu He to see Master Mozi. Master Mozi spoke with Mu He. Mu He was greatly pleased and addressed Master Mozi, saying: "Your words, sir, are truly excellent, but our lord is a great king under heaven. Would he not say 'This is just what a low-born man makes' and not make use of it?"

Master Mozi said: "As long as it works, (he would make use of it,) like in the case of medicine. The Son of Heaven eats the root of one herb to cure his disease. Would he say 'This is just the root of one herb' and not eat it?" Now the farmer pays his taxes to the great officer, and the great officer make sweet wine and millet for sacrifices to the Thearch on High and to ghosts and spirits. Would he say 'These are just what a low-born man makes' and not present them? Therefore, even though I may be low-born, if you compare me above to the farmer and below to the medicine, am I not even as good as the root of one herb?

"Moreover, has our lord also heard about the story of Tang? Of old, when Tang was about to go to see Yi Yin, he ordered the son of the Peng family to drive the chariot. Halfway along the road, the son of the Peng

---

5 The compound posthumous title Xianhui 獻惠 has aroused suspicion among premodern commentators. Bi Yuan 畢沅 (1730–1797) notes that no Chu king has such a title in historical records, and the same line is quoted in the commentary section of the *Wen Xuan* 文選 *Selections of Refined Literature* as "Mozi presented books to King Hui of Chu" (*Mozi xian shu* Chu Hui Wang 墨子獻書楚惠王). Sun Yirang also suspects that "Xianhui" is a textual error for "*xian shu* Hui Wang" (presented books to King Hui). See Sun Yirang, *Mozi jiangu*, 440. Influenced by their commentaries, Johnston translates this line as "Master Mozi travelled south to Chu to present a document to King Hui." However, in excavated Chu bamboo manuscripts, King Hui of Chu is often regarded as King Xianhui of Chu, such as in the Tsinghua manuscript *Chu ju* 楚居 *Chu Dwellings* (slip 13). Mozi probably did present books to the king, but the compound title is not a textual error.

family asked, 'Where is my lord going?' Tang said, 'I am going to see Yi Yin.' The son of the Peng family said, 'Yi Yin is a low-born man under heaven. If my lord wishes to see him, just summon him here and ask him questions. (In that way) he will still receive a great favor (from you).' Tang said, 'This is not something you know about. Now there was this medicine which, if I took it, would make my hearing more acute and my vision sharper. Then I would certainly be happy to make myself take it. Now to my state, Yi Yin is just like a good doctor or an excellent medicine. If you do not wish me to see Yi Yin, this amounts to your not wishing me to become good.' As a result, he dismissed the son of the Peng family and did not allow him to drive the chariot. Our lord would have to be like this to make thing work."

Works Cited

Allan, Sarah. "On *Shu* 書 (Documents) and the Origin of the *Shang shu* 尚書 (Ancient Documents) in Light of Recently Discovered Bamboo Slip Manuscripts." *Bulletin of the School of Oriental and African Studies* 75.3 (2012): 547–557.

———. "'When Red Pigeons Gathered on Tang's House': A Warring States Period Tale of Shamanic Possession and Building Construction set at the turn of the Xia and Shang Dynasties." *Journal of the Royal Asiatic Society* 25.3 (2015): 419–438.

Anhui daxue hanzi fazhan yu yingyong yanjiu zhongxin 安徽大學漢字發展與應用研究中心 eds. *Anhui daxue cang zhanguo zhujian* 安徽大學藏戰國竹簡. Shanghai: Zhong Xi shuju, 2019.

Ban Gu 班固. *Han shu* 漢書. Beijing: Zhonghua shuju, 1962.

Baxter, William H. and Laurent Sagart. *Old Chinese: A New Reconstruction.* Oxford: Oxford University Press, 2014.

———. "Guanyu Qinghua jian (wu) san pian de yixie biji" 關於清華簡(伍)三篇的一些筆記. In *Qinghua jian yanjiu* 3. Shanghai: Zhong Xi shuju, 2019, 29–54.

Bubai 補白. "Qinghua jian *Yin gaozong wen yu san shou* yishuo size" 清華簡《殷高宗問於三壽》臆說四則. At http://fdgwz.org.cn/Web/Show/2497. Posted 16 April 2015.

Cai Zhemao 蔡哲茂. "Xia wangchao cunzai xinzheng — shuo Yin buci de 'xiyi'" 夏王朝存在新證——説殷卜辭的"西邑". *Zhongguo wenhua* 中國文化 44 (2016): 47–51.

Cao Feng 曹峰. "Qinghua jian *Tang zai Chimen* yu qi xiangguan neirong yanjiu" 清華簡《湯在啻門》與氣相關内容研究. *Zhexue yanjiu* 哲學研究 2016.12: 35–41.

Cao Feng 曹峰. "Qinghua jian *San shou Tang zai Chimen* zhong de guishen guan" 清華簡《三壽》《湯在啻門》中的鬼神觀. *Sichuan daxue xuebao (zhexue shehui kexue ban)* 四川大學學報(哲學社會科學版) 2016.5: 33–40.

———. "Daojia 'di shi' lei wenxian chutan" 道家"帝師"類文獻初探. *Zhexue lunji* 哲學論集 49 (2018): 33–60.

Chan, Shirley 陳慧. "Shenti yu zhiguo—shidu Qinghua jian *Tang zai Chimen* jianlun 'ji'" 身體與治國——試讀清華簡《湯在啻門》兼論"疾". In *Qinghua jian yanjiu* 3, 171–182. Shanghai: Zhong Xi shuju, 2019.

Chang Yuzhi 常玉芝. *Shangdai zongjiao jisi* 商代宗教祭祀. Beijing: Zhongguo shehui kexue chubanshe, 2010.

Chen Jian 陳劍. "Qinghua jian (wu) yu jiushuo huzheng liangze"《清華簡(伍)》與舊說互證兩則. At http://www.fdgwz.org.cn/Web/Show/2494. Posted 14 April 2015.

———. "Qinghua jian ziyi lingzha liangze" 清華簡字義零札兩則. In Fudan daxue chutu wenxian yu guwenzi yanjiu zhongxin 復旦大學出土文獻與古文字研究中心 eds. *Zhanguo wenzi yanjiu de huigu yu zhanwang* 戰國文字研究的回顧與展望, 190–203. Shanghai: Zhong Xi shuju, 2017.

———. "Shi Shangbo zhushu he Chunqiu jinwen de 'geng' zi yiti" 釋上博竹書和春秋金文的"羹"字異體. At http://www.gwz.fudan.edu.cn/web/show/295. Posted 6 January 2008.

——— ed. "Zhouyi jingzhuan" 周易經傳. In Hunan sheng bowuguan 湖南省博物館 and Fudan daxue chutu wenxian yu guwenzi yanjiu zhongxin 復旦大學出土文獻與古文字研究中心 eds. *Changsha Mawangdui Hanmu jianbo jicheng* 長沙馬王堆漢墓簡帛集成 vol. 3. Beijing: Zhonghua shuju, 2014, 3–162.

Chen Ligui 陳麗桂. "*Tang zai Chimen* de qihua taichan shuo yu tian ren lunshu"《湯在啻門》的氣化胎産説與天人論述. In Fudan Daxue chutu wenxian yu guwenzi yanjiu zhongxin eds. *Chutu wenxian yu chuanshi dianji de quanshi* 出土文獻與傳世典籍的詮釋. Shanghai: Zhong Xi shuju, 2019, 97–112.

Chen Mengjia 陳夢家. *Shang shu tonglun* 尚書通論. Beijing: Zhonghua shuju, 1985.

——— . *Yinxu buci zongshu* 殷墟卜辭綜述. Beijing: Zhonghua shuju, 1988.

Chen Minzhen 陳民鎮. "Qinghua jian *Yin zhi* jishi" 清華簡《尹至》集釋. At http://www.fdgwz.org.cn/Web/Show/1647. Posted 12 September 2011.

——— . "Qinghua jian *Zhi zheng zhi dao Zhi bang zhi dao* sixiang xingzhi chutan" 清華簡《治政之道》《治邦之道》思想性質初探. *Qinghua daxue xuebao (zhexue shehui kexue ban)* 清華大學學報(哲學社會科學版）35.1 (2020): 48–52.

Chen Qiyou 陳奇猷. *Lüshi chunqiu xin jiaoshi* 呂氏春秋新校釋. Shanghai: Shanghai guji chubanshe, 2002.

Cheng Hao 程浩. "Gushu chengshu yanjiu zai fansi — yi Qinghua jian shu lei wenxian wei zhongxin" 古書成書研究再反思——以清華簡"書"類文獻為中心. *Lishi yanjiu* 歷史研究 2016.4: 132–143.

——— . "Cong 'mengfu' dao 'xingtan' xian-Qin shu lei wenxian de shengcheng, jieji yu liubian " 從"盟府"到"杏壇"：先秦"書"類文獻的生成、結集與流變. *Qinghua daxue xuebao (zhexue shehui kexue ban)* 清華大學學報(哲學社會科學版）36.6 (2021): 85–106.

——— . *You wei yan zhi: xian-Qin "shu" lei wenxian de yuan yu liu* 有為言之：先秦"書"類文獻的源與流. Beijing: Zhonghua shuju, 2021.

Cook, Constance A. and Paul R. Goldin. *A Source Book of Ancient Chinese Bronze Inscriptions*. Berkeley, The Society for the Study of Early China, 2020.

——— . "Contextualizing 'Becoming a Complete Person' in the *Tang zai Chimen*." In *Qinghua jian yanjiu* 3. Shanghai: Zhong Xi shuju, 2019, 183–193.

Cook, Scott. "Qinghua zhujian wu *Tang zai Chimen* zhaji" 清華竹簡(伍)

《湯在啻門》札記. In *Qinghua jian yanjiu* 3. Shanghai: Zhong Xi shuju, 2019, 144–145.

Du Yong 杜勇. "Qinghua jian *Yin gao* yu wanshu *Xian you yi de* bianwei" 清華簡《尹誥》與晚書《咸有一德》辨偽. *Tianjin shifan daxue xuebao (shehui kexue ban)* 天津師範大學學報(社會科學版) 2012. 3: 20–28.

Du Zhengsheng 杜正勝. *Gudai shehui yu guojia* 古代社會與國家. Taipei: Yunchen wenhua, 1992.

Durrant, Stephen, Wai-yee Li, and David Schaberg trans. *Zuo Tradition*. Seattle: University of Washington Press, 2016.

Els, Paul van. "Tilting Vessels and Collapsing Walls: On the Rhetorical Function of Anecdotes in Early Chinese Texts." *Extrême-Orient, Extrême-Occident* 34 (2012): 141–166.

——— and Sarah A. Queen eds. *Between History and Philosophy: Anecdotes in Early China.* Albany: SUNY Press, 2017.

Fang Shiming 方詩銘 and Wang Xiuling 王修齡. *Guben* Zhushu jinian *jizheng* 古本竹書紀年輯證. Shanghai: Shanghai guji chubanshe, 1981.

Feng Shengjun 馮勝君. "Qinghua jian Yin zhi 'zi nai rou da ying' jie" 清華簡《尹至》"兹乃柔大縈"解. In Zhongguo wenhua yichan yanjiuyuan 中國文化遺産研究院 eds. *Chutu wenxian yanjiu* 出土文獻研究 13. Shanghai: Zhong Xi shuju, 2014, 310–317.

——— . "Du Qinghua san *Chi hu zhi ji Tang zhi wu* zhaji" 讀清華三《赤鵠之集湯之屋》札記. In Qinghua daxue chutu wenxian yanjiu yu baohu zhongxin 清華大學出土文獻研究與保護中心 eds. *Chutu wenxian yu Zhongguo gudai wenming* 出土文獻與中國古代文明. Shanghai: Zhong Xi shuju, 2016, 251–254.

Fudan daxue chutu wenxian yu guwenzi yanjiu zhongxin yanjiusheng dushuhui 復旦大學出土文獻與古文字研究中心研究生讀書會. "Qinghua jian *Yin zhi Yin gao* yandu zhaji" 清華簡《尹至》《尹誥》研讀札記. At http://www.fdgwz.org.cn/Web/Show/1352. Posted 5 January 2011.

Gentz, Joachim and Dirk Meyer eds. *Literary Forms of Argument in Early China*. Leiden: Brill, 2015.

Gentz, Joachim. "Defining Boundaries and Relations of Textual Units: Examples from the Literary Tool-Kit of Early Chinese Argumentation." In Joachim Gentz and Dirk Meyer eds. *Literary Forms of Argument in Early China*. Leiden: Brill, 2015, 112–157.

——— . "Literary Forms of Argument in the Tsinghua University Manuscript *Tang Zai Chimen*." In *Qinghua jian yanjiu* 3. Shanghai: Zhong Xi shuju, 2019, 194–221.

Grundmann, Joern Peter. "The Term min 民 as a Political Concept in Western Zhou Thought." *Bulletin of the Jao Tsung-I Academy of Sinology* 4 (2017), 111–135.

Guo Yongbing 郭永秉. "Qinghua jian *Yin zhi* 'lu zhi zai Tang' jie" 清華簡《尹至》" 𤔡至在湯"解. In *Guwenzi yu guwenxian lunji xubian* 古文字與古文獻論集續編. Shanghai: Shanghai guji chubanshe, 2015, 248–253.

——— . "Shi Qinghua jian zhong daoshanxing de 'fu' zi" 釋清華簡中倒山形的"覆"字. In *Guowenzi yu guwenxian lunji xubian* 古文字與古文獻論集續編. Shanghai: Shanghai guji chubanshe, 2015, 262–274.

Grebnev, Yegor. "Numerical lists of foundational knowledge in early Chinese and early Buddhist traditions." *Asiatische Studien/Études Asiatiques* 74.4 (2020): 453–484.

Harper, Donald. *Early Chinese Medical Literature: The Mawangdui Medical Manuscripts*. New York: Kegan Paul International, 1997.

He Ning 何寧. *Huainanzi jishi* 淮南子集釋. Beijing: Zhonghua shuju, 1998.

Hou Naifeng 侯乃峰. "Ye shuo Qinghua jian *Chi jiu zhi ji Tang zhi wu* pian de 'zhou'" 也説清華簡《赤鳩之集湯之屋》篇的"洀." *Zhongguo wenzi yanjiu* 中國文字研究 24 (2016): 64–67.

Huang Jie 黃傑 (a.k.a. Musilang 暮四郎). "Qinghua wu *Tang chu yu Tangqiu* chudu" 清華五《湯處於湯丘》初讀 #17. At http://

www.bsm.org.cn/forum/forum.php?mod=viewthread&tid=3247. Posted 11 April 2015.

———. "Qinghua wu *Tang zai Chimen* chudu" 清華五《湯在啻門》初讀 #2. At http://www.bsm.org.cn/forum/forum.php?mod=viewthread&tid=3248. Posted 11 April 2015.

———. "Qinghua wu *Yin gaozong wen yu san shou* chudu" 清華五《殷高宗問於三壽》初讀. At http://www.bsm.org.cn/forum/forum.php?mod=viewthread&tid=3249. Posted 10 April 2015.

Hunan sheng bowuguan 湖南省博物館 and Fudan daxue chutu wenxian yu guwenzi yanjiu zhongxin 復旦大學出土文獻與古文字研究中心 eds. *Changsha Mawangdui Hanmu jianbo jicheng* 長沙馬王堆漢墓簡帛集成. Beijing: Zhonghua shuju, 2014.

Huang Dekuan 黃德寬. "Qinghua jian *Chi hu zhi ji Tang zhi wu* yu xian-Qin "xiaoshuo" — lüe shuo Qinghua jian dui xian-Qin wenxue yanjiu de jiazhi" 清華簡《赤鵠之集湯之屋》與先秦"小説"——略說清華簡對先秦文學研究的價值. *Fudan xuebao (shehui kexue ban)* 復旦學報(社會科學版) 55.4 (2013): 81–86.

——— ed.-in-chief, *Qinghua daxue cang Zhanguo zhujian jiaoshi* 清華大學藏戰國竹簡校釋 (Beijing: Shangwu yinshuguan, forthcoming).

Huang Kuan-yun 黃冠雲. "Shuo *Tang zai Chimen* lun qi yi jie wenzi" 說《湯在啻門》論氣一節文字. In *Qinghua jian yanjiu* 3. Shanghai: Zhong Xi shuju, 2019, 159–170.

Huang Rener 黃人二. "Qinghua daxue cang Zhanguo zhujian (wu) *Tang zai Chimen* tongjie — jianlun ren huaitai shiyue ge jieduan mingcheng" 清華大學藏戰國竹簡(五)《湯在啻門》通解——兼論人懷胎十月各階段名稱. In Paul Fischer and Lin Zhipeng 林志鵬 eds. *Zhiqi yangxin zhi shu: Zhongguo zaoqi de xiushen fangfa* 治氣養心之術：中國早期的修身方法. Shanghai: Fudan daxue chubanshe 2017, 106–112.

Huang Ruxuan 黃儒宣. "Zuozhong qiju ji bosai youxi xiangguan wenti yanjiu" 左冢棋局及博塞遊戲相關問題探究. *Zhongyang yanjiuyuan lishi yuyan yanjiusuo jikan* "中央"研究院歷史語言研究所集刊

93.2 (2022): 273–330.

Huang Tianshu 黃天樹. "Yinxu jiaguwen suojian yejian shicheng kao" 殷墟甲骨文所見夜間時稱考. In *Huang Tianshu guwenzi lunji* 黃天樹古文字論集. Beijing: Xueyuan chubanshe, 2006, 178–193.

Jia Lianxiang 賈連翔. "Fanyin moji yu zhushu bianlian de zai renshi" 反印墨迹與竹書編連的再認識. *Chutu wenxian* 出土文獻 6 (2015): 229–245.

———. "Qiantan zhushu xingzhi xianxiang dui wenzi shidu de yingxiang — yi Qinghua jian ji chu wenzi bushi weili" 淺談竹書形制現象對文字釋讀的影響——以清華簡幾處文字補釋為例. *Chutu wenxian* 出土文獻 1 (2020): 82–90.

———. "Qinghua jian *Yin zhi* shushou ziji de kuoda ji xiangguan wenti tantao" 清華簡《尹至》書手字迹的擴大及相關問題探討. *Chutu wenxian zonghe yanjiu jikan* 出土文獻綜合研究輯刊 13 (2021): 79–100.

———. "Tang Qinghua jian suojian shushou ziji he wenzi xiugai xianxiang" 談清華簡所見書手字迹和文字修改現象. *Jianbo yanjiu* 簡帛研究 2015 Fall and Winter: 38–52.

———. *Zhanguo zhushu xingzhi ji xiangguan wenti yanjiu: Yi Qinghua Daxue cang Zhanguo zhujian wei zhongxin* 戰國竹書形制及相關問題研究——以清華大學藏戰國竹簡爲中心. Shanghai: Zhong Xi shuju, 2015.

Jiang Guanghui 姜廣輝. "*Bao xun* yiwei xinzheng wuze" 《保訓》疑偽新證五則. *Zhongguo zhexueshi* 中國哲學史 2010.3: 30–34.

———. "'Qinghua jian' jianding keneng yao jingli yige changqi guocheng — Zai tan dui *Bao xun* pian de yiwen" "清華簡"鑒定可能要經歷一個長期過程——再談對《保訓》篇的疑問. *Guangming ribao* 光明日報, 8 June 2009.

——— and Fu Zan 付贊. "Qinghua jian *Yin gao* xianyi" 清華簡《尹誥》獻疑. *Hunan daxue xuebao (Shehui kexue ban)* 湖南大學學報 (社會科學版) 2014.3: 109–114.

———, Fu Zan 付贊 and Qiu Mengyan 邱夢燕. "Qinghua jian *Qi ye*

wei weizuo kao" 清華簡《耆夜》為偽作考. *Gugong bowuyuan yuankan* 故宮博物院院刊 4.168 (2013): 86–94.

Jiang Shanguo 蔣善國. *Shang shu zongshu* 尚書綜述. Shanghai: Shanghai guji chubanshe, 1988.

Jiao Xun 焦循. *Mengzi zhengyi* 孟子正義. Beijing: Zhonghua shuju, 1987.

Jin Dejian 金德建. *Sima Qian suo jian shu kao* 司馬遷所見書考. Shanghai: Shanghai renmin chubanshe, 1963.

Jing Lingling 荆鈴鈴. "Xian Qin shiqi Yi Yin xingxiang de yanbian" 先秦時期伊尹形象的演變. *Chutu wenxian* 出土文獻 11 (2017): 184–193.

Jingmen shi bowuguan 荊門市博物館 eds. *Guodian Chu mu zhujian* 郭店楚墓竹簡. Beijing: Wenwu chubanshe, 1998.

Johnston, Ian trans. *The Mozi: A Complete Translation.* Hong Kong, The Chinese University Press, 2010.

Knoblock, John and Jeffrey Riegel trans. *The Annals of Lü Buwei.* Stanford: Stanford University Press, 2000.

Kong Yingda 孔穎達 ed. *Li ji zhengyi* 禮記正義. In Ruan Yuan 阮元 ed. *Shisan jing zhushu* 十三經注疏. Beijing: Zhonghua shuju, 1980.

Krijgsman, Rens. "Cultural Memory and Excavated Anecdotes in 'Documentary' Narrative: Mediating Generic Tensions in the Baoxun Manuscript." In Paul van Els and Sarah A. Queen eds. *Between History and Philosophy: Anecdotes in Early China.* Albany: SUNY Press, 2017, 301–330.

Kuo Li-hua 郭梨華. "Qinghua jian (wu) guanyu wei zhi zhexue tanjiu" 清華簡（伍）關於味之哲學探究. In *Qinghua jian yanjiu* 3. Shanghai: Zhong Xi shuju, 2019, 222–236.

Lai Guolong 來國龍. "Shi 'e' yu 'xie': jianlun 'yi xing wei zhu' yu 'yin xing yi zonghe' liangzhong butong de guwengzi kaoshi fangfa" 釋"乡"與"离": 兼論"以形為主"與"音形義綜合"兩種不同的古文字考釋方法. *Bulletin of the Jao Tsung-I Academy of Sinology* 6 (2019): 187–224.

Li Ling 李零. Sunzi *shisan pian zonghe yanjiu*《孫子》十三篇綜合研究.

Beijing: Zhonghua shuju, 2006.

Li Meichen 李美辰. "Qinghua jian Wuding lei wenxian jishi yu yanjiu" 清華簡武丁類文獻集釋與研究. M.A. thesis: Jilin University, 2016.

Li Shoukui 李守奎. "Handai Yi Yin wenxian de fenlei yu Qinghua jian Zhong Yi Yin zhupian de xingzhi" 漢代伊尹文獻的分類與清華簡中伊尹諸篇的性質. *Shenzhen daxue xuebao (renwen shehui kexue ban)* 深圳大學學報（人文社會科學版） 32.3 (2015): 41–49.

———. "'Yu' zi de chanshi ji kaoshi: Shuowen yilai de hanzi chanshi" "俞" 字的闡釋及考釋:《説文》以來的漢字闡釋. In Jia Jinhua 賈晉華, Chen Wei 陳偉, Wang Xiaolin 王小林, and Lai Guolong 來國龍 eds. *Xin yuwenxue yu zaoqi Zhongguo yanjiu* 新語文學與早期中國研究. Shanghai: Shanghai renmin chubanshe, 2018, 260–278.

Li Shuang 李爽. "Qinghua jian Yi Yin wu pian jishi" 清華簡"伊尹"五篇集釋. M.A. thesis: Jilin University, 2016.

Li Songru 李松儒. "Qinghua wu ziji yanjiu" 清華五字迹研究. *Jianbo* 簡帛 13 (2016): 79–89.

———. "*Qinghua daxue cang Zhanguo zhujian* (liu) zhi *Guan Zhong* ziji yanjiu"《清華大學藏戰國竹簡》（陸）之《管仲》字迹研究. *Shufa yanjiu* 書法研究 2016.4: 34–45.

Li Songru 李松儒. "Qinghua jian *Nai ming* de shuxie, zhizuo yu bianlian" 清華簡《廼命》的書寫、製作與編聯. *Chutu wenxian* 出土文獻 1 (2020): 75–81.

Li Tianhong 李天虹. "Hubei chutu Chu jian (wuzhong) geshi chuxi" 湖北出土楚簡（五種）格式初析. *Jiang Han kaogu* 江漢考古 2011.4: 102–106.

Li Xiangfeng 黎翔鳳. *Guanzi jiaozhu* 管子校注. Beijing: Zhonghua shuju, 2004.

Li Xueqin 李學勤, Sarah Allan, and Michael Lüdke, eds. *Qinghua jian yanjiu* 清華簡研究 3. Shanghai: Zhong Xi shuju, 2019.

———. *Chongxie xueshushi* 重寫學術史. Shijiazhuang: Hebei Jiaoyu chubanshe, 2002.

——— . "Yigu sichao yu chonggou gu shi" 疑古思潮與重構古史. *Zhong-guo wenhua yanjiu* 中國文化研究 1999.1: 2–4.

——— . *Zouchu yigu shidai* 走出疑古時代. Shenyang: Liaoning daxue chu-banshe, 1994.

——— ed.-in-chief, Qinghua daxue Chutu wenxian yanjiu yu baohu zhongxin 清華大學出土文獻研究與保護中心 ed., *Qinghua daxue cang Zhanguo zhujian (yi)* 清華大學藏戰國竹簡（壹）. Shanghai: Zhong Xi shuju, 2010.

——— ed.-in-chief, Qinghua daxue Chutu wenxian yanjiu yu baohu zhongxin 清華大學出土文獻研究與保護中心 ed., *Qinghua daxue cang Zhanguo zhujian (san)* 清華大學藏戰國竹簡（叄）. Shanghai: Zhong Xi shuju, 2012.

Liao Mingchun 廖名春. "Qinghua jian *Yin gao* yanjiu" 清華簡《尹誥》研究. *Shixueshi yanjiu* 史學史研究 2011.2: 110–115.

Liu Bo 劉波. "Qinghua jian Yin zhi 'tong wang dian' bushuo" 清華簡《尹至》"僮亡典"補説. At http://www.fdgwz.org.cn/Web/Show/1421. Posted 4 March 2011.

Liu Chengqun 劉成群. "Qinghua jian yu Moxue guankui" 清華簡與墨學管窺. *Qinghua daxue xuebao (zhexue shehui kexue ban)* 清華大學學報(哲學社會科學版) 32.3 (2017): 131–138.

Liu Chuanbin 劉傳賓. "Qinghua wu *Yin Gao Zong wen yu san shou* jian 1–8 jiexi" 清華五《殷高宗問於三壽》簡1–8解析. *Guwenzi yanjiu* 古文字研究 31 (2016): 391–396.

Liu Guozhong 劉國忠. *Introduction to the Tsinghua Bamboo-Strip Man-uscripts*. Christopher J. Foster and William N. French, tr. Leiden: Brill, 2016.

Liu Jiao 劉嬌. "Qinghua jian *Chijiu zhi ji Tang zhi wu* 'shi shi wei pi' yu 'Jie zuo wawu' chuanshuo" 清華簡《赤鳩之集湯之屋》"是始為埤"與"桀作瓦屋"傳説. *Guwenzi yanjiu* 古文字研究 32 (2018): 387–383.

Liu Zhao 劉釗 ed. "Taichan shu" 胎産書. In Hunan sheng bowuguan 湖南省博物館 and Fudan daxue chutu wenxian yu guwenzi yanjiu zhongxin 復旦大學出土文獻與古文字研究中心 eds. *Changsha Mawangdui Hanmu jianbo jicheng* 長沙馬王堆漢墓簡帛集成 vol. 6. Beijing: Zhonghua shuju, 2014, 93–102.

Lu Puping 魯普平. "Qinghua jian *Yin gao* pianming niding zhi shangque" 清華簡《尹誥》篇名擬定之商榷. *Ha'erbin xueyuan yuanbao* 哈爾濱學院院報 35.2 (2014): 72–74.

Luo Genze 羅根澤. "You *Mozi* yin jing tuice ru mo liang jia yu jingshu zhi guanxi" 由《墨子》引經推測儒墨兩家與經書之關係. In Luo Genze ed. *Gu shi bian* 古史辨, vol.4. Shanghai: Shanghai guji chubanshe, 1982, 278–299.

Lü Yahu 呂亞虎. *Zhanguo Qin Han jianbo wenxian suo jian wushu yanjiu* 戰國秦漢簡帛文獻所見巫術研究. Beijing: Kexue chubanshe, 2010.

Ma Chengyuan 馬承源 ed. -in-chief *Shanghai Bowuguan cang zhanguo Chu zhushu (yi)* 上海博物館藏戰國楚竹書（一）. Shanghai: Shanghai Guji chubanshe, 2001.

Ma Nan 馬楠. "Zhou Qin liang Han Shu jing kao" 周秦兩漢書經考. Ph.D. dissertation, Tsinghua University, 2012.

Ma Ruichen 馬瑞辰. *Maoshi zhuanjian tongshi* 毛詩傳箋通釋. Beijing: Zhonghua shuju 1989.

Ma Teng 馬騰. "Lun Qinghua jian *Zhi bang zhi dao* de Mojia sixiang" 論清華簡《治邦之道》的墨家思想. *Xiamen daxue xuebao (zhexue shehui kexue ban)* 厦門大學學報（哲學社會科學版）2019.5: 63–73.

Marubbio, Mayvis L. "Yi Yin, Pious Rebel: A Study of the Founding Minister of the Shang in Early Chinese Texts." Ph.D. dissertation, University of Minnesota, 2000.

Meyer, Dirk. *Documentation and Argument in Early China*. Berlin: De Gruyter, 2021.

———. "'Patterning Meaning': A Thick Description of the Tsinghua Manuscript '*Tāng zài Chì/Dì mén*' (Tāng was at the Chì/Dì Gate) and What It Tells Us about Thought Production in Early China."

Bulletin of the Jao Tsung-I Academy of Sinology 5 (2018): 139–167.

———. *Philosophy on Bamboo: Text and the Production of Meaning in Early China*. Leiden: Brill, 2012.

Pang Pu 龐樸. "Ying Yan shu shuo: Guodian Chu jian Zhongshan san qi xin pang wenzi shi shuo" 郢燕書説: 郭店楚簡中山三器心旁文字試説. In Wuhan daxue Zhongguo wenhua yanjiuyuan 武漢大學中國文化研究院 eds. *Guodian Chu jian guoji xueshu yantaohui lunwenji* 郭店楚簡國際學術研討會論文集. Wuhan: Wuhan Renmin chubanshe, 2000, 37–42.

Perkins, Franklin. "*Yin Gaozong Wen Yu San Shou* 殷高宗問於三壽: Content and Context." In *Qinghua jian yanjiu* 3. Shanghai: Zhong Xi shuju, 2019, 279–297.

Qinghua daxue chutu wenxian dushuhui 清華大學出土文獻讀書會. "Qinghua jian diwu ce zhengli baogao buzheng" 清華簡第五冊整理報告補正. At https://www.ctwx.tsinghua.edu.cn/info/1081/2214.htm. Posted 8 April 2015.

Qinghua daxue chutu wenxian yanjiu yu baohu zhongxin 清華大學出土文獻研究與保護中心 eds. *Qinghua daxue cang Zhanguo zhujian (shiyi)* 清華大學藏戰國竹簡（拾壹）. Shanghai: Zhong Xi shuju, 2021.

Qiu Xigui 裘錫圭. "Chutu wenxian yu gudianxue chongjian" 出土文獻與古典學重建. *Chutu wenxian* 出土文献 4 (2013): 1–18.

———. "Zhongguo gudianxue chongjian zhong yinggai zhuyi de wenti" 中國古典學重建中應該注意的問題. Beijing daxue Zhongguo guwenxian yanjiu zhongxin jikan 北京大學中國古文獻研究中心集刊 2 (2001); See also, Qiu Xigui 裘錫圭. *Qiu Xigui xueshu wenji: Jiandu boshu juan* 裘錫圭學術文集: 簡牘帛書卷. Shanghai: Fudan daxue chubanshe, 2012, 334–344.

Raz, Gil. "Birthing the Self: Metaphor and Transformation in Medieval Daoism." In Jinhua Jia, Xiaofei Kang, and Ping Yao eds. *Gendering Chinese Religion: Subject, Identity, and Body*. Albany: SUNY Press,

2014, 183–200.

Ruan Yuan 阮元 ed. *Shisan jing zhushu* 十三經注疏. Taipei: Yiwen, 2001.

——— ed. *Li ji zhushu* 禮記注疏. In *Shisan jing zhushu*, vol. 5. Taipei: Yiwen, 2001.

——— ed. *Shang shu zhengyi* 尚書正義. In *Shisan jing zhushu*, vol. 1. Taipei: Yiwen, 2001.

Shan Yuchen 單育辰. "Qinghua daxue cang zhanguo zhujian (wu) shiwen dingbu"《清華大學藏戰國竹簡(伍)》釋文訂補. In Fudan daxue chutu wenxian yu guwenzi yanjiu zhongxin 復旦大學出土文獻與古文字研究中心 eds. *Zhanguo wenzi yanjiu de huigu yu zhanwang* 戰國文字研究的回顧與展望. Shanghai: Zhong Xi shuju, 2017, 204–210.

——— . *Xinchu Chujian* Rongcheng shi *yanjiu* 新出楚簡《容成氏》研究. Beijing: Zhonghua shuju, 2016.

Shaughnessy, Edward L. *I Ching (The Classic of Changes)*. New York: Ballantine Books, 1996.

——— . *Rewriting Early Chinese Texts*. Albany: SUNY Press, 2006.

——— . *Unearthing the Changes: Recently Discovered Manuscripts of the Yi Jing (I Ching) and Related Texts*. New York: Columbia University Press, 2014.

Shen Jianhua 沈建華. "Qinghua jian *Tang chu yu Tangqiu* yu *Mozi Guiyi* wenben" 清華簡《唐(湯)處於唐丘》與《墨子‧貴義》文本. *Zhongguo shi yanjiu* 中國史研究 2016.1: 19–23.

Shi Xiaoli 石小力. "Ju Qinghua jian (qi) buzheng jiushuo si ze" 據清華簡(柒)補證舊說四則. At https://www.ctwx.tsinghua.edu.cn/info/1081/2232.htm. Posted 23 April 2017.

——— . "Qinghua jian *Yin gao* 'gai' zi xin shi" 清華簡《尹誥》"慁"字新釋. *Kaogu yu wenwu* 考古與文物 2019.1: 110–113.

——— . "Qinghua wu *Yin gaozong wen yu san shou* chudu" 清華五《殷高宗問於三壽》初讀 #14. At http://www.bsm.org.cn/forum/forum.php?mod=viewthread&tid=3249. Posted 11 April 2015.

Sima Qian 司馬遷. *Shi ji* 史記. Beijing: Zhonghua shuju, 2014.

Smith, Adam and Maddalena Poli. "Establishing the text of the *Odes*: the Anhui University bamboo manuscript." *Bulletin of the School of Oriental and African Studies* 84.3 (2022): 515–557.

Škrabal, Ondřej 石安瑞. "Lun Xi Zhou jinwen zhong de xiaochen ji qi zhiwu yanbian" 論西周金文中的小臣及其職務演變. *Beida shixue* 北大史學 20 (2016): 1–23.

Sterckx, Roel. *Food, Sacrifice, and Sagehood in Early China*. Cambridge: Cambridge University Press, 2011.

Su Jianzhou 蘇建洲. "Qinghua jian (yi) kaoshi shiyi ze" 《清華簡 (壹)》考釋十一則. In *Chuwenzi lunji* 楚文字論集, 343–396. Taipei: Wanjuanlou, 2011.

Sun Feiyan 孫飛燕. "Du *Yin zhi Yin gao* zhaji" 讀《尹至》《尹誥》札記. In Zhongguo wenhua yichan yanjiuyuan 中國文化遺産研究院 eds. *Chutu wenxian yanjiu* 出土文獻研究 10. Beijing: Zhonghua shuju, 2011, 38–41.

Sun Peiyang 孫沛陽. "Jiance bei hua xian chutan" 簡冊背劃綫初探. *Chutu wenxian yu guwenzi yanjiu* 出土文獻與古文字研究 4 (2011): 449–462.

Sun Yirang 孫詒讓. *Mozi jiangu* 墨子間詁. Beijing: Zhonghua shuju, 2001.

Schwartz, Adam. *The Oracle Bone Inscriptions from Huayuanzhuang East*. Berlin: De Gruyter, 2019.

Tang Pui-ling 鄧佩玲. "Qinghua jian (wu) *Yin gaozong wen yu san shou* youguan 'zhi' 'li' 'xin' sanduan jianwen kaoshi" 清華簡 (伍)《殷高宗問於三壽》有關"智""利""信"三段簡文考釋. *Chutu wenxian* 出土文獻 11 (2017): 194–204.

Van Norden, Bryan W. trans. *Mengzi: With Selections from Traditional Commentaries*. Indianapolis, IN: Hackett Publishing Company, 2008.

Vogt, Paul Nicholas. "Consumption, Knowledge, and the Limits of the Body in the Xiaochen Texts." In *Qinghua jian yanjiu* 3 (Shanghai: Zhong Xi shuju, 2019), 237–260.

Wagner, Rudolf G. "Out-put Driven Proposals in the Transcription, *shiwei* 釋文, of Chinese Excavated Texts: A Study of *Yin Gaozong wen yu san shou.*" In *Qinghua jian yanjiu* 3. Shanghai: Zhong Xi shuju, 2019, 298–327.

Wang Guowei 王國維. *Gu shi xin zheng: Wang Guowei zuihou de jiangyi* 古史新證——王國維最後的講義. Beijing: Qinghua daxue chu-banshe, 1994.

Wang Jinfeng 王進鋒. "Yin Shang shiqi de xiaochen" 殷商時期的小臣. *Gudai wenming* 古代文明 8.3 (2014): 35–53.

——— . "Qinghua jian (wu) *Yin Gaozong wen yu san shou, Tang chu yu Tangqiu, Tang zai Chimen* san pian jishi" 清華簡（伍）《殷高宗問於三壽》《湯處於湯丘》《湯在啻門》三篇集釋. In *Qinghua jian yanjiu* 3. Shanghai: Zhong Xi shuju, 2019, 392–497.

Wang Ning 王寧. "Du Qinghua jian san *Chi hu zhi ji Tang zhi wu* sanzha" 讀清華簡三《赤鵠之集湯之屋》散札. At http://www.bsm.org.cn/?chujian/5995.html. Posted 16 January 2013.

——— . "Du *Tang zai Chimen* sanzha" 讀《湯在啻門》散札. At http://www.fdgwz.org.cn/Web/Show/2513. Posted 6 May 2015.

——— . "Du Qinghua wu *Tang chu yu Tangqiu* sanzha" 讀清華五《湯處於湯丘》散札. At http://fdgwz.org.cn/Web/Show/2501. Posted 21 April 2015.

——— . "Du *Yin gaozong wen yu san shou* sanzha" 讀《殷高宗問於三壽》散札. At http://www.fdgwz.org.cn/Web/Show/2525. Posted 17 May 2015.

——— . "Qinghua jian *Yin zhi Yin gao* zhong de 'zhong' he 'min'" 清華簡《尹至》《尹誥》中的"衆"和"民". At http://www.fdgwz.org.cn/Web/Show/1396. Posted 4 February 2011.

Wang Tingbin 王挺斌. "Qinghua jian *Yin gao* 'yuan bang gui zhi' kao" 清華簡《尹誥》"遠邦歸志"考. At http://www.fdgwz.org.cn/Web/Show/2082. Posted 30 June 2013.

——— . "Tantan guwenzi ziliao zhong cong er hua de zi" 談談古文字資料中從二化的字. *Chutu wenxian* 出土文獻 10 (2017): 79–84.

Wang Xianqian 王先謙. *Shi sanjia yi jishu* 詩三家義集疏. Beijing: Zhong-hua shuju, 1987.

——— . *Xunzi jijie* 荀子集解. Beijing: Zhonghua shuju, 1988.

Wang Xianshen 王先慎. *Han Feizi jijie* 韓非子集解. Beijing: Zhonghua shuju, 1998.

Wang Zhizhong 王枝忠. *Han Wei Liuchao xiaoshuo shi* 漢魏六朝小説史. Hangzhou: Zhejiang guji chubanshe, 1997.

Wen Haoyue 温皓月. "Chutu wenxian yu chuanshi wenxian zhi Yi Yin cailiao zhengli ji xiangguan wenti yanjiu" 出土文獻與傳世文獻之伊尹材料整理及相關問題研究. M.A. thesis: Jilin University, 2016.

Wu Kejing 鄔可晶. "*Yin Zhi* 'wei zi nue de bao chong wu dian' ju shi jie"《尹至》"惟戠虐德暴曈亡典"句試解. *Chutu wenxian* 出土文獻 9 (2016): 166–172.

Wu Yujiang 吳毓江. *Mozi jiaozhu* 墨子校注. Beijing: Zhonghua shuju, 2006.

Wu Zhenfeng 吳鎮烽. "Si qi mingwen kaoshi" 獣器銘文考釋. *Kaogu yu wenwu* 考古與文物 2006.6: 58–65.

Xia Dazhao 夏大兆 and Huang Dekuan 黃德寬. "Guanyu Qinghua jian *Yin zhi Yin gao* de xingcheng he xingzhi—cong Yi Yin chuanshuo zai xian Qin chuanshi he chutu wenxian zhong de liubian kaocha" 關於清華簡《尹至》《尹誥》的形成和性質——從伊尹傳説在先秦傳世和出土文獻中的流變考察. *Wenshi* 文史 2014.3: 213–239.

Xiao Yunxiao 肖芸曉. "Shilun Qinghua zhushu Yi Yin san pian de guanlian" 試論清華竹書伊尹三篇的關聯. *Jianbo* 簡帛 8 (2013): 471–476.

——— . "Qinghua jian shoujuan yanjiu juli" 清華簡收捲研究舉例. *Chutu wenxian* 出土文獻 7 (2015): 172–186.

Xiong Xianpin 熊賢品. "Cong jiagu wen 'xian wei Cheng Tang' tan Qinghua jian *Yin gao* 'Yin ji ji Tang xian you yi de'" 從甲骨文"咸為成湯"談清華簡《尹誥》"尹既及湯咸有一德". *Jianbo yanjiu* 簡帛研究 2021 Fall and Winter: 1–9.

Xing Wen 邢文. "Beida jian *Laozi* bianwei" 北大簡《老子》辨偽. *Guang-

ming ribao 光明日報, 8 August 2016.

———. "Bianzheng zhi mei yu sandian toushi—Beida jian *Laozi* zai bianwei" 辯證之美與散點透視——北大簡《老子》再辨偽. *Guangming ribao* 光明日報, 12 September 12 2016.

———. "New Light on the *Li Ji* 禮記: The *Li Ji* and the Related Warring States Period Guodian Bamboo Manuscripts." *Early China* 37 (2014): 519–550.

Xu Baogui 徐寶貴 and Wu Kejing 鄔可晶 eds. "Jiu zhu" 九主. In Hunan sheng bowuguan and Fudan daxue chutu wenxian yu guwenzi yanjiu zhongxin 復旦大學出土文獻與古文字研究中心 eds. *Changsha Mawangdui Hanmu jianbo jicheng* 長沙馬王堆漢墓簡帛集成 vol. 4. Beijing: Zhonghua shuju, 2014, 97–106.

Xu Weiyu 許維遹. *Lüshi chunqiu jishi* 呂氏春秋集釋. Beijing: Zhonghua shuju, 2009.

Xu Wenxian 許文獻. *Qinghua jian Yi Yin wu pian yanjiu* 清華簡伊尹五篇研究. Taipei: Wanjuanlou, 2021.

Xu Yuangao 徐元誥. *Guoyu jijie* 國語集解. Beijing: Zhonghua shuju, 2002.

Yan Ruoqu 閻若璩. *Shang shu guwen shuzheng* 尚書古文疏證. In Wang Xianqian 王先謙 ed. *Huang Qing jingjie xubian* 皇清經解續編. Jiangsu: Zoushe shuju, 1888.

Yan Zhenyi 閻振益 and Zhong Xia 鍾夏. *Xinshu jiaozhu* 新書校注. Beijing: Zhonghua shuju, 2000.

Yang Bojun 楊伯峻. *Chunqiu Zuozhuan zhu (xiuding ben)* 春秋左傳注（修訂本）. Beijing: Zhonghua shuju, 1990.

Yang Tianyu 楊天宇. *Zheng Xuan san Li zhu yanjiu* 鄭玄三禮注研究. Tianjin: Tianjin renmin chubanshe.

Yao Sujie 姚蘇傑. "Qinghua jian *Yin gao* 'yi de' lunxi" 清華簡《尹誥》"一德"論析. *Zhonghua wenshi luncong* 中華文史論叢 2013.1, 371–404.

Yao Xiaoou 姚小鷗. "Qinghua jian *Chi jiu* pian yu Zhongguo zaoqi xiaoshuo de wenti tezheng" 清華簡《赤鳩》篇與中國早期小説的文體特征. *Wenyi yanjiu* 文藝研究 2014.2: 43–58.

Yates, Robin D. S. *Five Lost Classics: Tao, Huanglao, and Yin-Yang in Han China*. New York: Ballantine Books, 1997.

Yu Wanli 虞萬里. *Shanghai bowuguan cang Chu zhushu* Zi yi *zonghe yanjiu* 上海博物館藏楚竹書《緇衣》綜合研究. Wuhan: Wuhan daxue chubanshe, 2009.

Zeitlin, Judith T. "*Xiaoshuo*." In Franco Moretti ed. *The Novel, Volume 1: History, Geography, and Culture*. Princeton: Princeton University Press, 2006, 249–261.

Zhang Fuhai 張富海. "Shi Qinghua jian *Tang zai Chimen* de bianji" 釋清華簡《湯在啻門》的褊急. *Chutu wenxian* 出土文獻 12 (2018): 130–134.

——— . "Li yong xiesheng gouni shanggu yin yinggai zhuyi de jige wenti" 利用諧聲構擬上古音應該注意的幾個問題. *Chutu wenxian* 出土文獻 2021.1: 132–139.

Zhang Hanmo 張翰墨. "*Tang zai Chimen*, shi yue huaitai yu zaoqi Zhongguo shushu shijieguan"《湯在啻門》、十月懷胎與早期中國術數世界觀. *Bulletin of the Jao Tsung-I Academy of Sinology* 4 (2017): 173–212.

Zhang Huaitong 張懷通. "You 'yi shu wei ji' kan 'Hong fan' de xingzhi yu niandai" 由"以數為紀"看《洪范》的性質與年代. *Dongnan wenhua* 東南文化 2006.3: 51–57.

Zhang Chongli 張崇禮. "Qinghua jian *Yin gao* kaoshi" 清華簡《尹誥》考釋. At http://www.fdgwz.org.cn/Web/Show/2400. Posted 17 December 2014.

Zhao Boxiong 趙伯雄. "Lun xian Qin wenxian zhong de 'yi shu wen ji'" 論先秦文獻中的"以數為紀". *Wenxian* 文獻 1999.4: 25–32.

Zhao Ping'an 趙平安. "Guai de xingyi he ta zai chujian zhong de yongfa—jian shi qita guwenzi ziliao zhong de guai zi" 夬的形義和它在楚簡中的用法——兼釋其他古文字資料中的夬字. In *Xinchu jianbo yu guwenzi guwenxian yanjiu* 新出簡帛與古文字古文獻研究. Beijing: Shangwu yinshuguan, 2009, 332–338.

Zhao Xiaobin 趙曉斌. "Jingzhou Zaozhi jian *Wu Wang Fuchai qi shi fa*

Yue yu Qinghua jian *Yue Gong qi shi*" 荊州棗紙簡《吳王夫差起師伐越》與清華簡《越公其事》, in *Qinghua Zhanguo Chujian Guoji xueshu yantaohui lunwenji* 清華戰國楚簡國際學術研討會論文集, Beijing, November 2021, 6–11.

Zhongguo shehui kexue yuan kaogu yanjiusuo 中國社會科學院考古研究所 eds. *Yin Zhou jinwen jicheng (zengbu xiuding ben)* 殷周金文集成（增補修訂本）. Beijing: Zhonghua shuju, 2007.

Zhou Boqun 周博群. "Qinghua wu *Yin gaozong wen yu san shou* bushi" 清華五《殷高宗問於三壽》補釋. *Chutu wenxian* 出土文獻 (forthcoming).

Zhu Qianzhi 朱謙之. *Xin jiben Huan Tan Xin lun* 新輯本桓譚新論. Beijing: Zhonghua shuju, 2009.

Zhuang Tianshan 莊天山. "Lun Tiangou, Wangshi de shizhi ji qita" 論天狗、枉矢的實質及其他. In Zhongguo tianwenxue shi zhengli yanjiu xiaozu 中國天文學史整理研究小組 eds. *Kejishi wenji* 科技史文集 10. Shanghai: Shanghai kexue jishu chubanshe, 1983, 151–169.

Index of Proper Names

Index of Text Titles

Images of the Manuscripts

圖片來源: 北京，清華大學出土文獻研究與保護中心。

Source: Research and Conservation Center for Unearthed Texts, Tsinghua University, Beijing.

Chi jiu zhi ji Tang zhi wu 赤鳩之集湯之屋

A Red Pigeon's Alighting on Tang's Hut, recto

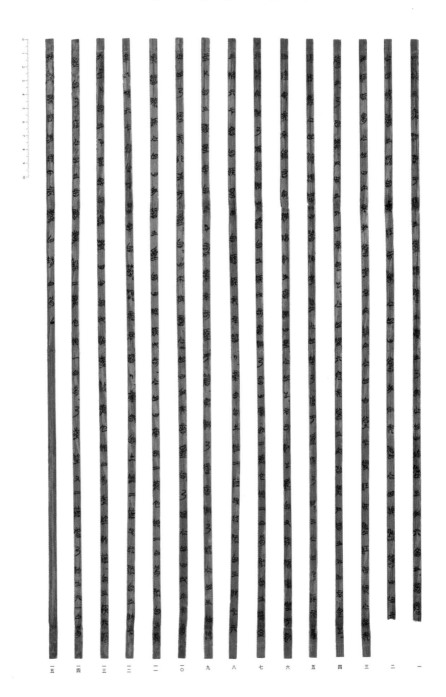

一五　一四　一三　一二　一一　一〇　九　八　七　六　五　四　三　二　一

Chi jiu zhi ji Tang zhi wu 赤鳩之集湯之屋
A Red Pigeon's Alighting on Tang's Hut, verso

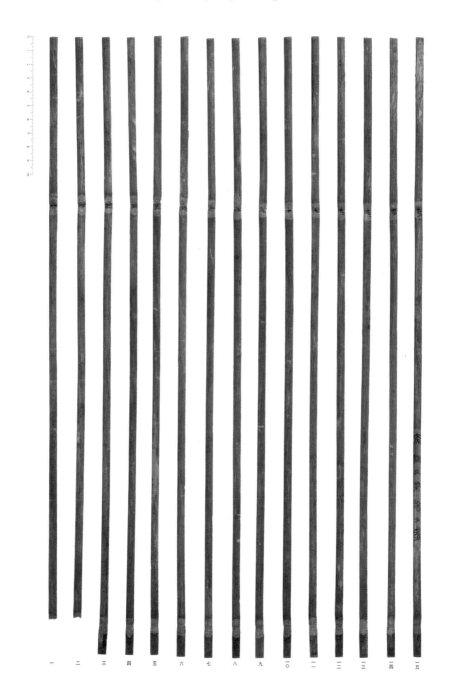

一　二　三　四　五　六　七　八　九　一〇　一一　一二　一三　一四　一五

*Yin zhi 尹至 *Yin's Arrival, recto

五　四　三　二　一

Yin zhi 尹至 *Yin's Arrival,* verso

一　　二　　三　　四　　五

Yin gao 尹誥 *Yin's Announcement,* recto

四　　　三　　　二　　　一

*Yin gao 尹誥 *Yin's Announcement, verso

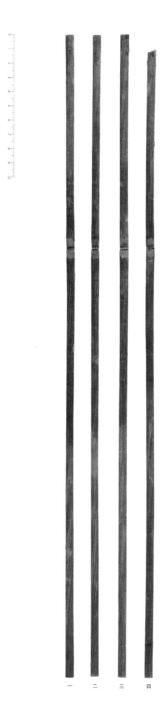

一　二　三　四

Tang zai Chimen 湯在啻門

Tang at the Gate of the Thearch, recto

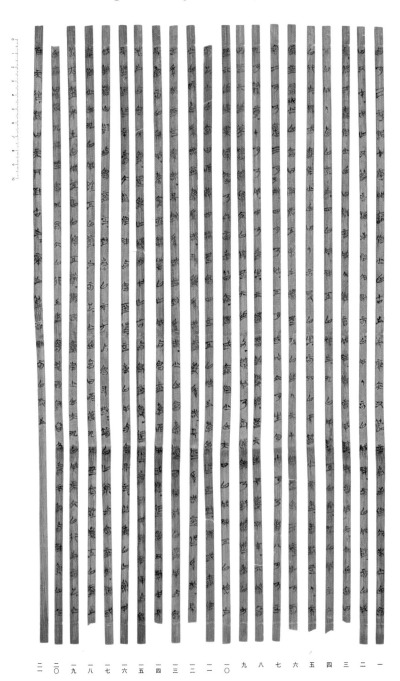

三　〇　九　八　七　六　五　四　三　二　一　〇　九　八　七　六　五　四　三　二　一

*Tang zai Chimen 湯在啻門

*Tang at the Gate of the Thearch, verso

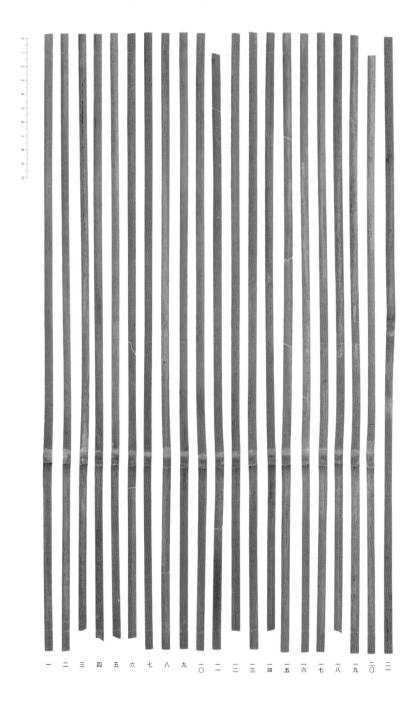

一 二 三 四 五 六 七 八 九 一〇 一一 一二 一三 一四 一五 一六 一七 一八 一九 二〇 二一

271

Tang chu yu Tangqiu 湯處於湯丘

Tang Resided at Tang Hill, recto

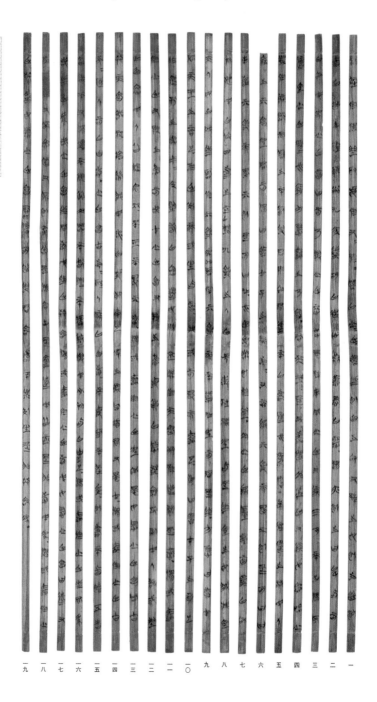

Tang chu yu Tangqiu 湯處於湯丘

Tang Resided at Tang Hill, verso

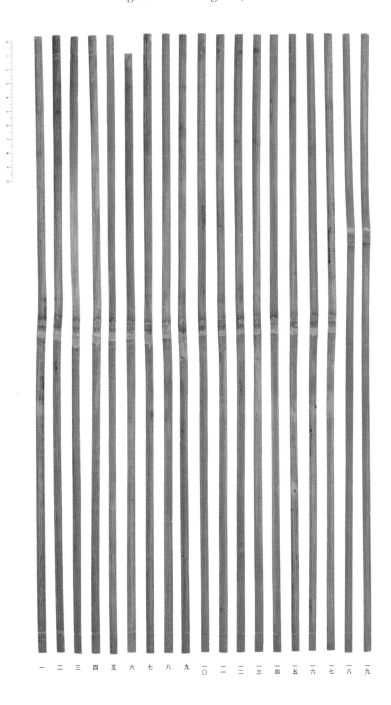

一　二　三　四　五　六　七　八　九　〇　一　二　三　四　五　六　七　八　九

Yin Gaozong wen yu San Shou 殷高宗問於三壽
The High Ancestor of Yin Asked the Three Long-Lived Ones, recto

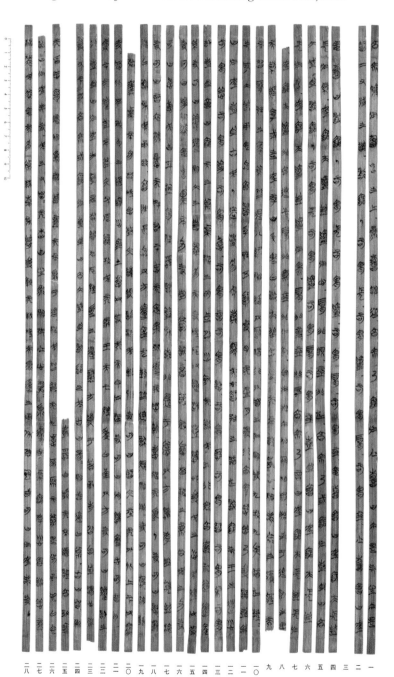

二八　二七　二六　二五　二四　二三　二二　二一　二〇　一九　一八　一七　一六　一五　一四　一三　一二　一一　一〇　九　八　七　六　五　四　三　二　一

274

Yin Gaozong wen yu San Shou 殷高宗問於三壽

The High Ancestor of Yin Asked the Three Long-Lived Ones, verso

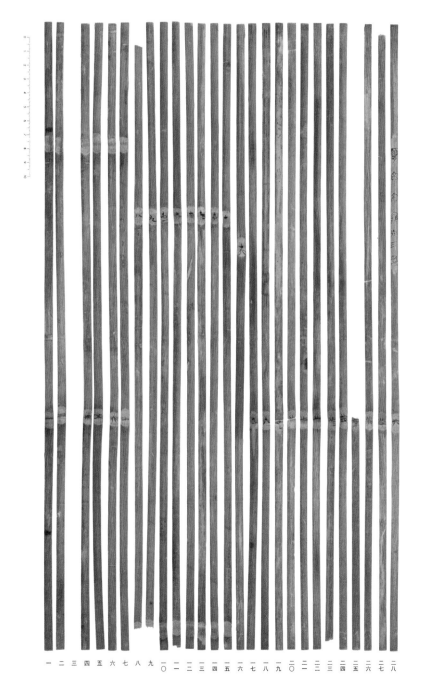

一 二 三 四 五 六 七 八 九 〇 一 二 三 四 五 六 七 八 九 〇 一 二 三 四 五 六 七 八

275